12/2010 A Gift to Bellefaire School from Max Edelman

Two Plus Four Equals One

Celebrating the Partnership of People with Disabilities and Their Assistance Dogs

Kathy Nimmer

Two hands/feet/eyes/ears, four paws, one magical union.
The stories of people with disabilities and their canine partners await telling.
May our voices now be heard.

First published by Dog Ear Publishing
4010 W. 86th Street, Ste H
Indianapolis, IN 46268
www.dogearpublishing.net

ISBN: 978-160844-716-9

This book is printed on acid-free paper.

Printed in the United States of America

Dedication

To those who came and went: June, Lindy, GraceAnn, Elena, and Raffles
To those who came and are still here: my family, friends, students, Prancer, and Elias
To those who are still to come: new friends, new students, guide dogs #4 and beyond, and Prince Charming?
To the One who is always present: my Lord and Savior Jesus Christ

Table of Contents

*Indicates contributors who elected to have their experiences written about by Kathy Nimmer.

+Submission written by Chazz Glaze.

Foreword

I have had the good fortune to have worked in the guide dog field for over thirty years and have been privileged to help blind people and their guide dogs develop a truly special relationship. This is a relationship in which the two partners are fully dependent upon each other. The guide dog is dependent upon the blind person for taking care of its most basic needs: food, shelter, vet care, grooming, exercise. The blind person needs and depends upon the guide dog to keep them safe from traffic, obstacles (small or large, moving or stationary), stairs which may appear out of nowhere, and a myriad of other potential hazards in their environment, all of this based upon a foundation of unconditional love and mutual trust in each other. They have complete faith in each other. They simply need each other.

One of the many joys of this profession is being able to watch this relationship grow, from the moment the blind person meets their dog to when they walk out of the training school. As in any relationship, there are the ups and downs as they learn to communicate with and understand each other, but ultimately the relationship begins to truly take form as they grow in their confidence in each other, knowing that they can fully trust each other. It is a source of wonder, and I doubt it will ever lose its magic for me.

Throughout this book, you will read happy stories, funny stories, sad stories, stories of bravery and courage, and perhaps stories of redemption. You will, however, find one common thread: all of this happens because of unconditional love. And isn't it wonderful what can take place in the space of such great love?

Kathy Zubrycki, Director of Training and Admissions
Guiding Eyes for the Blind

I have the privilege of working in the assistance dog industry, the best job in the world. Every day I am surrounded by exceptional dogs and exceptional people. I have a window on the everyday miracles that are created by the bonds of service. I regularly witness the unconditional love the canines share with their human partners as an assistance dog team.

Imagine being privy to a disabled child's first spoken words when the joyful delight of cuddling his dog unlocks the silence of his first six years. Embrace the triumph of a disabled adult who goes confidently into public situations with her dog by her side to pull the wheelchair if she tires or pick up her car keys if she drops them. Highly trained assistance dogs provide entrée to a world of independence and inclusion that is truly life changing.

The universal goal for all assistance dog organizations is to enhance the lives of disabled people by matching them with well-trained dogs. At our training facility, we understand the science of breeding dogs with the best possible physical composition and temperament to become assistance dogs. We invest in turning individuals with a passion for helping others and a love of dogs into talented trainers. We have perfected a program that consistently works to create highly effective assistance dog teams.

But, once the eyes of a disabled person lock onto the soulful gaze of their new best friend and canine helper, science and theory become mere background to the real stories. Enjoy the exploration of everyday miracles about to unfold for you.

Linda Valliant, Executive Director
Canine Companions for Independence, Southwest Region

A Note from the Author

Hundreds of writings were submitted for this project through http://www.servicedogstories.com over a five-month period in 2009. A panel of six judges narrowed down the entries to a pool of finalists. The stories and poems you will read here were then selected as the best representation of disabilities, breeds, writing genres, content, and tone. Many of the entries were written by individual authors. Others were written by me or my assistant after interviewing individuals by phone and email.

In this book, the term "assistance dogs" refers to all dogs trained to help people with all types of disabilities. While "service dogs" is still often used to mean the same thing, I have opted in this book to follow the newer designation of "assistance dogs," leaving "service dogs" to refer to those dogs trained to help people with needs other than visual or auditory. Individual authors within the anthology may hold other standards. Various specific labels are applied to dogs, depending on their certification and skills. You will also find some authors refer to "guide dogs" and others to "dog guides." Both references are to canines who guide blind or visually impaired individuals. Approximately half of the entries in this book showcase this type of assistance dog. The other half is comprised of dogs who assist with numerous other disabilities. This proportion is reflective of the abundant submissions that came in for this book from around the world and is loosely reflective of the number and type of teams working today.

Many of the dogs in this book were trained by specific schools, though some are owner-trained dogs (attribution for training follows each entry in italics). The ADA allows for such variety and gives the right for the dogs to have access to public places. Specifications of such access are explained in the text of the ADA. Among schools, some offer the dog and training at no cost to the client while others require a set fee.

Breed capitalization is a fluid issue with few consistent treatments in magazines, books, and other publications. I have chosen to follow the capitalization guidelines used by the American Kennel Club, capitalizing all breeds in almost every situation except when references are extremely broad.

The training methods, viewpoints, procedures, and working conduct presented in this book are wide-ranging and do not necessarily represent my opinion as author/editor.

Lastly, this volume is a labor of love, sometimes excruciating labor made manageable only because of immense love. Nothing can adequately capture every angle of the assistance dog reality, but by compiling these pieces in one place, I think we've done a pretty good job of it. You may visit http://www.servicedogstories.com to share your thoughts. May these pages bless your life with the fluff, fuzz, and fur that the authors in this anthology know and appreciate so well.

Acknowledgements

I would like to thank the following people for helping me with the creation of this book:

My mom and dad, Mary Ann and Bill Hiller, for standing by me as I juggled this project, teaching, selling a house, building a new house, having major surgery, and trying to stay marginally sane throughout!

Assistants Chazz Glaze (2010) and Katie Robinson (2009) for being all that I needed when I needed it.

Linda Valliant and Kathy Zubrycki for lending their voices and expertise in the forward.

Judges Jim Hand, Abigail Heath, Bev Klayman, Shirley Kraemer, Denise Lanier, and Beth Muehlhausen for reading through the hundreds of submissions and helping narrow down the pool.

Sidney Bolam for creating the stunning cover art. We are unlikely, unshakable soul sisters.

Matthew Voorhees for the author photo on the back cover. He's only in high school and is that good already!

Ines Almeida, Nagi Fugie, and Gabriele Giuliani for translation help with the foreign submissions.

The eleven contributors to "Paw Prints of Wisdom" whose insights launch each chapter so beautifully.

Amanda Barnett, De Bush, Karen Pond, Megan Sietsma, and Catherine Staszewski for technical support.

Detra Bannister, Alysa Chadow, Heidi Fernandez, and Deborah Wagner for being contributors and helpers at the same time.

My own dear creative writing students Jill Bowman, Rachel Dark, Percy Davis, Kaylee Hughes, Keely Korstanje, Roshan Krishnan, Paige Pearl, and Mallory VanMeeter for suggesting titles for some of the pieces I wrote. Your creativity has just begun to shine.

Paige Cantwell and Rytha Geyman for reading the full manuscript to catch any last-minute errors. Any that remain are my responsibility alone.

Paula Carver for creating http://www.servicedogstories.com, where the project took wing.

The Lilly Endowment for naming me a 2009 Lilly Distinguished Fellow so that I might pursue the dream that is this book.

Chapter 1

At First

Puppy Raisers and Trainers Get Things Started

Paw Prints of Wisdom

"The dreadful day came when we had to return Kate to Leader Dogs for the Blind. And it was a dreadful day, the first Sunday in November: cold, damp, cloudy, windy, spitting rain. After putting our empty leash in the car, we walked to the dorm to deliver something to our friend who was training with a new dog. The halls were full of happy people and their happy dogs. We left our pain outside in the gloom."

—Dick and Isabel Atcheson,
puppy raisers for Leader Dogs for the Blind and Paws with a Cause

"Until my pup is four months old, it thinks its name is 'No.' At six months old, its name changes to 'Leave It.' As it goes off for training at about fifteen months, it has become 'Good Boy' or 'Good Girl.'"

—Marilyn Valder,
volunteer puppy raiser for Guide Dog Services New Zealand

Puppy raising is a monumental undertaking with moments of frustration, laughter, and victory. Linda Elmore Teeple shares her experiences raising Grace.

Loving And Letting Go

by Linda Elmore Teeple

Dog lover that I am, I'm always on the alert for opportunities to increase my lap time with the canine community. One spring I found myself drawn to a Leader Dogs for the Blind booth at the Lion's Club Home Show, an annual event in my community. Every year I would stop at this booth to admire the Labrador Retrievers, German Shepherds, and Golden Retrievers sporting blue bandannas and jackets declaring, "Future Leader Dog."

I began entertaining the notion of becoming a puppy raiser and convinced my husband to join me in this venture. In June 2003, Grace Marie, an adorable, seven-week-old yellow Lab, came to live with us.

"How on Earth are you ever going to give Grace up?" everybody wanted to know. Even though I knew that Grace was the property of Leader Dogs for the Blind and I signed an agreement to bring her back when they recalled her litter, I loved her as my very own. I reminded myself daily that Grace had a destiny, and that it was my role—my temporary role—to prepare her for her life of service.

It had been years since my husband and I had housebroken a puppy. We'd forgotten what it's like to be rudely awakened in the middle of the night to the pathetic, heart-wrenching, irritatingly high-pitched howls of a baby. Totally erased from our minds were the chilly treks outside to feign excitement over a few dribbles and plops, only to return to the house to clean up puddles and piles of "oops, didn't-make-it-to-the-door-in-time!" messes, as an energized whirlwind of fur whipped around us, nipping at our frigid feet.

Like all puppies, Grace had a mischievous nature and a proclivity toward destruction. Gracie loved pushing our buttons and hearing us shriek, "No! I mean, leave it!" (proper Leader Dog vernacular). "Grace," I said, "Leave it! Good puppy! Good leave it!"

Grace was most endearing in her "unendearingness." It was hard not to laugh at her when she stole socks and unmentionables from the bedroom, and, with a twinkle in her eye, engaged us in a lively game of keep-away. Panda, our family Goldendor (half Golden Retriever, half Labrador Retriever), would launch into retriever mode, tackling Grace so we could confiscate the illicit item.

Gracie's most memorable heist occurred one morning when I was hurriedly preparing food and gathering up things I needed for a very busy day. I was running late and making numerous trips to the garage to load items into the van. For some unknown reason, the van alarm kept going off and the doors kept locking. I was growing increasingly more frustrated by the minute, that is, until I happened upon Grace in the dining room, contentedly munching on my husband's remote van key that she had lifted from his nightstand. My frustration immediately evaporated and I chuckled out a less-than-convincing, "Leave it!"

As a first-timer Leader Dog puppy raiser, I was overly anxious about being a good foster parent. Unlike all the other Leader Dog puppies that I heard fellow puppy raisers proudly bragging about, Grace was not content to lie quietly at my feet, walk obediently by my side, or keep her trap shut in church. One Sunday, she joined in on the anthem as the choir sang. On another occasion, she could not restrain from expressing her opinion regarding the pastor's sermon. "What am I doing wrong?" I wondered. "If I were a good mother, my baby would be better behaved."

In time, I learned to accept Grace for who she was (active, verbal, stubborn, creative, sneaky) and not worry about ironing out all her personality wrinkles. Just between you and the uptight, inhibited part of me, I take devious delight in Grace's antics, wishing I too could occasionally let myself "bark" during the sermon, chew holes in someone's favorite new sweater, and pig out on the dessert designated for company.

While I wanted Grace to become a model Leader Dog, I secretly hoped that her trainers would not be able to extinguish all of the quirks that made Grace so exasperating and yet so entertaining. In truth, I also wanted her future partner to realize just what we went through to raise this dog for him or her ("Grace can be so ornery sometimes; her puppy raisers must have been absolute saints!").

One Saturday evening, the night before the children at church were to celebrate Grace's first birthday, the birthday girl helped herself to ten of the twenty-four cupcakes cooling on the kitchen counter, paper liners and all. Several remaining cupcakes bore nose smudges, but evidently did not pass the sniff test. I fully expected a puppy tummy ache to ensue, but Grace tolerated her sugar binge extremely well.

That Sunday, as the children sang "Happy Birthday" to Grace, their cone-shaped, Sponge Bob hats askew atop their heads, I realized that this was also a good-bye party. That nagging question, "How on Earth are you ever going to give Grace up?" caused butterflies in my stomach.

A few weeks later, several carloads of puppy raisers, with their gangly, one-year-old pups squeezed between legs and bags of puppy supplies, caravanned to Leader Dogs for the Blind in Rochester Hills, Michigan. We were a solemn group, yet full of excitement and expectation. Tearful good-byes to pups were accompanied by mutually comforting hugs between the grieving puppy raisers, many of whom would journey back to Leader Dogs in a few weeks or months to collect another puppy.

Six months later, when I had the opportunity to see Grace again and meet her partner, I cried tears of joy. I was thrilled to learn her destination was Costa Rica. I had recently been on a mission trip with Volunteer Optometric Services to Humanity in Costa Rica. Despite the language barrier, our mutual joy transcended all barriers.

"How on Earth would I ever give Grace up?" I now knew the answer: it was for this moment that I raised her and let her go.

Leader Dogs for the Blind

Dick Shafner couldn't have anticipated what happened when he took his puppy Elias with him to renew his driver's license.

Elias at the Registry of Motor Vehicles

by Dick Shafner

If you lived in Massachusetts, you would know that the state's Registry of Motor Vehicles has historically had a very bad reputation for dealing with its public. However, over the years it has gotten better, as they now try to go out of their way to be nice to their customers. But their reputation still haunts them.

One year I had to make the trip to the registry with the first guide dog we were raising for Guiding Eyes for the Blind (GEB), Elias. My trip that morning was to renew my driver's license. So I took Elias, wearing his official GEB jacket indicating he was a GEB puppy in training, and went to the local registry office.

Elias and I sat down after taking a numbered ticket for service. While I waited I enjoyed my morning Starbucks coffee, and Elias intently watched customers come and go. Eventually my number was called, and Elias and I were sent into one of the many numbered rooms located down the main hall.

As I walked in with my coffee in my right hand and Elias at a heel position on my left, the grumpy attendant, who sat at his desk behind a couple of machines and did not look up, asked me what I wanted.

"I need to renew my driver's license."

"Put your face in that machine," he muttered, still not looking up. "Read the second line of text."

I read the line flawlessly, which did not impress him at all, if his continued scowl was any indication.

"Okay, sit down." He motioned to a chair by the open door. As I started to walk toward it, Mr. Anti-Sunshine finally looked up.

"What?" he choked. I watched his lips move as he read the words on Elias's jacket. "Guiding Eyes for the Blind!" he belched out. "How did you do that?"

Being the wise guy that I am I said, "How did I do what?"

"How did you read that line in the machine?"

"I can see just fine."

By then, I noticed other people in the area watching our exchange. Continuing the fun, I said, "I guess you do not see too many guide dogs in here!"

The scowl finally retreated as the attendant admitted he had not, that this was the first one. After we all had a good laugh, I finally told him and the onlookers the truth about being a *puppy raiser* for GEB, not a visually impaired handler. With that admission, I successfully renewed my license.

Guiding Eyes for the Blind

Monika Miller-Neumaier's life changes when Pace comes trotting into it with a personality the size of a football field.

Raising Pace

by Monika Miller-Neumaier

My journey into being a "dog girl" began June 30th, 2006, at the Milwaukee Airport. My husband Michael, our two-year-old son MacKai and nine-year-old daughter Madz, and I had all excitedly driven up from Illinois to Wisconsin to pick up Pace, the newly assigned furry member of our family. We pulled up to the cargo area of Midwest Airlines, walked into the building, and immediately heard him: a high pitched constant barking/whining echoing from the other room.

"Looks like you have a noisy one!" the airport worker exclaimed. He smirked and I swore I heard a bit of an evil chuckle as he handed the tiny kennel over to me. He continued, "Seen a lot of these service dog trainees come and go. Good luck with this one." Not really sure how to interpret his comments, my excitement was immediately squashed. I suddenly realized my vulnerability; never having had a dog in my life, I had no idea what to do with this furry baby. A puppy was entirely new to my life experience and now, I was really nervous.

We carried the travel kennel outside to an area of grass where we had water and a bit of food waiting. As we opened the kennel door and gazed in, the barking instantly stopped. There our eight-week-old Pace stood in all his glory. A fuzzy, black, big-bellied pup strutted out of the kennel with no hesitation. He stopped, stared at us as if to say, "How *dare* you!" and then proceeded to find a spot to poop. It was in those first few moments with Pace where I learned not only about "dog attitude," but also, the need for poop bags! Within those first few moments, Pace had us laughing, and my nervousness began to subside.

The "World According To Dog" kicked into full gear the next fifteen months as I learned about the usual "dog stuff": potty training, puppy proofing, commands, training classes, etc. Unexpectedly, however, were the eye-opening lessons in patience, acceptance, and the truth behind a dog's unconditional love. I realized what I had been missing the first forty years of my life and why a dog is considered, in this case at least, a *woman's* best friend.

Before Pace, true blue dog people had always been a bit of a mystery to me. Holiday photos with dog and Santa, seeking just the right dog Halloween costume, going to a specialty bakery for that perfect dog birthday cake, saving puppy teeth when they fall out—this all seemed, well, a bit odd. Yet soon, I found myself guilty of all those things—and more! I would refer to Pace as my "furry son"; before turn-in I planned a "going to college" party for Pace. We had a family photo taken (Pace included of course), and with each case of doggy diarrhea Pace encountered, my family was doomed to frozen pizza for dinner while I slaved over a hot stove creating my magical "system soothing rice and chicken dinner" for His Majesty.

Although I never had a dog before, I knew Pace was going to graduate to be a service dog; there was something unique, special, and almost innately human about Mr. Handsome. His deep burnt-sugar color brown eyes would connect to mine with intellect and understanding; he never ceased to amaze me with how quickly he could learn. Impressively, he even mastered the ultimate human male trait of selective hearing, choosing to ignore me just about every time when puppy playtime was over at training class. From the first time I picked him up, cuddling him like a baby, it was love at first sight. He had me morphing into a "dog girl" from the moment I opened that kennel door.

Raising Pace was my privilege and yet a sacrifice I had freely chosen; this was something I could not have completely grasped until I released his leash from my hand and into that of another for the last time. As *our* story ended August 18, 2007, on turn-in day, I realized *his* story was truly just beginning. I walked away thinking that the next time I saw him, he would be a different boy, no longer my little goofball, but the handsome, loyal, incredible dog he was bred to be. He would change.

Before Pace, I never knew that puppies snore or suckle in their sleep like a newborn baby. I never knew that puppies cry when first taken from their litter or that they have such depth to their emotions and souls. But most of all, I never remotely knew how a big-bellied, black Lab-Golden Retriever mix would eventually, and thoroughly, change me.

Canine Companions for Independence

Saying goodbye to Trisy was a bittersweet sacrifice Emily Overcarsh knew she had to make.

I Send You Like a Prayer

by Emily Overcarsh

I send you like a prayer
To shine in a land without sun
Where scents and sounds bloom
Like thunder over the expanse
Of the impossible black horizon
Could you have known where you were headed?
That all along you were a hero?
You were never mine to keep
So I held you just long enough
For you to grow into a savior
For the lost
And now I let go

I send you like a prayer
Like a fulfilled promise
I hang on to your scent in your blanket
That you're too big for now
And as the tears every mother has wept fill my eyes
Know that you carry my heart with you
To the land without sun
So don't look back now
Instead, look ahead
To the impossible black horizon
And shine with the knowledge
That you were born for this moment
Where you set a blind man free

Southeastern Guide Dogs, Inc.

Shannan Dumke's heart was breaking as she drove toward the school where Zen's new life would begin. What happened next was totally unexpected.

The Gift of Zen

by Shannan Dumke

Looking into the rearview mirror I could see his big brown eyes staring at me from the back of the station wagon. Trusting and soulful, he was a beautiful dog. As much as he was a part of the family, he wasn't really ours. Zen had arrived seventeen months earlier, a fluffy and chubby ten-week-old black Lab puppy. It was love at first sight, despite the fact that we were raising him to be an assistance dog and would only have him for a short time.

Now, here we were, driving him to Santa Rosa to deliver him to the training facility where they would finish his education and determine if he had what it took to be a partner for someone.

As we drove, mostly in silence for those two days, I wondered how I would ever be able to let go of his leash and relinquish him to total strangers. I thought of the hundreds of times I had been asked that question by others. Each and every time I had confidently responded that we were like foster parents and that we had always known our time with Zen would be limited. I also reminded them that hopefully Zen was going to go out in the world and help someone live a more independent, happy life. I spent countless hours convincing other people that this was a great thing to do. Now all I had to do was convince my breaking heart the same thing.

The state-of-the-art facility was impressive beyond words. The staff had organized a tour of the warm and comfortable environment in which our dog would be living and learning for the next six to nine months. As we walked through one of the buildings we saw where Zen's name was written on a feeding board to let others know his needs. The lump in my throat grew to the size of a small boulder. "Turn-in" would happen tomorrow, and ready or not we were going to have to drive home without him.

A graduation ceremony the next day was a time to celebrate the dogs who had been turned in before ours. These dogs were the success stories. They had beaten the odds and made the cut. Only about thirty-five percent of all puppies that are raised and returned actually have all the attributes a service dog needs. Health and temperament in graduates must be perfect. The ones that don't make it became "change of career" dogs, either going back to their puppy raisers or to another family that wants to adopt a well-trained pet.

We watched as the recipients received their new partner's leash from the person who had raised him. Witnessing this emotional ceremony renewed our desire to be the ones who had raised one of these special dogs. The reception following was full of laughter and stories as puppy raisers, recipients, trainers, breeder caretakers, and other volunteers interacted, sharing a tangible common bond. The desire to fulfill Canine Companions for Independence's mission of "raising miracles one puppy at a time" was apparent in the faces of each and every person.

We still had the "feel good" emotions as we left the graduation and headed back to the training facility. We agreed not to delay the inevitable any longer than necessary. We each took a moment to say goodbye. My daughter rubbed his exposed belly, whispering sweet nothings and encouragement into his ear. My husband "shook" his paw and ruffled Zen's fur, his eyes wet with tears. I gave him the biggest bear hug I could and sank my nose into his fur to try to place his scent permanently in my memory.

After giving us some time to take a few pictures, the trainer asked us if we were ready to send Zen off to college. We slowly nodded. As she took his leash and walked off I expected Zen to look inquiringly at us...but he proudly and confidently pranced away and never looked back. He was ready. We had done our job well, and the knowledge that he could enrich another life was all I needed to let him continue walking. My heart didn't break after all, but swelled with considerable pride and love.

Now the waiting game began. Would Zen make it or would he be coming home to us? The trainer sent us a progress report after the first ten days, informing us of Zen's perfect health. After a month, we received an in-depth evaluation of Zen's progress. They assured us that he was excelling in his training. At this point I had a gut feeling that Zen would not be returning to live with us. I felt he had a calling to do something more than be a wonderful pet. Little did I know at that point just how big his calling would be.

At the two month anniversary of Zen's turn-in we received a phone call from one of the breeding coordinators. They had chosen him as one of the "best of the best" and decided to make him a breeder. This honor is only given to about four percent of all the male puppies born into the program. He would be placed with a local family that had applied for a breeder dog. There he would be a much loved family pet with some additional responsibilities.

As Zen moved in with his new family, our lives felt like they were in Limbo. Our task was finished and Zen's new life had begun. We attended his graduation for new breeders and handed his leash to his new family. They promised to stay in touch, and I knew they would.

At that point a decision was made to honor Zen and to share our love, time, and skills with another. Within six months Aris joined our lives. Zen's firstborn son arrived at the airport, an eight week old, fluffy and chubby, black Lab. Once again our hearts were filled with puppy love.

Canine Companions for Independence

Suzanne Ferguson's commitment to puppy raising is profound, as are the differences it has made in her life.

A Life of Lives

by Suzanne Ferguson

In retrospect, each of the last ten years has been defined by one special "Future Leader Dog for the Blind" in my care. Puppy raisers are motivated and called to service for different reasons. Mine was a selfish one: I did not want to bury another dog. At age fifty, I was ready for all the wonders of puppyhood and none of the sadness of old age; and in the process of fostering a puppy, I would be able to feel I had made a difference in the life of an individual who would ultimately become the recipient of my charge. Little did I know that I had opened emotional doors which I would never be able to close.

There had been no puppy in our household for thirteen years, so excitement and anticipation of a "fur baby" spilled over to friends and relatives. We puppy-proofed the house and office, sent announcements throughout the community, and as a grand finale had a puppy shower. Sandwiches, cookies and cakes were all shaped like dog bones, and gifts ranged from pooper scoopers to designer collars. A good start, but it did not prepare me for what lay ahead.

The awesome responsibility of what had been undertaken dawned on this first-time raiser somewhere between a one A.M. potty break in twenty degree weather and the first accident in public. Everything during that puppy's first year impacts his demeanor as a working dog in the field, success or failure—the ultimate goal being to bring as many real life experiences as possible into that first year in order to prepare the dog for life with a visually impaired or blind individual.

Life became a series of adjustments. The puppy in residence became attached to us twenty-four-seven, going everywhere we went from the World Trade Center Memorial in New York to Disneyland in California, from Jimmy Buffett's stomping grounds in Key West, Florida, to the Iditarod Trail Headquarters in Alaska. Our commitment was simple: if our puppy couldn't go, neither did we.

Having had a tailless dog for many years, our first Lab puppy taught us the strength of this appendage. During the year, breakables were raised to at least a foot above tail level and remained there throughout the next decade. Every errand became an educational session with the public—no more darting in and out of a store. In even the finest restaurants, children resided under our table with the puppy; my husband and I expertly took turns eating and answering questions. Our wardrobe became a walking advertisement for Leader Dogs for the Blind in Rochester, Michigan, and our pockets were equipped with clean-up bags, our puppy's business card, and brochures from the school. The end-table in the bedroom became a glass-topped crate, and our carpet was removed in favor of wood flooring. The yard was fenced and the frog-pond removed since puppies, frogs, and water plants do not ecologically co-exist.

During the puppy years, the fact they were not "mine" was always elusive. All too quickly when the dreaded card came in the mail announcing their return date to the school, all the initial, noble intentions and warm, fuzzy feelings of doing something good were replaced with the gripping sensation that I may never see this wonderful dog again. Such heartache never gets easier—only harder. That last walk to the kennel is the longest walk of all walks. Everything turns surreal, and the year replays itself in slow motion. There is no going back—what's done is done. Emotions are laced with worry—worry about adjustment to kennel life, worry about the rigors of up-coming training, worry about falling short in preparing our puppy for this new life as a Leader Dog.

Two Labrador Retrievers, two Golden Retrievers, four German Shepherds, and multiple visiting puppies have tempered me with an abundance of dog wisdom. Moments are cherished more than years. Fortunately, Kodak froze many of those treasured moments which we revisit often: the snow storm at Mount Rushmore, hiking the White Sands of New Mexico, surprise encounters like the clown on the pogo stick, and of course the countless faces of smiling children hugging, holding, and kissing our traveling puppy. I don't take myself so seriously anymore and can laugh easily at mishaps—cleaning up dog poop with a dollar bill (forgive me George) and going through the Albuquerque Airport with a vomiting eighty-pound German Shepherd can do that. My patience is eternal knowing that a low, soft voice and consistency will calm a puppy temper tantrum in record time.

Disappointment of a career change is not the end but can become a new beginning with different successes. Hearts are big enough to encompass the puppies, graduate dogs, their new handlers and families; our family grows with every assigned puppy we have raised. Understanding expands the love, respect, and awe for those with visual disabilities and all they can accomplish with a service dog. Destiny called for them to leave us, but the doors to our home and heart remain always open.

There is no greater pride than seeing my puppies as professional dog guides. We have witnessed a goofy Golden transformed in harness to a serious representative of the Leader Dog School for the Blind. Bred as a show dog but donated to the school, our black Labrador's intelligence was nurtured and developed so that as a working Leader Dog his assessment of danger kept his active professional partner out of harm's way more than once. Their new homes are throughout the U.S., Canada, and Spain; along with our love and best wishes, each took a photographic chronicle of that first special year.

As one handler shared, "Until I met you, I assumed their life began when I took the leash, never thinking about them having a life before me." For my part, I cannot imagine having a life before them.

Leader Dogs for the Blind

Stephen Rodi knew far more about being in prison than he did about puppies, but the chance to raise Rugby while incarserated changed everything.

Saying Goodbye to My Best Friend Rugby

by Stephen G. Rodi

As I sit here in my cell, I find myself confronted by conflicting emotions, knowing that within a few days, I will have to say goodbye to my best friend Rugby—a sweet, happy-go-lucky Labrador Retriever I have been privileged to raise and train from the time he was twelve weeks old. I'm looking down at him now as he rests at my feet, quiet and well-behaved. He raises his head, bumps against me with his wet nose, and puts his chin back down on his forelegs. As I watch him, I am affectionately reminded of how he came bouncing into my life that first day he arrived on the prison compound.

An adorable little fluff ball of black fur, he looked up at me as if I were the most important thing in his life. In that instant, he made my heart smile and nudged emotions I never thought I would experience again. It only took moments of cuddling and scratching behind his soft, floppy ears for us to bond immediately. And when I took hold of his leash for the first time, I knew my life would never be the same. I would now have a mission, a genuine opportunity to do something so important and special.

Still, I have to admit for a few weeks following Rugby's arrival, I was overwhelmed with worry that I wouldn't be able to handle the responsibility needed to raise and train a puppy. Having been incarcerated most of my life, I became accustomed to a system steeped in the thinking that prison inmates could not be trusted, nor given responsibility to contribute to the welfare of themselves or others. Now, here I was being afforded the opportunity to prove that I could be. Of course, I knew the stakes would be high and challenging; I would need to put my best foot forward and make it happen.

So, with a renewed sense of purpose, I was determined to put every ounce of effort in providing the best of care and training for Rugby, connecting and creating a solid working relationship with him. I'll never forget that first week I started training; I was completely lost. I had zero experience as a trainer, and, of course, Rugby didn't make things any easier for me. There were moments he could be unruly, putting the brakes on when we walked, or refusing to listen. I spent the better part of several weeks building my confidence and establishing leadership with him. However, it wasn't long before everything started coming together. I began to recognize that it was all about being benevolent and having clear communication with him. And following through with what I expected from him, even if it took a thousand times. But mostly, it was about forming a partnership.

Many hours were devoted toward building Rugby's confidence and preparing him to learn all the skills he would need to become a great service dog. As week after week, month after month passed, I was truly delighted to witness his progress. I found myself becoming motivated and inspired to work even harder. Every day promised something new to learn and fascinating to watch as he began to excel and show great potential. Every session of his training gave me an enormous sense of pride.

My relationship with Rugby has taught me many things about myself, about being a better person, and achieving a greater degree of patience, sensitivity, and compassion. Spending a small part of my life with him has helped me to grow and mature emotionally, and to find the inner goodness within myself. But mostly, I was able to make a connection with humanity again. I would have never imagined my life could change so much simply by sharing space and time with a dog. But having done so, I now know the true meaning of unconditional love.

It has been an extraordinary journey. And now, as I prepare to hand over his leash for the last time and say goodbye, I find myself overwhelmed with mixed emotions. It's going to be difficult having to sever the bond I so carefully and harmoniously nurtured during our time together, as well as trying to imagine my life without my "Good Boy," my best friend. But, although it's going to be a painful experience for me, I will also experience an overwhelming sense of pride knowing that every ounce of effort and commitment put into Rugby's training will ultimately yield enormous benefit as he goes on to provide an invaluable service to a disabled adult or child.

Rugby has emerged as a wonderfully gentle and loving service companion who will enrich the quality of someone's life. As much as I am going to miss him, clearly I will enjoy the memories I made with him. I will remember the simple pleasures of his morning greetings—which were always loving and affectionate—, how he would roll over on his back looking to be rubbed on his belly, how he played with me and amused himself with his favorite toys. I will remember how he would fall asleep curled-up like a donut and snore, and how he would look up at me with his soft, brown eyes filled with excitement and joy. But mostly, I will always remember how amazing he is and the love in my heart I've felt for him. I have spent many blessed moments with Rugby, and in doing so, I have been honored and privileged to be a part of something remarkable and noble.

You're my Good Boy, Rugby.

National Education of Assistance Dog Service

When your life revolves around dogs as with Pat Dolowy, every part of your existence is touched by them, even the house where you live.

Thirteen Little Puppies

by Kathy Nimmer

Puppy fur was everywhere! All types, too. Stiff and black, stiff and yellow, wispy and golden, even short and incandescent, not easily attached to an identifiable breed. It was a house of fur and fluff and love.

Thirteen puppies had marched in with wobbly legs and untamed spirits. Thirteen dogs had marched out with strong legs and disciplined spirits. But they left behind their fur, glued onto the underside of the couch cushions, woven into the fibers of the carpet, even mysteriously consorting in air-tossed clumps behind the appliances that stood guard around the kitchen, a room that recorded the click-click-click of puppy toenails, walking to and fro, running and scampering and investigating.

Their personalities were as mixed as their fur. Kelsey, the smooth coated Collie, was gentle and quiet, light on the leash, and a perfect lady. Sergei bounded into the furry home, a donated ten-month-old with no manners, but his intellect saved the day as he caught up to training and then some in record time. Mystic was an independent sort, not seeking attention. The crew of ebullient Golden Retrievers was much different. Mocha, Trina, Hunter, Clover, Krickit, Cinder, and Jordan wiggled and waggled until the fur flew, sweeping away all frowns and frustrations in one mighty swirling golden funnel cloud. Complete with the perpetual question from the public of "what breed is that?" came Charger and Java, Australian Terriers who made up for their modest size with notable brilliance. And, bringing up the rear in the puppy parade was Temple, a dainty Papillion whose obedience couldn't be beat and whose busy nature made him alert to even the tiniest detail in the world around him.

Yes, the fur flew and settled, resting on everything in the home and everyone. It spun spastically while the pups learned to sit and stay. It floated freely while they added to their repertoire of other commands. It danced in the daylight as the dogs reached the age when they were ready to leave the fuzzy home and enter official training, to test their abilities in professions that would ameliorate deafness or mobility challenges or seizure disorders. And, as they pranced into futures whose destinies showcased different skills, the fur wove its way into a lingering tapestry, upon which was written the noble pronouncement, "Puppy Raiser."

Paws With A Cause

Even the heavens wept the day that Emily Overcarsh had to say goodbye.

My Heart for Their Eyes

by Emily Overcarsh

She didn't know it was the last day of her childhood and the first day of the rest of her life. There was no celebration to announce the rite of passage that we had been working toward since the day I met her, small and clueless and ecstatic for the adventure we were about to embark on. The last night we had her, I pulled a comforter and a pillow onto the floor and slept by her kennel with the door open, her body hot on my arm, her breath soft in my hair. When I woke up, her nose was touching mine in sleep, and I wondered if she knew that this was it and was kissing me goodbye.

We took a short walk on the beach where she got to watch the birds swooping nervously over the sand. For the last time we had all eyes on us as we made our way, I with her leash in hand and she with her jacket on proudly, and I tried to imagine the next day, when I would walk through a store or a church or wherever my life took me, and I would fade into the crowd with no dog at my side. It still seems strange to not be reciting commands for every move that I make.

By the time we got to the school, I had abandoned my wad of tissues and was instead crying into her fur, clutching her to me, knowing only minutes stood between us and the inevitable. A shower was passing through, but when we hopped out of the car we took our time saying goodbye. We could care less about getting wet. This was it. This was the moment I had been dreading since the day I realized this dog had become my very heart. I held my heart close, and then I let her go. A fissure rippled through my chest, sending choking, repressed sobs rolling through my lips. She gazed up at me with certainty and confidence, and I knew then that she was ready to be a hero for someone else that deserved her more than I did.

The ceremony was brief. We shook hands with one of the staff members, and then she slipped a new collar onto my dog and I slipped her old one off. She was officially enrolled now. They took her away, and she did not look back. I like to believe that she was excited about this new chapter in her life and that she forgot me swiftly. After all, I am not the one she was meant to love.

Occasionally, I can feel my heart beating across the expanse that separates us, and I know that she is happy. After her training, she will meet her soul mate, her new partner for life, and they will fall in love. She will be the eyes they have gone too long without. She will guide them when they are lost, be a source of comfort by their side when they are scared, and be their best friend when they are lonely. She will give them the unconditional love that I gave her. She is my heart, after all.

Southeastern Guide Dogs, Inc.

Training dogs was a passion for Sarah Broderick. She never could have guessed that a dog she trained would soon be supporting her own special needs.

Luna: My Moon and Stars

by Sarah Broderick

In 2000, when I became the first volunteer for Summit Assistance Dogs in Anacortes, Washington, I started training potential service dogs under the tutelage of the founder. We used positive reinforcement/clicker training methods only, and I quickly became proficient training using the clicker and treats. My first two dogs graduated. The first—a sweet, gentle, calm Golden Retriever named Butter—went to a little girl in Bellingham, Washington, who was born prematurely and as a result had multiple disabilities. The second—a Border Collie mix—was rescued, mud-covered and hungry, from the side of a busy country road by another Summit volunteer. Her name was Marble for her black and white coat, and she went to work as a facility therapy dog at an elementary school in Vancouver, Washington. "Hey, this isn't so hard," I thought. "Soon I'll have many graduates under my belt as a trainer." How naïve I was! It was soon to change… albeit in a most delightful way with a serendipitous turn of events involving my next canine student.

She was a lovely, small, light blonde Golden Retriever name Luna. She came full of antics and her favorite game was lying at the top of the basement stairs and nudging a tennis ball with her nose. The ball would bounce down the stairs and Luna would fly down after it, trying to retrieve it before it hit the basement floor. Then she would grab it, run up the stairs, and start all over again, keeping herself (and me!) amused for ages.

Training her, however, was a completely different matter. No matter what I tried, she simply would not perform tasks with the same zeal she exhibited in her games with the ball. For a while, I wondered whether I had lost my training touch. However, it soon became apparent that it was not my inabilities or her lack of intelligence or ability that was derailing her progress. The fact was that she had absolutely zero motivation. "Hey, Mom," she would look at me as if to say. "Why are you asking me to pick up a pen you dropped when you are perfectly capable of picking it up yourself?" Oh boy… trainer versus logical Golden Retriever resulted in trainer, zero, Golden Retriever, one!

A failure? Well, maybe, in the most rudimentary and shallow definition of the word. But not for me. This dog had a wonderful temperament and as much as she frustrated me with her lack of a work ethic she got under my skin with her gentle, mellow, loving nature. Then we got creative at Summit. How about if we played to her strengths and found a place for her to simply spread her love without any need for complicated tasking? Good idea, we all thought, and when Seattle's Children's Hospital showed interest in acquiring their very own resident facility dog, I was thrilled. What better destiny and future for my lovely Luna than to help children with cancer find some moments of joy and love. Unfortunately, it was not to be. For reasons I have never understood, the pilot program for a resident therapy dog was turned down by the Board of Directors. Once again I despaired about Luna's future as a working dog. It seemed such a waste to simply release her from Summit's training program and adopt her out as a pet, although she was sure to thrive. Something kept pushing me to find her a "job," a special way to share her special soul as a working dog.

It was not long after that my personal life began to unravel. My husband changed jobs and spent half of every week out of town. And then our son was diagnosed as bipolar. He was out of control and the situation at home was filled with stress. I had to be strong. I had to do everything I could to help my son. I had to keep the house going in my husband's absences. As I struggled to maintain control and keep myself together emotionally, I began to realize how much I was depending on Luna. One day, as I sat hugging her and letting my own grief and worry pour out onto her strong shoulders, I realized that I didn't know where I would be emotionally if it wasn't for Luna. She was a huge comfort to me. She was there, always, to let me bury my face in her hair and cry. She demanded little from me and gave so much. Even in my darkest moments, she could bring a softening to my heart and a smile to my lips. The bond that had started when she was just a little blonde puppy had grown into an attachment and dependency that finally showed me the light: Luna and I were *destined* to be together, and more than just as an owner and pet; she was indeed my *assistance* dog already…a *psychiatric* assistance dog.

I too have bipolar disorder and suffer mostly from depression and anxiety manifestations. Luna was there to calm me by laying her soft, golden head on my lap. Thanks to her, I was able to go out more. She went with me everywhere, giving me more confidence to interact with people and even continue to work. Bipolar is one of the "invisible disabilities." Like deafness and often blindness, psychiatric disabilities are not visible to others. So many people assumed that Luna was still in training. Because of the stigmas so often attached to psychiatric disorders, sometimes I found it easier to simply say "yes, she is still training" in order to avoid explaining what she did for me. At other times I would simply say I suffer from panic attacks and leave it at that.

But having Luna there to care for me was just the beginning. I wanted to share her gentle nature with others who would benefit from her therapeutically, just as I do. So together she and I went through the process to become a *certified* therapy dog team. As a certified assistance dog, she didn't need this additional certification to work; it was just one more way she and I could work together and share. As graduates of the Love on a Leash national therapy dog certifying organization, we began our "second career." Together we visited nursing homes and Alzheimer facilities where Luna's gentle love reached many who had so little joy left in their lives. But, what we both enjoy best is participating in the Tales for Tails reading enhancement programs in our community. These programs target reading-challenged second graders. Because these children have difficulty reading, they are often embarrassed enough to avoid it, and without practice they fall even farther behind. Because dogs never judge or criticize but instead give confidence and encouragement, the children feel comfortable reading to them. Luna snuggles up beside them, resting gently as she listens to their young voices struggle to read. She never reacts negatively and her unconditional acceptance, affection, and love encourage them to keep reading. At times I "interpret" for her, telling the children how much she is enjoying listening, and the looks of pride and delight on their faces are enough for us both to know how much we are helping.

Some time ago a regional artist offered to paint portraits of Summit dogs as part of a fundraiser. Eagerly I stepped forward and ordered one of my dear Luna. When it came time for a title for the portrait I didn't hesitate. "Luna… my moon and stars," I said. Because she is that and more. She means everything to me, and I count my lucky stars to have her in my life.

Summit Assistance Dogs

Chris Muldoon, a Scot who lives in Australia, knows a thing or two about training guide dogs. However, he meets his match with Jarvis.

Jarvis the Golf Pro

by Chris Muldoon

The moment I looked into the dog run and saw Jarvis, I knew things were not going to go well. He sat in the yard all by himself while all the other dogs were playing. When I looked in, he looked out, and a clear understanding about rights of entry was established: I could come in if he was okay about it. There would be days of negotiation and some of virtual siege, but on others he would be at ease.

A Labrador Retriever by birthright but a Great Dane in mentality and size, Jarvis's body was a couple of sizes too big for him. He, by sheer power to weight ratios and application of force against force, could turn a simple training walk under harness into the famous Iditarod cross-country sledge pull. On a wet day a Guide Dog Cadet Instructor such as myself could come back to the office with the left arm that holds the harness noticeably longer and lacking in function for the remainder of the day.

This pitting of dog against human was his mantra, and the successes of numerous victories over me were sweet nectar to be savored. It was by definition, fun to run me ragged and watch my frustration: a blissful interlude to see me whipped around a corner like a water skiing champion on a barefoot slalom or glorious ecstasy to crash me into every overhanging tree and bush that, with a slight step to the left, might have been avoided.

The Scot in me came out with the resolution of a national heritage that has seen us thumped by everyone who has visited our country since the Roman occupation. I gritted my teeth and set about the challenge. I told my boss John that we would work it out, learn each other's tolerances and grow into a team. John could obviously see the humor in this ludicrous belief and left me to my task of turning Jarvis into a guide dog.

Our favorite game was a variation on the popular dance hall song "The Hokey Pokey." When approaching a curb, a perfect guide dog will stop at the curb, alerting the handler to the presence of the road and a step. For Jarvis, this action was an opportunity to play mind games and show that he made the decisions in this team. We would carefully approach a curb, and I would warn Jarvis I would not accept errors. "Careful, Jarvis, up to the curb. There's a good lad." Jarvis would draw me into the game by stepping cleanly up to the curb with a great demonstration of his alleged concern about not stepping over. Just when he knew I was about to say "good boy," he would, while looking straight up at me, place his right front foot squarely into the road. "NO! Bad boy, don't do that," I would growl at him. For emphasis and to demonstrate how important it was to get this right, I would walk back five paces, turn him around and approach the curb again. On the second attempt, perfection personified, like there had never been a problem. Merrily we would continue along the street until the next intersection. As we stood perfectly aligned with curb and footpath, I felt we had connected. A millisecond before I gave Jarvis his praise he would, with meticulous cruelty, look up at me and place his left foot in the road. And so the Hokey Pokey went all round the streets of North Balwyn to the undying mirth of other instructors. With head bowed in shame I watched as they would come out on breaks to see Jarvis perform his dance with me on the curbs. Some days Jarvis got sick of the game and for variation would launch *both* feet onto the road as the ultimate defiance: "I'm gonna do it and you try and stop me."

The end for Jarvis as a guide dog came about halfway through his training, even though we were still working out the dance steps to the Hokey Pokey.

Part of the guide dog's training involves traveling on public transport. To everyone's amazement, including my own, Jarvis excelled in this task. He found the door of the bus easily, took the necessary care to allow me to get on safely, and found me a seat every time with flawless determination. I was so impressed with Jarvis that I would tack onto other instructors' travel sessions on buses, showing them how good he was in negotiating public transport and how by my perseverance and support the big fellow was now on track for guide dog duties.

One fateful day I was working with my colleague Pete and his dog Banjo, traveling the local Kew area bus route. We got on with no incident, Jarvis doing his best impression of a guide dog. I was watching the little Asian driver's face in his rearview mirror, and it was clear that he didn't know quite what to make of this big dog. In fact, the more he was watching in his rearview mirror the less he concentrated on the road ahead, and we squealed around some of the more sedately driven corners in Kew. "He doesn't like dogs," said Pete. "He was really jumpy yesterday too."

"Oh good," I said. "Then Jarvis is all he needs to contend with to compound his fears." Dogs have an uncanny way of assessing fear, and Jarvis had the poor little driver summed up in a flash.

I never noticed it as we sped along, but another factor was looming on the horizon, one that was to put the icing on the cake. A young lad had gotten on the bus with a golf bag. As there is a local golf course nearby there was nothing unusual about this. He sat directly opposite Jarvis and me. The lad placed the bag full of clubs in front of his feet—upright so the tops of the clubs were near his head—and began to be distracted by events outside the window. At my feet where Jarvis was sitting there began a low rumbling, like the bus was going over corrugated iron. When I looked down Jarvis's hackles were fully erect and he had riveted his gaze onto the golf bag. I looked across and saw to my horror the source of his aggression. In the golf bag were a number of clubs with covers on them. The club covers were in the form of cute cartoon characters with fluffy heads and little arms. As the dog began to audibly growl, the driver unconsciously applied more throttle to the already heaving bus, which in turn, made the little heads of the clubs in the bag dance a jeering tarantella in front of poor Jarvis who was giving them his best "stop staring at me" look.

The faster we went the more the heads danced, and the more Jarvis felt he was losing control—and the more I knew I didn't have any. I saw the headlines "Guide Dog Eats Golf Bag on Bus" and my career slipping away from me. Jarvis sat bolt upright and gave the most thunderous bark at the laughing, bobbing heads in the golf bag. Their little fluffy tops and arms goaded him as we tumbled around while the driver tried to get further away from the problem by driving faster, creating more problems as the clubs began to lift out of the bag. This seemed to Jarvis an overt attempt to have a go at him as they were now suddenly coming for him. Like Custer at Little Big Horn he sounded the charge in a baleful wolf-like howl and stood to his full height with me on the end trying for all I was worth to hold him back.

The lad took this look and stance as an act of aggression from Jarvis personally and attempted to cower behind the bag, shoving it further away from him—and closer to the now furious Jarvis.

Confucius says if mad dog eats all the fluffy heads of the golf clubs then the next thing that looks a bit like a fluffy head in a golf bag is going to be eaten too, and that was the person driving the bus. He was jabbering and gesticulating wildly, which did nothing for his control of the vehicle or the situation in general.

We ground to a begrudging halt at the next stop, and Jarvis and I were bundled off the vehicle. All the time Jarvis was trying to get at the little heads, baying and barking at them like a drunk in the pub who wants to fight the bar. With the little Asian driver still gesticulating wildly and the heads in the golf bag waving goodbye and my colleague Pete still on board, I watched any chance of Jarvis becoming a guide dog roll away with the bus like the tears of laughter streaming down Pete's face.

Guide Dogs Victoria

Puppy raisers don't always get the opportunity that Joan O'Neill had to see one of her puppies all grown up and on the job. Multiply that excitement by a trip to Spain, and the answer is pure magic.

Changed Lives

by Joan O'Neill

There is a cathedral on a hill outside the walled city of Avila, northwest of Madrid. Next to the cathedral is a café with expansive views of the city and surrounding area. It is at that café where Isidro, a middle-aged Spanish gentleman, meets his friends for coffee each morning after hiking up the hill from town. He navigates the narrow city streets and rugged dirt path with his Leader Dog, Buddy, a small yellow Lab.

We raised Buddy for the Leader Dog School for the Blind in Rochester, Michigan. He came home with us when he was just eight weeks old. We loved and nurtured him for the first year of his life and returned him to the school when he was old enough to learn how to guide someone who was visually impaired. That someone turned out to be Isidro, a man with four children who lost his sight due to a genetic illness he didn't know he had until he was in his forties.

Isidro invited our family to visit him in Spain in a Christmas letter, in which he instructed our children, Stacey and Alexei, to "tell your parents to come and see the people who love you and want to thank you." Pat and I had never been to Spain and were excited by the opportunity to meet Isidro. And we felt lucky that our kids would get to see Buddy at work. I took Spanish classes in preparation for the trip, and we boarded a plane eight months later.

Isidro and his wife were the perfect hosts, taking us to their weekend home in an ancient village set in the mountains and to a festival that lasted late into the night. Isidro escorted us to Segovia, a nearby city famous for its Roman aquaducts, and showed us around Avila. Prior to losing his sight, Isidro owned a restaurant, so he knew many people in town. We often stopped on a street corner while he chatted with a friend or neighbor and introduced us as "Buddy's American friends." It became obvious to us that the two of them got around. Pat called Isidro's companion "Buddy the Bar Hound" because when he walked past the open door of a bar or restaurant, Buddy would glance in to see if Isidro's friends were inside.

We have many fond memories from our visit, but the one that will stay with me forever was when Isidro took us to that special spot on top of the hill and showed us the path that led from the edge of town to his meeting spot at the café. At that moment, standing next to Isidro on that hill under the hot summer sun, I understood the freedom that Buddy provided for this sweet, kind man. For without Buddy, it would be nearly impossible for Isidro to hike that mountain trail, to sit with his friends at the café and talk about plans for the day, to be a part of the community where he had grown up.

Perhaps the reason this was such a dramatic revelation for me was that I had never known anyone visually impaired until I met Isidro. Our puppy-raising adventures stemmed from a desire to find a fun family-oriented community service project for our two children. I never expected it to become such a big part of our lives. Lynn and Tom, our puppy counselors, organized monthly events in Illinois and Indiana designed to socialize our puppies and get them used to unusual environments. We experienced a simulated flight hosted by American Airlines at O'Hare airport, visited the Field Museum in Chicago, went Christmas shopping at a mall, toured a fire station, and attended a minor league baseball game. In between events, we took Buddy to art fairs and concerts and fireworks. And he ran errands with us to the bank, post office and pharmacy, becoming more and more confident with each new experience.

After Buddy left for Spain, we raised three more dogs for the Leader Dog School—two handsome German Shepherds and an adorable Golden Retriever. With each puppy, we looked for novel situations to test their adaptability. Kendall, the Golden, had the greatest adventure of all, riding a gondola in Colorado. But we learned that for puppies, there is novelty in everyday situations as well. I often thought about what a blind woman told us when we first got Buddy: "I once had a guide dog that refused to leave the hotel where I was speaking because it was pouring outside." After hearing that, I introduced Buddy to water in my shower and put on my rain jacket to walk him around the block in thunderstorms. And I sought out other potential obstacles, such as bridges, train tracks, and scaffolding, which our puppy might confront later in life.

Through the years, I have often been asked, "How can you give him up?" And each time I tell the inquirer about visiting Buddy and Isidro, standing on that special hilltop in Avila, looking down on the path that they traverse together. I tell them how at that very moment I realized that raising a Leader Dog puppy is about giving a very precious gift to another person. Some people get that, but to be honest, not everyone does. But those that do nod with a knowing smile, for they understand how great it makes me feel.

Leader Dogs for the Blind

Chapter 2

And Then

The Partnership Begins

Paw Prints of Wisdom

"I began working with my dog when I noticed he was actually trying to help me. He loves to learn, so it was a pleasure for both of us. He really knew what he was doing; wish I could say the same for me!"

—Kay Bennett,
handler of an owner-trained service dog

"The most rewarding part of working with dogs is seeing the independence and quality of life they offer clients. The clients I work with come alive again, have access to their community, and have confidence in their mobility—life changing experiences."

—Kim Ryan,
guide dog mobility instructor, Royal Guide Dogs, Tasmania

Some disabilities make communication difficult or impossible. Sixteen-year-old Jake Jones, who has Cerebral Palsy and a seizure disorder, finds his voice in this poem as he speaks to his service dog Bodie.

Ghost Chaser

by Kathy Nimmer

Can't imagine life without you now.
Never knew it could be this way.
Found strength that I didn't believe existed.
It's all about purpose, a reason for being here on this earth.

Never knew it could be this way.
Me, set free from the confines of body and mind.
It's all about purpose, a reason for being here on this earth.
It's all about how you help me, how you fill my empty places.

Me, set free from the confines of body and mind,
Both tainted irrevocably by mistakes doctors made.
It's all about how you help me, how you fill my empty places
And chase away the ghosts of malpractice that haunt what could have been.

Both tainted irrevocably by mistakes doctors made,
My body rebels often, my mind fails to spread its wings
And chase away the ghosts of malpractice that haunt what could have been,
But you are my ghost chaser, and I need no other.

My body rebels often, my mind fails to spread its wings,
And I am bound by limitations that shout "nothingness" in hideous shrieks.
But you are my ghost chaser, and I need no other.
The shouts have become whispers, and now silence, with you at my side.

And I am bound by limitations that shout "nothingness" in hideous shrieks,
But we defy that chorus and say, "Life is good."
The shouts have become whispers, and now silence, with you at my side.
So much what I needed and didn't know I could have.

But we defy that chorus and say, "Life is good,"
Each and every time pity paints isolating fences that lock me out.
So much what I needed and didn't know I could have:
That's you, my precious friend, that's you.

Each and every time pity paints isolating fences that lock me out,
You lay your gentle head upon my shriveled lap.
That's you, my precious friend, that's you,
Looking up at me, absorbing and reflecting my love, my hero.

St. Francis of Assisi Service Dog Center

Stacy Fry's diary covers the days leading to her five-year-old daughter Ehlena's union with her service dog.

Hope for Independence: A Diary Excerpt

by Stacy Fry

September 30, 2009

With every up there is a down I guess. I got an email today to call Karen, the founder of the training center. The matches are coming out on Friday, and she wanted to pre-warn me. When we filled out our match form for the dog I stated very blatantly that my family did not like the Poodle mixes. Karen knew that we would be having a reporter there when we opened up the "Dear Ehlena letter" from the dog introducing itself. She wanted me to know that Jeremy, the trainer and dog match-maker, is agonizing over our match. Karen told me that the "perfect" dog for Ehlena was indeed a Poodle mix, and that it was really tearing Jeremy up because he knew that that is exactly what we didn't want. I will not be shy in saying that I am devastated. There is no other word to describe how I feel. She could not share which Poodle mix we were getting but didn't want me to have a bad reaction in front of the reporter. I am very disappointed, but we did always say we wanted the *best* dog for her, so I will have to put my big girl pants on now and have faith that this will be the perfect dog for our family and for Ehlena. In every aspect of Ehlena's life, and my boys for that matter, I have had to learn that I do not have full control, that there is a higher power up there. Still, that is hard to digest and scares me to death.

October 2, 10 pm

"Dear Ehlena,

Hey Ehlena. My name is Wonder because I am Wonder the Wonder Dog! And also, yes, I do wonder a lot, like I have been wondering who my new best buddy is, and now I know it is you! How cool is that?! It does one good to have the name Wonder. Like sometimes, "Isn't that dog WONDERful?" LOL. I have one up on all the other dogs. I feel like I know you because my friend Baloo filled me in about you and your whole family and how all of you need me, even your brothers. How cool is that to be needed by more than one kid? I must be special like my name! I was in the first Goldendoodle litter born at 4 Paws. We were the litter of Hope. We all have cool names like Treasure, because he is a treasure, and Promise, because he promises to be the best service dog ever. My birthday is 4-27-2007, and my Mom is MJ and my Dad is Hobo! Well friend, I so can't wait to be your best, best, best friend.

Love, hugs, and Kisses,

Wonder the Wonder Dog!"

So there he is, the newest member of our family. Part of me is still disappointed, but I am sure that will soon fade.

October 3

Wonder is a hard name for Ehlena to get but we are working on it. I will ask her the name and when she cannot remember I simply state, "I *Wonder* what your dog's name is?" Slowly but surely she is starting to pick it up. I also put a picture on our kitchen table to help us make him feel like a part of the family. Everyone thinks he looks like a wonderful dog. His hairy look is growing on us, as it is definitely not something we are used to.

I guess working so hard to raise the money for the dog I never anticipated being disappointed about the dog match. I was told, however, that this dog has been doing mobility work for a year already, and that is reassuring. I am excited about the fact that he will not shed and is hypoallergenic. The more I look at his face the better I feel about it. I also feel it is fitting for our dog to have come from the litter of *Hope*. It is interesting the small things that bring comfort, helping things to seem like the puzzle is coming together.

So I guess the moral of the story is I have to have faith that Wonder is *our* hope.

October 12

I can't believe we are almost there! It has been such a long journey that it was starting to feel like the day we would meet her service dog would never come, that it was just a someday. After fundraising for six months and waiting another five, that someday is TOMORROW! We are all so excited and Ehlena keeps asking when we are going to meet him. We are leaving after school.

October 13, 2009

When we walked in the door of the training facility Ehlena, the little lady who just months prior was scared to death of dogs, kept asking, "Where is my Wonder?" The trainers brought the dogs out one-by-one to meet the kids. Ehlena was low on patience but as cute as can be, looking around and asking, "When am I going to meet *my* dog?" The fourth dog was him, this huge, fluffy ball of, well, hair.

Ehlena was in her wheelchair and it seemed as though she was going to jump out of her seat with excitement. She could not hold still. She was a little nervous at his size for a few seconds, but then it was all love.

Ehlena kept asking "Can we keep him, can we take him back to the hotel with us?" "Yes, he is your dog," they responded. She finally has her dog.

All I could think was, *Point made, God*. All disappointment that may have loomed dissipated. I think we have the coolest dog, fur and all.

The kids were overjoyed to meet him and I think Wonder also relished all the hugs, kisses, and treats that his new family bestowed upon him. He was very well behaved, and everyone thought he was just, well…Wonder-full! He settled in like he belonged with Ehlena, like this match was meant to be.

So as one journey ends another begins. Our journey to independence has now become a Wonder-filled journey of Hope.

4 Paws for Ability

Alysia Wells writes from the point of view of her guide dog Heidi in this story, showing what the beginning of a new partnership might be like from the dog's perspective.

First Lady: Heidi's Story

by Alysia Wells

Alyse is excited! She is calling her brother from the Leader Dog School, where she is in class. It is a clear, glorious, early spring day in Michigan. "I just got my new dog today," Alyse gushes to her older brother. "Yes, she is a beautiful German Shepherd." As you can imagine, my Shepherd ears perk up. After her call, Alyse turns and reaches out for me. "Come, Heidi, it's time for our meeting." I obey, passively; I'm quiet and demure now because I think my trainer, Dan, has abandoned me. We have worked together for months and I've been a quick learner, so eager to please him and hear his praise as we walked, stopped at curbs, crossed streets, maneuvered around obstacles, and found different locations. I basked in his enthusiasm about my performance; I'd do anything for him, anything!

Yesterday, he brought me to Alyse, here in the dorm room, telling me to stay by her. "Good girl," he reassured me and then disappeared unceremoniously. Alyse was sitting on the floor. Her long, auburn hair fell forward as she greeted me, petting my sleek head. "Good girl, Heidi," she chirped. "Sit! Let's get to know each other." I sat, but at some distance from her. I was facing the room door, looking longingly for Dan. Alyse held my leash; she had it when Dan escorted me here and fastened it to my collar. Alyse smiled and cooed to me. "Oh, Heidi, this is so exciting! I've been looking forward to this day for a long time and now you have come, just for me!" She moved closer to embrace me, and I stiffened a little bit. She smelled good, like daisies in a field, and her voice was lilting and soothing, but where was Dan, my buddy? Dan was tough and strong, and I knew what he expected; this young lady seemed soft.

Now we exit the room and join other people and dogs for some kind of powwow. Hey, here's Hobo, King, and Molly! Strange humans are corralling them with leashes like mine, one person to one dog. But it's chaos. Alyse moves toward someone she calls Brian. "I have Heidi," she announces. "This is Hobo," Brian says. "Oh, what a cute name," Alyse exclaims. Hobo, my pal in training, glares at me, shunning the idea of cute. He stretches dramatically and gazes up at his tall human companion. Our eyes are full of questions. Every person takes a seat, and every dog is instructed to rest at the person's feet.

Dan enters the room, and my heart skips a beat. I'm suddenly up, bounding to him, dragging my leash, tail waving, dancing with delight. He's back for me and the others—but wait, they're all still sitting with their humans, regarding me with chagrin. "Alyse, call your dog," Dan advises firmly, not looking at me. "Heidi, come." She is tentative; I hesitate. "Call her like you mean it," he insists. "Heidi, come!" Now her voice is authoritative. Dan remains still, dismissive. I slink to Alyse, regretfully, hurt and embarrassed. "Good girl," Alyse encourages, and only then Dan looks at me kind of like he used to and echoes, "Good girl." Then I notice tears emerging in Alyse's eyes; she brushes them away, impatiently. We experience this strange unease together, lost in a new time and space.

Yes, dogs have emotions. And I'm too smart for my own good, because I can't express myself in words. I sense things and vocalize, but I can't laugh or cry. This moment is confusing. Dan speaks confidently to all of us, about all of us, about the immediate days to come and days in the future away from the school. A new reality begins to register with me. Dan is transferring me to this other person who admits that I am her very first dog and who also soon admits bewilderment and some disappointment as she cries, "Heidi doesn't like me!" More tears spill quietly from her eyes. "Oh, she will," Dan states calmly.

The next few weeks are hectic and tumultuous with activity, learning more about being a guide dog, experiencing many ups and downs. I practice leading Alyse in a straight line, trying to ignore distractions as I focus on my job, responding to many requests and commands. I am trained to be sensitive and obedient, but sometimes I resort to intelligent disobedience if I am told to do something which is incorrect in the current situation. If we are walking along and I see a car pulling out of a driveway in front of us, I must stop, with absolute conviction, until the path is clear.

Suddenly, the exhausting but safe practice period and training is over. It's time to leave. Alyse and I board a plane. We are traveling into a new life, unknown to me. In her fancy journal, Alyse writes that we are like uncertain actors in a developing drama of partnership. I'm just scared. She's in college, and I'm just growing out of puppyhood. I'm so full of nervous anticipation (I don't know how I let this happen!), I poop in the airport! I've never done this before in public! I am a proud dog, well trained, and this is mortifying! Fortunately, Alyse's dad, who has come to pick us up, defuses the moment and acts quickly to clean up the mess. "We just won't tell your mother," he jokes.

It is noisy as we leave the airport and climb into a silver car. Alyse seems happy now, recovering from the unmentionable incident. Her pretty mother turns around to check me out in the back seat where I sit straight and alert. "She is a beauty, Alyse, but so big!" she regards me cautiously, as Alyse's dad laughs easily.

When we arrive at the place they call home, he pats me gently on the head and ruffles my immaculate fur. Something about his voice, his face, his hands—

he isn't Dan, but something about this guy is reassuring. Alyse assumes responsibility then, showing me around the house and the yard. I have a place to be, a bed, food and water bowls just for me.

Soon, I am wearing the harness, leading Alyse down neighborhood sidewalks, crossing streets, entering a grocery store. Alyse laughs often, and I don't see any more tears. Besides my acute senses of eyesight, hearing, and smell, I am surprised by a new sense of purpose. My trainer, Dan, never needed protection, but Alyse is more vulnerable. At school, Dan criticized her for some unconvincing interaction with me and I was tempted to resist and rebel. But now as she gets stronger, I change too. This isn't a game or an exercise. She depends on me for real; I can tell she doesn't know about this flight of steps and stops when I do to absorb the information. She is serious about me as an essential partner in her independent adult life. Soon, our adventures will multiply as Alyse moves into her own apartment and we explore the world together. I am her first lady, and she is most certainly mine.

Leader Dogs for the Blind

Tragedy almost takes the life of Ricky Jones as he crosses a street with his white cane. Less than a year later comes his unforgettable first training walk with Pearson.

First Walk

by Kathy Nimmer

The harness handle rattles in his grasp. Tears well in the corners of his eyes. The first walk with a guide dog, ever. "What will it be like?" He hears the reassuring voice of his trainer, but his mind flickers backward in time.

Less than a year ago, it had happened. He was hit by a car while crossing a street with his white cane. Severe injuries left scars, none deeper than those gouged into his confidence. He had become afraid of even the sound of traffic, let alone the prospect of walking beside it or crossing in front of it.

Now, he stands beside a congested urban road with countless cars rushing past him and a still unfamiliar dog panting at the end of the harness handle. He speaks in a whisper. "Pearson, forward." The dog shifts in slight acknowledgement but doesn't step ahead.

"Louder, Ricky."

"Pearson, forward." His voice cracks but is convincing enough for the black Lab to believe the intent. The dog steps ahead. Ricky follows. His fingers clinch spasmodically on the leather handle. The trainer walks two steps behind Ricky and Pearson, her leash securely fastened to the dog's collar as is customary for first-time outings.

A delivery truck speeds past. Ricky flinches. A police car flies by with siren screaming. Ricky gasps. Two convertibles with roofs down roar by in tandem, the heavy throb of rap music vibrating the sidewalk below his shuffling feet. Ricky closes his eyes, wrestling with memories once more.

It had been October the previous year when the accident happened. The driver was fully at fault, but the consequences were Ricky's to bear. Thrown twenty yards into a pile of torn flesh and broken bones, Ricky had wondered what it would ever take to feel whole again.

Pearson stops. Ricky's foot moves forward to detect the edge of the curb. He finds it instantly. "Good boy, Pearson." His grip relaxes minutely. "Pearson, left." Ricky steps back. The dog pivots. They resume their journey.

"You're doing well." The trainer is calm. "Keep it up."

Three more curbs. Three more turns. Dozens more motors and brakes and screeching tires and pounding drumbeats. Ricky's mind stays in the present. His pace increases. Shuffles are replaced by steady, even steps. Fingers ease into a gentle, rounded curve around the harness handle. Pearson listens astutely to

Ricky's voice which no longer shakes or cracks. Ricky notices nothing.

"We're here." The trainer places a hand on Ricky's shoulder. "We're back to where we started."

Ricky tenses as a car's horn sounds. A warm, soft weight pushes against Ricky's leg. Back to where they started today, but not back to where it all started last October. Ricky pets the broad head of the black Lab, beginning to realize that he has just navigated a busy city route safely with his new guide for the first time. As traffic speeds by, he begins to smile.

"Ricky, may I tell you something?"

The trainer's voice erases Ricky's smile. He is sure he is about to receive a reprimand, a critique, a blow as staggering as that given by the reckless car last October.

"Ricky, for the last two blocks,… Ricky…?"

He curls inward, protecting himself against her words as he could not protect himself against the car that had stolen his independence and security.

"…Ricky, you were doing it without me. Ricky, I unhooked my leash. It was just you and Pearson. You made it, the two of you. You made it."

Guiding Eyes for the Blind

Sophie seems less suited to service work than any other dog in the class. Then, Wendy Enos figures out the real issue.

Service Dog In Training

by Wendy Enos

"Put all your dogs on a down stay, walk to this side of the room, and call them to come one by one."

"Oh, please," I prayed silently, plodding to the far end of the room, "let her do it right this time!" Already, I was cringing at the thought of yet again being humiliated by my dog.

Keeping focused on a rugged service dog training program, in which Sophie and I trained together as a team, was a lot to ask of a flighty, fourteen-month-old Golden Retriever with the attention span and unlimited energy of a toddler in the throes of a sugar rush.

Sophie fidgeted nonstop while the other three dogs in the class sat quietly on the other side of the room. A classmate successfully called his dog and returned to the table. So did another. Sophie was next. It was just as I feared. The instant her name was called, she broke her stay, bounded over with a wagging tail to the black Boxador next to her, offered up a few vivacious licks, and took off the other way when she saw me coming.

She ducked under the table to roll around with the Dal-Pointer and flirt with the Flat-Coated Retriever on the end while I, with a crimson-flushed face, tracked her down and brought this screwball back under control.

"We'll never make it,“ I told myself with absolute certainty. Who was I trying to kid? Sophie would never be service dog material. At the end of every class, I half-expected to be kept after school to be formally dismissed from the program.

Graduates of the program offered as much encouragement as they could. "She's not a robot, she's a dog. She's going to do dog things.“ But that didn't help my morale any when, at every dog event we attended, Sophie acted as though I had laced her kibble with a double shot of espresso.

"Here it comes," I worried as our trainers let us know one Saturday that they had formed a new beginners' class and were advancing our class to the next level. "At best, I'll be kept back with the beginners…but I doubt it. This is where we'll be pink-slipped and sent packing."

Amazingly, we weren't dismissed at all. Instead, one of our trainers kindly but honestly informed me, "The only problem with Sophie is you." My anxiety, impatience, frustration, and outright anger were traveling right down the leash into this ordinarily free-spirited and happy-go-lucky Golden puppy. (Goldens are puppies till they're two years old, or three, or maybe four.) The trainers were right. When

I settled down, began acting human, and took a close look at Sophie's very heart and soul, something amazing happened: we enjoyed a bond like we had never really known before. She began understanding me, and I her. A special kind of love was born.

Does this mean the rest of the training was a breeze? Hardly! It was a gradual change. Sophie still had a lot of maturing to do and, even at nearly fifty years old, so did I. But now we were growing up together. I halted the unreasonable demands and expectations and allowed Sophie to be who she was. And she surprised me!

As advanced class neared its end and our lead trainer began discussing "The Test," all my fear and anxiety burst forth, causing her to declare, "If I could give Sophie the certification test without you around, I would." Sophie was fine; I was a wreck!

Then our trainer proposed a plan. The president of the organization was in town and, as long as she was here anyway, we'd arrange a mock test…"just to see how far you can go with it and find out what else you need to work on. It won't count."

I could do that; it was a great idea. The first third of the test was done at home and, though Sophie had a few little distractions, she did very well. Next, on a walkabout through the neighborhood, she did even better, stopping only to wildly wag her tail at the honking goose our neighbors were keeping in their back yard.

Then... (insert *Dragnet* theme here) ...Wal-Mart! Sophie was always great in public; I hadn't any worries there, even when children came up to her to pet her and fawn over her. She loved children and just ate that up!

Our lead trainer met us at an in-store restaurant to discuss "The Test." Sophie had done well, and we went over the trivialities of the points she had taken off.

"I have to admit something to you," she told me. "This wasn't a mock test. It was real."

My heart fell. "You said it wouldn't count!"

"It wouldn't have, if she didn't pass." She had to tell me twice. "She passed."

The trainers and testers laid the lovely turquoise cape over Sophie's back and pronounced her "CERTIFIED" as tears welled up in my eyes. My little fruitcake had blossomed into the protector, rescuer, companion, and helper she was born to be.

I looked into her eyes and could barely see them because of the tears in mine. Her eyes danced as her face gave off a special kind of glow. We did it! She made it! I was proud of her, and life just couldn't get any better than that!

Happy Tails Service Dogs, Inc.

Kelly Randall couldn't wait to introduce her new emergency medical alert/seizure alert dog to her grandmother whose reaction is immortalized in this poem.

From A Grandmother

by Kathy Nimmer

I held you when you were a baby,
Wishing endless joy for a granddaughter
Who was as precious as a flawless diamond,
And the eternal light of my life.

I watched you grow up,
Struggling with such medical nightmares,
Wishing for a normal life
That I would have sold my soul to give to you.

You became a woman, so strong,
But still battling the demons of illness,
Pinning you down from becoming all
That you would have dreamed of being.

Then you spoke of a companion,
A four-legged friend to walk beside you,
Someone who could do for you what I could not,
Someone else for you to love.

I prayed and waited and watched,
And when you stood again in my doorway
With the velvet black coat of your new friend
Shimmering in the glow of the lamp,

I was grateful, so grateful,
For my beautiful granddaughter
Now stood taller and prouder than before
With a partner to love forever.

My days became fewer,
Vicious cancer draining away my strength.
But oh the cherished moments when my suffering
Was cloaked by the nuzzle of your friend's cold wet nose,
Pressed into my shriveled old palm.

Time was not my ally,
As it shrank into a pinprick of light
In a midnight black sky,
Then extinguished altogether.

I slipped away from this world,
Sad to leave the granddaughter I loved,
But at peace to know
That cold wet nose would be
Pressing into your strong, young hand Tomorrow.

Great Plains Assistance Dogs Foundation, Inc.

Returning to Poland from America with her first guide dog, Malgorzata (Maggie) Galbarczyk did not know what to expect.

Breaking the Ice

by Malgorzata (Maggie) Galbarczyk

Am I going to be accepted with my guide dog in shops, restaurants, hospitals, university, churches, and other public places? How soon am I going to receive help if I happen to experience some difficulties with my new dog? In what way will my family, friends, teachers, and people who I simply meet on the streets react to my new way of traveling? Is my guide dog going to manage to cope with such a different environment from the one he was trained in? All of these questions were making me very anxious in September 2005, when I was getting ready to go back from the United States—where my first guide dog, Ingmar, was born and trained—to Poland, where I live.

Since Ingmar is one of the very few guide dogs in Poland, initially the local community was completely unfamiliar with the concept of the blind person traveling with the help of the four-legged companion. In the beginning I experienced many difficulties trying to access public places and use public transportation. Occasionally, due to problems with access, I even had to resign from some activities or completely alter my plans. Furthermore, as I was no longer using a white cane, many people did not view me as a blind person, which caused many potentially dangerous situations and misunderstandings. Over the first couple of months I had to constantly explain to many different people what the role of my dog was, in what ways he was helping me, why he shouldn't be patted, and so on.

Very helpful to me and our transition to acceptance was the fact that Ingmar was shown a couple of times on national TV and a few articles about him were published in the local press. Yet the most powerful tool that allowed me to promote the positive image of the guide dog in my local community was Ingmar's irresistible charm and the fantastic way in which he always performs his work. Fortunately—still a long time before the access law for service dogs will be established in Poland—people in my neighborhood warmed toward Ingmar, and my life has changed completely.

Now Ingmar is the most popular dog in Lublin, the town where I live. By many people he is treated as a true hero. Still, for me the most rewarding thing of all is the fact that a few of my friends who've had a chance to observe how much my everyday life has improved thanks to Ingmar have decided to apply for guide dogs themselves. It is my hope that now more and more people in Poland will have a chance to have service dogs and that, thanks to the adventures that I have had with Ingmar to pave the way before them, their lives will be at least a little bit easier.

Guiding Eyes for the Blind

Psychiatric service dogs can stabilize the lives of individuals with mental illness. Katherine Walters knows this firsthand.

Canine Relief

by Katherine Walters

The term psychiatric service dog was not something anyone in my area knew. However, after a psychotic break and the onset of paranoid schizophrenia left me disabled, the thought of a service dog gave me much needed hope.

My fiancé provided me with information on psychiatric service dogs while I was staying in the hospital, adjusting to my new medication. I was thrilled to learn that dogs could be trained to help people with all sorts of mental illnesses. Dogs for people with schizophrenia could be used for reality testing—proving that a hallucination or delusion is not real. A dog would also be able to help me with my anxiety about being in public. Since the start of my illness, I had begun to isolate myself at home almost constantly. Hopeful that a service dog would help me, I presented the information to my psychiatrist. Thankfully, she thought it would be a great idea and gave me her support.

Unlike guide dogs and many other types of service dogs, there are no schools that raise and train psychiatric service dogs. That meant that I would have to find a trainer that could train a dog I already owned. Luckily, I did have a dog that I felt would be a perfect candidate for the job. Within a week I located a nearby trainer. I got up the guts to email him, asking if he would be willing to help me train my dog, Sheriff. It took a few weeks, but we worked out the details and decided that my dog could be trained.

The trainer, Kevin, was an animal control officer in my city. He arranged for me to begin lessons at Animal Control. I fretted over having to get out into public and meet someone new but decided that this was an opportunity I did not want to miss. Kevin also mentioned that I could possibly begin volunteering at Animal Control, allowing me to spend time with animals. This encouraged me because I had previously been a dog trainer before I found that I could no longer work with my illness.

Sheriff's training began and so did my volunteering. Since I was so concerned about being in public, Kevin decided that we could train Sheriff to "cover" me. If someone approached that made me tense, Sheriff would move in front of me and physically block the person from getting too close. Sheriff became a natural at this, easily sensing when I was anxious. He also began accompanying me to Animal Control as I volunteered, allowing me to do so with considerably less anxiety.

Within three weeks, Kevin decided that it was time for our first outing in public: the mall. I was extremely nervous. I hadn't been to the mall since before I became ill. It was a long stretch from a fenced-in training yard to a crowded mall with lots of sights and sounds. Nevertheless, we went and the trip was a success. Sheriff was learning quickly and his presence was allowing me to become social again. Each week we ventured to the mall, and each week it became easier. I began to take trips to the grocery store and to the local book store. Sheriff went with me to therapy sessions and even on a vacation to the St. Louis Zoo.

Whenever I become nervous around people, Sheriff is there to remind me that I am not in danger and to stand in front of me, making sure that I always have enough personal space to be comfortable. Whenever I think I am hallucinating, I simply look at my dog and allow him to show me that he does not see or hear what I do. Whenever I have a panic attack or become paranoid, Sheriff helps me redirect my thoughts by helping me perform grounding techniques.

Sheriff graduated and became a real service dog after only six weeks of training. Nearly a year later, I have returned to college full-time and have begun to become more productive. He has given me the confidence to consider working again once I graduate. For now, with him by my side, we pursue volunteer opportunities to help other animals, help other dog owners train their pets, and advocate for those with psychiatric disabilities or service dogs. I owe so much of my current independence to Sheriff, and to Kevin for not judging me because of my diagnosis and helping me train the most amazing dog I have ever had the privilege of calling my companion.

Owner-Trained Dog

Joe Mauk welcomed Roxanne into his world as a trusted guide dog. However, in the first three months of their partnership, so much more was in store for them both.

What I Did on My Summer Vacation

by Kathy Nimmer

In June, I …
Finished my training to be a guide,
Met the man whose eyes I became,
Began loving this man at my side,
Worked well with him in sunshine and in rain,
Started believing that this bond would abide,
Saw that every hope was ours to gain,
Graduated with pleasure and boundless pride,
Realized our lives would never be the same.

In July, I …
Bonded even more with this person of mine,
Started waking him now and then at night,
Sensed that his sugar levels were in decline,
Tried to tell him that something wasn't right,
Was happy when he got the message over time,
Watched him chuckle with shock and pure delight,
Heard him say my ability must be divine,
Loved him yet more, with diabetes and no sight.

In August, I …
Refused to let him harness me one day,
Wriggled and cowered until he forced it on me,
Protested and whined every step of the way,
Saw him stagger as his sugar plummeted dangerously,
Walked him home, though his skin was pasty and gray,
Dragged him inside to where I knew some help might be,
Panicked with terror when he fainted away,
Woke him up by kissing him endlessly.

This summer, I …
Proved that I could guide with constancy and skill,
Began a career I'd always wanted to start,
Showed him that I had a devilishly strong will,
Became happiest when he and I weren't apart,
Unveiled a surprising second role I could fill,
Glowed brighter each time he bragged I was smart,
Saved his life so we could be together still,
Found the home I'll never leave, deep inside his heart.

Guiding Eyes for the Blind

Military service and numerous permanent traumatic injuries alter the course of James Falsken's life. Then comes a little dog with an unusual name and the power to change everything yet again.

My Ten-Dollar Hero

by James Falsken

In my younger days, I served my country with the United States Coast Guard and did three tours in Vietnam before eventually becoming disabled. It has been a very rough road trying to face life while suffering with disabilities, and for a period, I was even living on the street. While homeless, I fought back and even graduated from college. In 2005, Agent Orange raised its ugly head and shut down a few of my organs. My doctors at the Veteran's Hospital did not give me much hope or promise of surviving. We did not know what to expect after the kidneys shut down.

One doctor suggested that I get a dog. Just a few months before, I had buried my last dog. She had been with me through it all, covering a fourteen-year period, and had seen all the hard times, including living on the street. I did not feel I could ever replace her and learn to love another dog ever again.

I was going to the hospital every week for tests and treatments. The pain was unbearable at times, wearing me down and reducing my will to live. I had a big blanket of self-pity to wrap up in each minute of every day. I turned to booze to drown the pity and to help forget the pain.

One day, I went to the grocery store to pick up more of this self-prescribed medicine. Just before entering the store, I saw people fussing over a grocery cart with a cardboard box in it. Thinking little about it at the time, I just went about my business, only to find that I had left my wallet at home. So, I rushed home to retrieve it. Upon returning to the store, I again noticed the commotion around the shopping cart but hurried inside to complete my purchase.

On my way out of the store, I finally decided to stop and see what all the fuss was about. A family that was in need of money was trying to sell mixed breed puppies—Blue Heeler and, possibly, Pit Bull—to people entering the store. I asked the price and they said ten dollars. I asked if they had a female pup and they said that I would want a male instead. After a little more discussion, they showed me a female pup trying to hide in the bottom of the box. The puppy did not like all the handling and the noise going on around her. As I stood there, I thought about the fact that my kidneys were shutting down and that the dog would live longer than I would. Still, something made me reach into my wallet and pull out the ten dollars. All I could think about was the fact this dog might be signing on to a sinking ship, but I took her home. This would later prove to be a life-changing event and would be the best ten dollars I have ever spent.

From the very beginning, I could tell there was something special about my new friend. In a short matter of time, she won and healed my heart. I was at a loss for a name though; nothing seemed to fit this special dog. One day she wiggled free from her collar and darted away in the parking lot of PetSmart. I could not run after her because of the injuries to my legs. All I could envision was that she would be hit by some car with all the traffic rushing about. I quickly reached out and caught her by her tail. I told her it was a good thing her tail did not pop off like a lizard's does. It was then that her name was born: Lizard.

With each passing day, new problems arose and I found I did not want to leave the home without Lizard at my side. So began a long search for service dog training or a school. In my weekly visits to the hospital, I would inquire from my doctors if they knew anything about the subject, and I kept getting the same message from them: they would have the information by my next visit. Nothing ever came of it. A year and a half went by, and then one day I noticed an article in the *Disabled American Veterans* monthly magazine about service dogs. I quickly wrote to the editors of the magazine to see if they could help me. I got a letter back with a list of twelve places to call. I set about calling the companies but was really losing faith. Everyone wanted me to purchase a dog from their company, and the price of the down payment was out of my reach. Then there was also the balloon payment on delivery. I was only further discouraged after they told me about a waiting list that was seven years long, to which I would reply, "What if your doctor doesn't give you seven years to live?" I heard a lot of "sorry to hear that" and "wish you all the luck in finding a dog." My hope was quickly diminishing by the time I got to the end of the list. I called an organization named Top Dog that was well out of my location in the state. However, they put me in contact with a sister program in my area called Happy Tails Service Dogs Inc., which just happened to have a new class forming.

Suddenly, I found that for the first time in my life everything was falling into place. Lizard and I started classes in January of 2008. With each passing day, we worked toward our goal of her becoming a fully certified service dog. The doctors at the Veteran's Hospital were astonished at the changes she has made in my health and how Lizard has assisted in their ability to treat my injuries. Even my kidneys came back on-line.

It took us a year and five days, but Lizard did eventually pass her service dog test and is now fully certified. The school had thought we could not make it and were taking bets on which week we would drop out. I had to undergo surgery twice that year, so even I did not think we would make it. At times it was a struggle for me in trying to overcome my disabilities enough to train Lizard. But we made it simply because we both did not quit on each other. During the year there were times that my dog seemed to be teaching me. It was as if she knew what to do before I learned to teach it to her.

Now, Lizard can do over thirty skills including opening doors and turning on lights. She picks up things I drop, and when my hands are full, she helps me cook by opening and closing the refrigerator door. However, the biggest job she can do for me is call 911, which she learned just three days before her big test. She does not have days off or sick days that nurses and other healthcare staff have. Lizard works because she loves it and is only the happiest when she is working. Everywhere we go, I see people with their jaws wide open in amazement when they see her doing one of her many skills in public. I find Lizard is changing people's minds about why the disabled need service dogs.

Not bad for a ten dollar dog…

Happy Tails Service Dogs, Inc.

It is a myth that every moment of a partnership is perfect, as seen with Chris Chapman and Fellow.

Why

by Kathy Nimmer

It was a brisk winter day. Chris's tears might have chilled to rigid icicles had she been outside, but she was not outside. Instead, she sat sobbing at a table inside a restaurant, questioning her decision to get a guide dog. She had just battled for ten minutes with her new dog, Fellow, to stop him from scavenging for food underneath the table, a losing battle whose fallout was Chris's hopeless tears.

"You have to gain Fellow's respect," her husband said, reaching across the table to take her hand.

"I think I made a mistake," she choked. "I can't do this."

"No one ever said this would be easy, honey."

And they hadn't. She'd heard that some partnerships didn't gel into solid working teams for more than a year. She knew that dogs would always be dogs, interested in things such as the food scraps Fellow had quickly inventoried and disposed of when they sat down. She knew that they were a new team and had much learning about each other to do. But still, Chris wept.

"Maybe I won't take him to restaurants," she murmured. "Some people do it that way."

"You will take him to restaurants," her husband replied. "Why did you get a guide dog after all?"

Why do you get a guide dog? For more freedom, faster travel, companionship, independence. Your confidence can rise, and the social barriers that disability often erects can fall like wind-driven snow. You know that the equation that adds your abilities to the dog's abilities comes out with an answer that is greater than the sum of the two. And so you tough it out and stay consistent and find patience where there is no more and dry away the tears and learn an awful lot about your dog and even more about yourself. And you go to restaurants, because when all of these things are valued, the dog settles into his role little by little, and you learn what you are supposed to do little by little, and your partnership grows little by little, and it is worth it all.

It was a hot summer day six months later. Chris's smile would have warmed the coldest heart had there been any around, but there were no cold hearts around, nor was there any visible residue of the fallout from that battle months ago. What was left for anyone to see as they surveyed the woman and her dog was something definitely worth fighting for: a team.

Guiding Eyes for the Blind

Caitlin Lynch examines her early journey with Laser in this poem.

That Was Then

by Caitlin Lynch

I used to wake up each morning and worry about
who you would sniff, what you would eat, or where we might get lost that day.
That was before I became aware of the slight movement that lets me know
you're looking for a French fry or have just spotted a particularly pungent baby.

That was before I realized that getting lost with someone else
is so much better than getting lost alone.

I used to get upset when you would moan, yawn, and snore in the middle of class;
You would draw attention to us, and I mostly wanted to go unseen by the professor.
That was before I understood that you're always going to be loud, and
before I realized that my heart
really does melt every time I hear you vocalize.
I used to hate it
when people would say hello to you
and completely ignore me.

That was before I realized that
being known for having such a beautiful, kind, and gentle dog
is one of my best attributes.
I used to worry that
you would be better suited for someone else;
I used to worry that we were an awful team.
That was before our strides matched, and I was able to read your signals
like my favorite book.

That was before I understood that you're perfect for me, and that
there's nowhere else you would rather be than by my side.
I used to think that walking confident and tall was only for the sighted.
I used to think that flying
was reserved for gods and comic-book superheroes.
But, that was before I met you
and got my wings.

Judy Burch shares how her first dog led her to a very special discovery early in their partnership.

The Matchmaker

by Judy Burch

In the summer of 1974, at the age of nineteen, I attended my first blindness convention in Chicago, my first real trip alone away from my home of Macon, Georgia. Accompanying me was my beautiful Golden Retriever dog guide, Buffy. We had been a working team for two years, and she and I had already been places and done things which I would never have dreamed of doing before she and I met one another.

On this particular day, a friend and I decided to walk to a restaurant a block or so from the hotel for dinner. On the way there, Buffy and I took a little detour into an alley so she could take care of those personal things which dogs must take care of in order to be more comfortable. We walked a number of paces into the alley so that she could have some privacy.

As I removed her harness, Buffy began to wag her tail and pull on her leash a little, indicating that she saw something or someone in which she was interested. At the same time, I heard the jingle of collar and tags as another dog shook its body in greeting.

"Hello," I said. "I am Judy Herndon from Macon, Georgia, and I have my Golden Retriever Leader Dog, Buffy. Who are you and what kind of dog do you have?"

"Hello," said a very pleasant male voice. "I am Rick Burch from St. Louis, and I have my Seeing Eye dog. She's a German Shepherd and her name is Ruthi."

We exchanged a few pleasantries, and all the time I just couldn't get over the wonderful sound of that voice! We then went our separate ways, he with his friends and I with my friend.

After dinner, I decided to take a ride on an L-train. I had never been on a subway, or, for that matter, any type of train, so this would be a new experience for both Buffy and me.

Buffy guided me expertly through the turnstile, and as the train stopped in front of us and the doors opened, she walked onto the train as if she had been doing this for years. We enjoyed a very nice ride to the north end of the line, then rode back to where we had started our trip. Buffy and I disembarked and proceeded to walk to the front door of the hotel.

There was a crowd of people standing outside the door. As we were negotiating the crowd, Buffy began to wag her tail.

"Hello," I said.

"Hello," came that wonderful voice which I had heard not very long before.

"I think I'm going to take a walk around the block," I said.

"I'll come with you, if you don't mind," replied the voice.

As it happened, Rick had enjoyed an unusually long dinner with friends. Of thousands of people who could have been at the hotel's front door, who would have thought that we would have returned to the same door at the same time? It simply was meant to be, and I thank my wonderful little matchmaker for introducing me to my future husband-to-be!

Buffy and Ruthi were with us on our wedding day on November 6, 1976. And almost thirty-three years later, we are still sharing our lives with and being guided by wonderful dogs, now a pair of German Shepherds named Indy and Melvin.

Leader Dogs for the Blind

Rescuing a stray saves the animal's life, but one woman's rescue would go down in history in Japan.

One Fine Stray

by Chazz Glaze
Translation Assistance Provided by Nagi Fugie

Something about this stray was different, special, the woman just knew it. But when she found the three-month-old stray, cold and much-too-thin, in front of a grocery store in the Japanese prefecture of Ibaraki in January 1999, she had no idea the fate that was in store. "Mikan," the woman named the Shiba-mix, meaning "mandarin orange," like the color of her fur.

Far away in western Japan Yoshiko Kishimoto was letting another kettle of water boil dry, missing another package delivery. Yoshiko was deaf. The sounds of the everyday world, sounds that could save her life, were lost to her. Her family was constantly afraid to leave her alone, fearing for her safety, and she was depressed, withdrawn, an outsider in a world of hearing insiders.

Back in the north of Japan, Mikan had been welcomed into the woman's home as the fifth canine family member. One day, the woman remembered something she had seen on TV about Japan Hearing Dogs for Deaf People (JHDDP), and she had a feeling, like the feeling she'd had when she first saw the pup, that this was what Mikan was supposed to do. She loaded Mikan into her car and drove six hours to the organization.

One day in Yoshiko's life, her daughter came to her and told her about an ad she had seen: "free hearing service dog." At her daughter's encouragement, Yoshiko contacted JHDDP.

Moto Arima, president of JHDDP, had been training Mikan as the first hearing service dog in Japan when Yoshiko was accepted into the program. Mikan and Yoshiko were a match destined to be together, but not before having to overcome forces standing in their way.

The woman and dog team trained and passed accreditation through the school and were ready to take the public access test required by the Japanese railway company in order to be afforded access. In order to pass the test, the dog had to demonstrate how she would react in a number of hypothetical instances: getting her foot stepped on, being grazed by a bag, and refusing food. Mikan completed all tasks, demonstrating her calm and professional demeanor, except for refusing the food. Mikan ate the piece of bread which the examiner practically forced into her mouth. It seemed an act of blatant sabotage. Still, the team was not deterred. They continued training and were determined to pass the test the second time around.

In April 2001, Mikan became the first hearing dog to pass the test and be allowed access to the railway. Not only that, but Mikan was also the first hearing dog who is internationally accredited by the CEO of Britain's Hearing Dogs for Deaf People. Legislation for assistance dogs and their partners has since passed in Japan, changing public transportation access for such pairs, though there is still much work to be done for the general public to be accepting of service dogs, especially hearing dogs.

By touching Yoshiko's foot with her paw, Mikan has made Yoshiko an insider in this world. She signals Yoshiko to the sound of the kitchen timer, alarm clock, fire alarm, doorbell, and, for the first time, the sound of her name when it is called. Yoshiko, a former secluded housewife, is now a paid PR and hearing dog instructor for JHDDP.

Japan Hearing Dogs for Deaf People

Chapter 3

Yet Again

Daily Life Unveiled

Paw Prints of Wisdom

"Initially, most people thought of service animals as the dogs that guided the blind in public places. Service animals now assist with vision, hearing, mobility, seizures, and psychological well-being. These roles have one thing in common: they enrich the life for the service animal and increase independence for the human partner."

—Alan M. Beck,
School of Veterinary Medicine, Purdue University

"There is no greater feeling than to have one of my graduates send me an email or give me a call to boast about something new the dog has learned to help make that person's life a little easier. I choke up every time and remember once again why I do this."

—Carol Davis,
Co-founder and Program Director for Paws'itive Teams

Nancy Scott recognizes the beauty of independence in this story about shopping with a friend who has a guide dog.

Buses, Bones, Etc.

by Nancy Scott

I board the bus to the 25th Street Shopping Center. The driver congratulates me for being on time today. The last time I took this bus, I was late and dashing for it. (Have you ever seen an uncoordinated blind person dash? It's memorable.) I fold my white cane and mention that Pauline will join me later.

Pauline has a guide dog named Autumn. She licks my hand once before making sure her human is seated. Then she settles herself on the floor as much out of the way as possible, where she lies quietly as she was trained to do.

Several passengers ask about Autumn. Pauline explains that she and Autumn, a Retriever-Labrador mix, were trained at The Seeing Eye around four years ago. Pauline also cautions passengers not to pet the dog when she is in the guiding harness. She is a "working dog" and must not be distracted.

Sooner than we expect, the bus driver says we've arrived at the shopping center. Technically, guide dogs are not trained to guide two people, so I walk behind Pauline with a hand on her shoulder. I use my cane for my right-side clearance. I don't think this fools Autumn, who understands more than she lets on.

Our adventures involve errands and food. Today, Pauline chooses the place, in order to go to the pet store for little dog-bone treats. Autumn guides, with Pauline giving directions like "forward" or "left." Pauline can see just enough to recognize landmarks and find doorways.

Once in the store, Pauline says "Go to the counter." Autumn does. Pauline asks about the dog bones and a female employee goes to get them. Autumn stays still but her head is up, and Pauline can tell her eyes avidly follow the girl. I think Autumn knows what she's getting.

When the dog bones are paid for, Autumn never barks, jumps, or begs. She sniffs, though, and must know what Pauline is carrying. Autumn gets the command "outside" and heads obediently for the door. We are off to The New York Bagel & Deli for breakfast.

The counter people know us. They are always very patient when I ask them to name all the cheese and salad choices. They get our drinks and carry the tray. We follow our helper to a table. Autumn lies quietly underneath, and we eat and talk. I say that Autumn surely should have at least one dog bone now. Pauline promises to give her one before we leave the restaurant.

First, though, we ask about desserts. We both buy coconut macaroon cookies, and I also have to try the cinnamon sticks. The counter man is still patient. He even gives me a free cinnamon stick because it breaks in half. And Autumn gets her munchy too. She knows it's coming and sits with great dignity as if to say, "I know I deserve this."

We again go outside with Autumn's help. We walk toward the bus stop, but we are interrupted by a strange cry from above. Autumn looks up. I know it's a bird and say that it must be a seagull. I have heard gulls both near the ocean and, once, in the parking lot at K-Mart.

The bird cries again and Autumn cocks her head. I don't think Pauline believes that this is a gull. "There's never a sighted person around when you need one," I lament. I know the one at K-Mart was a gull. I was with a sighted person that time. Too bad Autumn can't talk.

We round the corner and settle on the bench. The gull does not follow and we do not hear it again. We eat the free, already divided cinnamon stick. It's very good. Autumn watches, but the intensity of her stare is wasted on us. We suspect that she stares more at me, since she knows Pauline won't usually give her people-food.

Another woman joins us. I ask if she saw the seagull. She says no, but she has seen gulls here before. I poke Pauline.

When the bus arrives, I am smiling over my gull victory. Autumn needs no commands and finds a seat for Pauline. I fold my cane, and the driver asks whether we are going home. (We ride this bus often and many drivers know us and are very helpful.)

Pauline again spends part of the ride answering questions about Autumn. Soon, the driver announces Pauline's stop. We say goodbye and she and Autumn leave at a brisk pace. Autumn will go home and the harness will be taken off. She will become a regular dog who is petted, loved, and played with rather than being disciplined and commanded.

I ride farther, paying attention to the turns. The driver does not forget, and I leave the bus at my stop. I am still smiling.

Close to home, I move faster. I want to tell the story of the seagull. Maybe I'll write about it while munching macaroons.

The Seeing Eye, Inc.

Jennifer Warsing's deafness hasn't kept her from having a fulfilling life that includes her hearing dog Hattie.

My Girl Hattie

by Jennifer Warsing

Merriam-Webster defines the word "hero" as someone possessing "superior qualities, courage and strength, nobility and acquiring a special skill." To me, my hearing dog, Hattie, a chocolate Lab, embodies all of the above. I am thirty-three years old and was deafened at the age of five by Meniere's Disease. Meniere's Disease is a vestibular disorder of the inner ear that destroys hearing and balance.

I can honestly say my life didn't begin until September 14, 2007. That is the date Dogs for the Deaf, Inc. arrived at my door with Hattie, my hearing dog. With Hattie at my side I have discovered that the possibilities for my life are never ending.

Since Hattie's arrival, she and her training have enabled me to take my hearing disability and turn it into an infinite ability. Before Hattie, silence pervaded my home. One could think of it as setting the volume to zero for one's life. That is, until she cut in: my link to the hearing world, to sound, my Hattie. With a tap of her nose, she alerts me to my surroundings, be it the alarm clock, oven timer, microwave, doorbell, smoke detector, telephone or someone calling my name. The lonesome quietude no longer consumes my every waking moment; awareness and sound now invade my soul.

The electrifying fear that the smoke detector's life-saving blare will go unheard no longer engulfs my nights. I no longer prance nervously about, wondering if the phone is ringing. Is someone trying to reach me? Hello? Hello? There's no one there. Or the telephone's friendly ring goes unanswered. The nauseating stench of burnt meals no longer pervades my home because the oven timer's urgent beep goes by ignored. Hattie, my hearing dog, has taken that life and transformed it into one of sound, awareness, peace and joy.

Not only has Hattie transformed my home life, she has transformed my outside world as well. While outside, I am tapped, alerted to look up, and there I see a flock of geese in formation flying south. I am aware of the life-flight helicopter flying urgently in for landing. I have "heard" birds territorially fighting over a newly built nest, an ambulance, a fire truck going dutifully by. Across the street a baby's cry becomes Hattie's alerting sound in my environment at that given moment.

"Hero" defines Hattie, my hearing dog. Courage, strength, nobility and acquiring a special skill are her special qualities, that "skill" being the gift of sound.

Because of Hattie, my nights are now filled with blissful peace and rest because I know she will alert me to any danger. My telephone is now greeted with an enthusiastic, "Hello!" because she has let me know someone was calling. My meals are edible and the smells of freshly baked cookies and Thanksgiving turkeys permeate my home. Sound now fills each crevice in every room, and laughter, joy and sound flood my soul. My gait is no longer one of nervous stagger; my step now contains independence and liveliness. Hattie has enabled me to blossom into being. She has laid the groundwork for a bright new future for me, one with sound, hearing and awareness, which I cherish with a smile. My ears have chocolate fur, a tail and a heart of gold.

Dogs for the Deaf

A day in the life of an active business woman in the heart of a big city is nonstop as demonstrated by Rebecca Bridges and Daisy.

Routine Confidence

by Kathy Nimmer

She is walking boldly. And, SHE is walking boldly. Both petite, both young, both strong. They are walking boldly together.

First it is a block-and-a-half walk to the nearest Metro station. They move quickly, black fur and blonde hair whooshing by. The quickness is the end product of confidence, and it is good.

Into the station and to the escalator, a fearful barrier for some teams since paws can be hurt by the hungry, grinding, ever-moving parts, but no fear descends the escalator with these two. Outstanding training, protective booties for the paws, and that bold, sure confidence speeds them on their way.

Another escalator, deeper into the bowels of the station, then a platform filled with waiting passengers. They move forward toward the edge, no rails to protect them from a pair of fatal falls, but rails aren't needed when outstanding training is engrained. Blocking her partner from the unseen edge, the dog curls backward and nudges her away. Sometimes, the woman tests the dog to see how reliable this curl-nudge is. It is as reliable as the sun that rises, though the woman can't see its golden rays. It is as reliable as this dog's Labrador zest for life, though its life hasn't been a long one yet at the tender age of two.

The train pulls in. They follow the crowd toward the open door. Boldness is needed again, if not speed this time. A little pushing and shoving, a little inserting of a stout black head between legs clad in slacks, skirts, khakis, and pantyhose. This opens a path for both of them, and they board the train for the next stage of the journey.

Another escalator whisks them from another station platform to yet another station platform and another train. The same menacing edge is defeated shamefully by the curl-nudge. The same stout head herds more self-possessed business travelers, wearing the same lower body adornments. And all that is left behind as the doors slide closed behind them are a few stray black pieces of dog fur and an impression that these two can do anything.

Nothing refutes that impression. Nothing would dare. Every day, they weave through chaotic places with pedestrians creating a constantly shifting barrier between them and their destinations. They thrive in an urban environment where horns, screeching brakes, speeding taxis, confusing roundabouts, historic monuments, tall buildings, and diverse neighborhoods paint a living kaleidoscope of impossibilities. And yet, it is possible. It can be done. They do it, every day.

The woman admits to passing anxieties. *What now? What if? What then?* The dog has her hesitations too. Perfection isn't what they want to prove through their daily journeys. So what is it? Dignity, vitality, and ability. Proven! Case closed!

She is walking boldly. And, SHE is walking boldly. The sun that the woman can't see is slipping below the Washington D.C. horizon. It glints briefly on black fur and blonde hair that whooshes by just a little more slowly than when the day was young. Their day's work is almost over. Home is near. It is time to rest. Tomorrow is not far away.

Guide Dogs for the Blind

Being deafblind is something Jennifer McEachen handles well with the help of Nixon, whose canine thoughts about how and why their partnership works are captured in this poem.

Through the Silent Shadows

by Kathy Nimmer

Your eyes—they do not focus well,
But mine see all there is to see.
Your ears—they do not hear some sounds,
But mine are sharp as sharp can be.

I sense you trusting me to guide
You safely down each busy street,
But it's my gift to you to add
A wag when someone's there to meet.

And when I see someone you love
Who's coming right toward you and me,
I take you there since you could not
Find them when you can't hear or see.

I send you signals with my moves
And know you understand them all,
For life without those sights and sounds
Has made you stand up proud and tall.

I know some folks would think that it
Could never work for dogs to guide
A person who is also deaf,
But in this job I take great pride.

And when the world begins to doubt
What you and I as one can do,
You put the harness on my back
While I stand proudly next to you.

And off we go into the world
That just may never understand
How disability retreats
When teamwork fuses paw and hand.

Guide Dogs for the Blind

It would take some effort to imagine how a visually impaired woman with CP who gets around in a motorized wheelchair could function on a daily basis. Kim Shepherd and Scooby have it figured out.

Forward

by Kathy Nimmer

When you think you can't, start believing you can. When you think you won't, start believing you will. When you think it's impossible, start believing you're wrong. When you think you're done, start believing you've just begun.

Kim could have given up many times, and the world would have said, "You're right to do so." After all, she is legally blind, not an easy reality to manage. Throw into the mix the fact that she is a functional quadriplegic from cerebral palsy and severe arthritis, and you have what most people would consider a deal-breaker. She is unable to see or move freely on her own. If asked, the world would avidly say, "I would give up too, so please do it, with our approval."

The world would have to hear from Scooby then, if that was the prevailing thought. A specially trained black Lab, Scooby is certified to guide Kim and to assist her with her physical limitations. Wearing a three-foot-long offset harness that keeps him far away from the wheels of Kim's electric wheelchair, Scooby guides her through the challenges of a world not very user-friendly for someone with Kim's physical limitations. He does his job with accuracy and flair, fulfilling this incredibly unique role with apparent ease.

How Scooby manages is nothing shy of amazing. He begins to slow about two feet from the edge of a curb, giving Kim indication of what is coming. He stops at a forty-five degree angle; Kim must trust him to do this since she can't feel for the edge of the curb with her foot as most guide dog handlers do. Kim carries a white cane to probe the ground in front of her when Scooby stops, to try to detect any dangers such as glass or broken pavement. When they are moving, she lightly rests the palm of her left hand on Scooby's harness handle, using the very limited sensation and strength that she still has to read his movements through her thumb. When turning, Kim maneuvers the wheelchair far enough away from Scooby so they can pivot together. Scooby locates wheelchair ramps automatically so that Kim can position her wheelchair directly down the slope.

Scooby also fulfills many traditional duties as a service dog, things that help Kim function more easily when at home or in public. He picks up dropped items and brings them to her. He can open or close doors when ropes or straps are connected to the door handles. Scooby can turn on and off lights by jumping up with his feet against the wall, then nudging the switches with his nose. In public, he can press the buttons on automatic door openers. Finally, when Kim transfers in and out of the wheelchair, he stands near her to help brace her so she won't fall.

The world would say to Kim that it is right and good to surrender. However, Kim would flatly disagree. Scooby himself would not just refute the world's judgment with his skills; he would refute it with his own will to live. In 2006, without warning or apparent cause, Scooby became dangerously ill with a 108-degree fever and an extreme allergic reaction. Severely dehydrated and near death, Scooby was rushed to an acute care veterinary hospital where he fought to stay alive in a ten-day battle that Kim still recalls with a shiver of horror.

He came through, depleted of energy, preexisting joint damage now magnified by his weakened condition. But, his first stop once he came home was the table where Kim kept his working harness. She knew then that he wasn't ready to quit. She would do whatever it took to restore his health and happiness. That she did, supporting him gently for months through his recovery until he was back at her side.

They make an incredible team, Kim and Scooby. The woman who believes "she can and will" is happiest when beside the dog who believes the same thing. Together, they erase "impossible" from the world's vocabulary. To observe four paws steadily padding down the street with the hum of an electric wheelchair whispering alongside, that same world must now surely agree, "Indeed, you have only just begun."

ProTrain Dogs

Kay Bennett was not eager to go shopping that day, but Rufus was ready.

I Only Have Eyes for You

by Kathy Nimmer

Autumn sunshine splashed through the leaves of the trees outside Sam's Club. It was a spectacular day with the crispness of the changing season. But Kay didn't feel the beauty around her. Instead, her heart hammered with rising dread.

Ever since Kay had been diagnosed with multiple sclerosis and cognitive difficulties, her life had become starkly different. She lost a long-time job, didn't go out much, and said goodbye to some of the independence that marked her existence before. But, Rufus had started to change much of that. A spunky Yorkshire Terrier, Rufus leapt into her world as a puppy, just a pet she thought, but soon showed a delightful attentiveness to Kay's needs. After displaying sensitivity to her rising emotions by licking her face or putting a paw on her cheek, Rufus entered a program from which he was certified as a psychiatric and medical alert service dog, to help Kay stay calm and focused. They'd been on a great path ever since.

This day was different, however. They were going to a store together for the first time. Rufus wasn't terribly fond of children, and Kay knew there was a high likelihood of kids being in Sam's Club. She was concerned about how he would handle the chaos. Since her own cognitive abilities were affected by tension and anxiety, she also worried about how she herself would do.

Stepping through the front door with Rufus in his service dog vest by her side, Kay grabbed a cart and took a deep breath. She placed Rufus in the front compartment of the cart facing her, where little children were meant to sit. Then, she began to shop.

Nothing could have prepared Kay for what happened next. While her own anxiety escalated with each hesitant step, Rufus sat erect as a soldier, staring straight into Kay's eyes. He was so intent on her that he didn't even turn his head when a pair of children darted past the cart toward a display of potato chips. He didn't interrupt his gaze with Kay when she put packages of food in the large compartment behind him. Not even a bag of his favorite dog treats made him break focus. The more anxious she became, the fiercer Rufus's effort was to keep her calm. Even as they checked out, Rufus had eyes only for Kay, not minding the large family in line behind them, nor the beeps and buzzes of the cash register, nor the admiring comments of the cashier. He had a job, and that was making sure Kay was okay.

Back in the car, Kay fought back tears and hugged Rufus as he slathered her face with kisses and bounced around the front seat, all dignity and reserve gone now that he had gotten Kay through the ordeal of shopping. His alert little face practically beamed with joy over a job well done, by both of them.

Owner-Trained Dog

One of Kathy Nimmer's former students was deeply touched by Kathy's first guide dog Raffles. Hear Sidney Bolam's impressions of the partnership from the outside looking in.

A Friend with Class

by Sidney Bolam

"Look, I have the class with the dog for English!" I said, delighted, as I perused my second semester schedule. "You mean the one with the blind teacher? She's good, my friend had her before. She won the Golden Apple Award last year." Even as my acquaintance and I compared our schedules my mind was on the dog who would be a resident in my English class. I had seen the pair padding along silently in the halls between classes and couldn't help but stare at the beautiful creature, long flaxen fur swishing as it went on its way. I took little notice of the teacher who followed the dog like a water skier in slow motion. Animals had always been better friends than people, and I regarded humans with a general feeling of mistrust and suspicion, teachers in particular. I didn't exactly have any expectations about the lovely dog's human cohort.

I took my seat on the first day and let my eyes pass around the room. I noted the dog pillow underneath the teacher's desk and felt my heart flutter with excitement. I had heard there were rules about how to behave with a blind person's dog, and I gravely thought of not being able to touch that forbidden golden fur.

The teacher entered the room with ginger steps, lead by the dog I had watched from a pensive distance. For the first time I sized this human up, noting she bore a strong resemblance to Amelia Earhart. Her ice blue eyes didn't see us, but something about the way she smirked told me that she knew we were all ready for class. Miss Nimmer told a little bit about her background and how she ended up as a blind high school English teacher. She introduced Raffles and explained some guide dog etiquette. I was delighted to learn that on rare occasion, as a reward, we might be able to pet him as long as he wasn't "working." I left that first class feeling excited by the prospect of making a new dog friend and a newborn curiosity to see how this teacher managed a class of irreverent ninth graders. I had no way of knowing that this would all eventually lead to one of the dearest friendships I have ever had.

Every day I would hurry to my seat and wait for Raffles to arrive. Instead of dreamily watching the clock like in my other classes, I enjoyed staring contests with the dog under the desk. His soulful amber eyes would twinkle at me, and occasionally I would get to run my fingers through that silky mane. It wasn't long before I found myself fascinated by the partnership of the teacher and dog. Wordlessly and with some unseen magic they would make their way around obstacles and to destinations. I couldn't help but respect and even like any human who got on so well with dogs.

It was unintentional at first, but soon I found myself really enjoying those classes. Miss Nimmer appealed to our sense of humor with silly antics and allowed us to express our understanding of the material through acting, artwork, or poetry. When we would end our work early she and Raffles would entertain us with funny tricks. Before I could stop myself I had really grown to like Miss Nimmer nearly as much as I liked her canine partner!

As the weeks turned to years I accepted an invitation to be Miss Nimmer's student aid. This was a wonderful arrangement because I got to spend more time with Raffles, whom I considered a close personal friend. He would greet me lovingly, show me whatever toy he had hidden in the English office, and ask for the usual belly rubs or rear-end scratches. Few people understood my deep affection for that beautiful dog, except one person who adored him more than I did: Miss Nimmer. Their relationship was a treat to watch, and they worked in such unified harmony and mutual understanding that I felt a trace of envy.

After high school things changed. I moved to college two hours away, and Miss Nimmer officially became Kathy to me. Professional student/teacher relationship became casual friendship, and I always made time during visits home to see my new friend Kathy and dear buddy Raffles. After I graduated I moved back to my hometown, and soon Kathy and I became closer than ever. She even helped me land a job as a receptionist at the vet clinic where Raffles was a patient.

In the course of our short friendship, Raffles had gone from a lively, enthusiastic pooch to a white-muzzled old man. It was time for him to retire his harness and enter the quiet life of a civilian dog. It was a hard process for Kathy, but she knew it was the best thing for her faithful friend. Just months after his retirement, it was discovered that he was very sick and had, at best, only months to live. Those of us who were closest to Kathy and Raffles were chilled to the core.

I worked at the very vet clinic where Raffles drew his last breath. It came about suddenly, as the winter took its toll on his already weakened body. I couldn't bear the loss or the thought of Kathy without her guide and dearest friend. I couldn't understand this most terrible of cosmic jokes, that the "people" we love the most might grow old and die in a tenth of the time it takes us. What was the use of loving someone so much if it would only cause us such unbearable sadness? The answer to this question is different for everyone, but my own answer soon became apparent.

Through our mutual admiration for that golden dog Kathy and I had formed a special friendship. We were remaining members of a fan club, left to comfort each other and remember our fallen friend. Raffles helped me lay down my emotional shield and open my heart to a friend I have been grateful for ever since. Kathy and I make a funny pair when we are out together: I'm a five foot tall, tattooed, dark haired bohemian and she is tall, fair, slender and conservative. I'm sure people marvel at how such an odd match ended up together getting coffee on a Saturday. If only they knew how a dog could unite people. Raffles is only a memory to us now, but he made a lasting paw print on my heart that I will never forget.

Pilot Dogs, Inc.

Airports are stressful for many people, not just those like Elaine Jordan who battle PTSD and other mental illnesses, but Destry makes the difference.

Guardian

by Kathy Nimmer

It had been a trying weekend but a positive one overall. Elaine and her psychiatric service dog Destry had flown on their own for the first time from San Antonio to Dallas where Destry had successfully taken and passed a temperament test and a public access test that underlined his suitability as a service dog. With a history of post-traumatic stress disorder, major depression, and generalized anxiety disorder, Elaine considered the weekend a huge success for both her and Destry. The flight, the connections, the tests … and now finally the return trip was near.

But not near enough! The friend who dropped Elaine and Destry at the airport had commitments during the day, so she deposited the pair at the main concourse several hours before their flight was to depart. Elaine was anxious about how they would pass their time in the less than serene environment of a busy international airport. The chaos of sound and motion was like sandpaper rubbing on her skin.

Destry, a tall black Belgian Sheepdog, was trained to alert Elaine about oncoming panic attacks and other crises, and he could do his job well. Strong nudges and full body pressure would tell Elaine to get ready, often giving her a chance to find a quiet place to relax or telling her that she needed to have her medicine handy.

Now, a sense of unease began bubbling in Elaine as she looked around the airport. Restaurants and lounges, meant for relaxing between flights, were crowded. Corridors were packed with travelers pulling heavy suitcases and baggage carts. Excited children screamed as they darted in and out of crowds. Courtesy carts beeped with their intrusive signal for people to get out of the way. Nothing was serene here, nothing at all.

Destry pushed close to Elaine, jamming his large black head firmly against her thigh. "Okay, let's find somewhere to be," Elaine whispered to Destry, rubbing his shaggy head.

As the pair walked through the airport, Elaine saw only one place that was quiet and free from the throbbing activity closing in on her: an empty gate with no flights listed for several hours. Rows of unoccupied chairs fronted a large picture window that looked out on the tarmac. Sun streaked the window, lighting the pocket of solitude with a warm glow that was somehow appealing this time, even though bright light usually bothered Elaine. "Let's go, Destry."

Elaine bypassed the chairs and went right to the corner where wall and window created a nook of safety. She sat on the floor, commanding Destry to sit beside her. As time passed, Elaine calmed and grew sleepy, slipping further down to the floor and curling up with her back to the world that had too often been a menacing foil to her happiness. Now, though, she was secure in the prospect of happiness being less elusive. With Destry by her side, things seemed more doable. Life seemed almost as bright as the Texas sun that enveloped her as she drifted off to sleep.

When she awoke a few hours later, Elaine was engulfed by warmth. The sun still sparkled on the window in front of her. Destry lay against her back, his strength and stability a barrier against the difficulties of the world. She stroked his fur, grateful for a guardian, not of her body but of her spirit. With him, she knew there was hope. And so there was.

Owner-Trained Dog

Paulette Wilson and Radar discover life lessons while on a simple picnic.

Bridge

by Kathy Nimmer

A gentle spring breeze rippled through the tufts of wild grass clinging to the rocks. The suspension bridge grasped each side of a deep canyon, swaying and serving as a precarious support for the group of home school kids charging in its direction.

"Slow down! Take it easy! Be careful!" But the children were deaf to the warnings, basking in their freedom, and registered not even fragments of the shouted words.

As if the invisible hand of Mother Nature had just grabbed their pumping arms, one child, then two and three, abruptly stopped their headlong plunge toward the bridge to stumble back to the adults, slipping and sliding over the loose gravel that led toward the bridge. They panted and paused, gasping out words of worry that didn't match the world-conquering courage that had fueled their flight just seconds before.

"You can't go across that bridge with Radar," one little girl cautioned.

"It bounces."

Another child, this one with red hair and glasses, nodded in agreement. "It will make you fall, and it's a long way down, even if you can't see it."

A third child, this one wizened with teenaged insight, touched Paulette's arm. "Really, it is narrow and unstable. It wouldn't be a good idea."

Paulette grasped Radar's harness. The picnic had been an unqualified success thus far. The children, all with a richness of understanding that surprised Paulette, had accepted her, her guide dog, and her blindness with equanimity. The two other adults had been great too, everyone treating her normally, without the "disabled" tag that so often hindered relationships. Even the weather had cooperated, offering a softness and freshness that Alabama humidity didn't always allow. But now, was this where the realities of disability would show up, unwelcome arrivals on this otherwise blissful day?

"He can handle it," Paulette pronounced, stroking Radar's sleek yellow back. "We'll take it one step at a time." Amid a chorus of protests, Paulette and Radar moved toward the bridge.

"Slow down! Take it easy! Be careful!" Paulette smiled to herself as she heard the very same words that the adults had shouted to the kids, now uttered by high, uncertain voices that had known no fear when it came to their own safety.

Paulette touched the rope rail of the bridge with her right hand, then stepped carefully to the left rail, three feet away at most. Radar stood patiently, sniffing the first wooden plank. "Forward."

Voices stopped, completely. Only the thud-thud-thud of footsteps broke through Paulette's concentration. There were the footsteps of the older children walking ahead of her, not cocky in their adolescent invincibility, but cautious and concerned, as they continually looked back over their shoulders. There were the footsteps of the two other adults, one before and another behind, ready to lend a hand if needed, but aware that Paulette now needed them most to recognize that she was an adult just like they were, walking the same bridge, the same journey. There were the footsteps of the little ones, believing in miracles still, accepting both fear and victory with wonderment, watching with thumbs in mouths and Velcro tennis shoes padding quietly behind Paulette and Radar, mimicking every foot placement with uncanny accuracy. There were the footsteps of Radar, four strong, firm thuds punctuated by the click-click of dog's nails on swaying wood. And, there were the footsteps of Paulette herself, slightly hesitant at first but gaining in boldness as each plank passed under her feet like the undulating surface of the sea.

The symphony of footsteps continued. Then, little by little, the thuds died away. Feet now scuffed gravel, not wooden planks. They had reached the other side of the canyon. The literal suspended reality was over. Paulette tensed. Now what?

"Hey, I'll race you to the woods!"

"Yeah, right! I'll blow you away!"

"Mommy, I'm thirsty."

"I have a rock in my shoe."

Footsteps and voices surged around Paulette as the rituals of youth, discovery, and life resumed. Normality. Acceptance. But victory still. She leaned down and stroked Radar's head. "Good boy."

Guide Dogs of America

How can a service dog help with daily tasks such as sorting laundry? Ask Lori Buffington and both her current and retired service dogs who make it a team effort!

Slapstick Retirement

by Lori Buffington

In the fall of 2003, I graduated from Canine Partners for Life where I was matched with a Standard Poodle named Fennec. Ironically, I truly loved Labs (the majority of those wonderful dogs were Labs); our household had always had a Lab as a pet, for as long as I can recall. But they felt that Fennec would be a good match for me. When my vet found out that I had been matched with a Standard Poodle, he said, "They are so smart, even smarter than your beloved Labrador Retrievers and my German Shepherds." Fennec amazed me from day one, not only for his excellent service skills, but also his devotion and loving personality. He won my heart, as well as the rest of the family's.

Then one day he woke and was limping, not badly but enough that I could see. It worsened as the day went on, so that night my vet wanted to see him after hours. Fennec would need x-rays and perhaps a slight sedation. When my vet came out with tear filled eyes, I knew it wasn't good news: Fennec had hip dysplasia. He had only been at my side for four years, and at six years old, I knew his work time with me was limited. We were able to work for another six months by limiting his tasks and giving him injections and pain medications. But then he began balking at the jump into my van and from the van floor onto his bench seat in the rear. With the look he gave me when I asked him to load up, I knew it hurt him; so at that point my vet suggested early retirement. After many tears, the wonderful support of my vet, and Canine Partners for Life's vet and staff, the decision was made. They had a little black Lab named Tinker lined up for me for that fall class.

After we completed a very emotional and tough three weeks of team training, Tinker and I graduated. She was very different from Fennec, and more comical, more like a clown. I was nervous about the homecoming; after all, Tinker would be meeting Fennec and the two other pet dogs we have. Fennec is "the top dog" and Tinker seemed very submissive, so I really didn't expect trouble. She was welcomed for the most part with open paws. Fennec was the only one of the four that really had issues; then again, he was going through retirement too, a huge change for a dog of his dedication. All of a sudden after Mom had left him for three weeks, she arrived with a little black Lab in "his spot," doing "his job"—how dare she!

The next day I began playing catch up in the laundry room. I sorted the piles of laundry according to colors, etc. I gave Tinker the command to "go take" the first pair of blue jeans on that pile; with pleasure she did as I asked and I placed them into the front loading washer. I told her to "go take" another pair, watching her as I pointed to the pile and she once again did as I asked. I took it from her and turned to put it in the machine when I noticed the washer was empty; now I *knew* I had already placed one pair inside. I looked to my right and there stood Fennec, his pom-pom tail wagging so proudly, the first pair of jeans in his mouth. I could tell this was going to be fun. I told him to give them to me and he did; so that I could get the wash going, I escorted him from the laundry room and shut the door, only to have him pop it open and re-enter. Tinker took more wash and brought it to me as asked. She was doing wonderfully. I noticed all of a sudden Fennec took off through the house. I thought, *Wow, that went pretty well. He's going to go lie down and let Tinker do her job now.* A few seconds later he reappeared with one of my shoes in his mouth; I couldn't help but laugh. Then I thought, *Well, perhaps if I keep Fennec busy retrieving my footwear, Tinker and I could get the laundry loaded into the washer.* So I sent him for shoe after shoe. Fennec knew about six pairs by name, so at the end of loading those jeans, I also had collected five individual shoes.

Fennec took retirement fairly well. It's been a year and a half, but he will still wait patiently at the laundry room door watching Tinker work with Mom. But that's okay. As my dad often told me growing up, every job needs a supervisor.

Canine Partners for Life

One train ride holds the unexpected for Alysa Chadow and Patsy.

Portrait of a Traveler

by Alysa Chadow

Day dreams are made out of solitude. That solitude, in turn, is comprised of commuter trains, morning darkness, and the silence of the sleepy.

I was no stranger to the solitude. I had taken the train numerous times prior to getting my first guide dog in 1998. I still took the train after that, and I was taking the train just as much in 2000, the year I began teaching at the California School for the Blind. It was also the year that I learned the hard way how to get off the train at its last stop.

It was that steel-encased solitude, silence, and day dreaming that did it. One stop became the same as another, one warning message to please stand clear of the closing doors sounded the same as another, and even the momentary pause in motion felt the same as another. It was only when I realized that the pause was more than momentary that I finally looked around and noticed that Patsy and I truly were the only ones left in the car. The final clue was the announcement that this was now a Richmond train, and the doors would be reopening in five minutes. It was more than once that I had missed the words "LAST STOP, FREMONT," and subsequently more than once that we were forced to spend an extra five minutes on the train.

There was, however, only one morning when solitude did not keep me on the train at LAST STOP, FREMONT.

I can no longer recall at just which stop the young man with the bag got on, but I do remember him sitting across from us and fixing his gaze on Patsy for quite a long time before saying, "That's a beautiful dog you've got there."

"Thank you," I said, obviously always very pleased when my girl received a compliment.

The young man continued to stare at Patsy with a lover's intensity before saying, "She's absolutely gorgeous. I've never seen a dog this beautiful."

"I feel very lucky to have her," I said, which was true. I was incredibly blessed to have this dog, cinnamon red ears and all.

Patsy was returning this enamored stranger's gaze with equal intensity when he suddenly asked, "Can I draw a picture of her? I'm an artist."

"Why...sure," I said with some hesitation. Somewhere in the background the train operator could be heard announcing a station two stops away from Fremont, along with the guide dog school's admonition not to let strangers photograph or in any other way record our dogs.

Perhaps it was his focus for such a long period of time, or perhaps it was even the bag at his side, but there was definitely something about this person that did not suggest an ulterior motive.

The young man drew a sketch pad and pencil from his bag and promptly sat on the train car's floor in front of Patsy. "I like the position she's in," he said as he flipped open his pad to a clean page. "I hope she doesn't move."

"She won't," I said. "I think she knows that you're about to sketch her." It was true; Patsy hadn't moved a muscle since first laying eyes upon her portrait maker, and she certainly wasn't showing any signs of doing so any time soon.

"LAST STOP, FREMONT." The train operator's voice was more an admonishment than an announcement. "THIS IS NOW A RICHMOND TRAIN." Neither one of us paid any attention.

"Darn!" the young man said. "I wish I had more time to draw in her body."

"PLEASE MAKE SURE TO TAKE ALL YOUR PERSONAL BELONGINGS WITH YOU," the voice continued to order.

The young man turned around his pad toward me and my mouth fell open. A perfect likeness of Patsy, pink nose splotch included, looked back at me. "This is beautiful!" I said in awe.

"DOORS WILL BE OPENING IN FIVE MINUTES," the overhead voice announced.

"Thank you," the young man said. He carefully peeled the page from its pad, rolled it up, and handed it to me. "Thank you," I said. "What's your name?"

"Wilson," he replied. "I used to be a student at the San Francisco Institute of Art. What's your dog's name?"

"Patsy," I answered, trying not to crush the picture as I slipped it into my backpack.

Wilson smiled. "You're a beautiful girl, Patsy. Take good care of your mother."

"RICHMOND TRAIN NOW BOARDING." A new voice had now taken up the admonishing.

"Man, this is a great picture of your dog," the young man at the frame shop said. "Who drew this?"

"Just an artist I met on the train," I replied, hoping to sound as Berkeleyish as I could.

"Whoever this was has great perspective," the framer continued, inspecting the work with admiration. "Too bad they didn't sign it."

"Yes, that is too bad," I agreed. I did not disclose Wilson's name. It felt just as Berkeleyish to do that too.

The drawing, sans signature and all, hung in my apartment in Berkeley and now graces my home in Alameda. Patsy's head is more than good enough.

Guide Dogs for the Blind

Katheleen Stagg has faced many obstacles, including questions about Summer's ability to be a service dog. The Bichon Frise finds her own words to answer critics.

Against All Odds

by Kathy Nimmer

I lie quietly beside your wheelchair,
Waiting for you to need the assistance I can give,
But hoping too that you won't need me,
Because when I'm needed, that means you aren't okay.

You live your life so bravely,
Travelling the world and coveting each breath.
And I am honored beyond the speaking of it
To be your very own cherished support.

But I see you struggle, see you grope
For strength, for relief from your pain,
For freedom from the seizures that plague you,
For a day when your "normal" matches how the dictionary defines that word.

I watch you battle the unkind questions too,
Those that doubt my suitability as your service dog.
Disbelief because of my size and my breed:
"That dog can't do anything," they say with a sneer.

But you are used to those empty expectations,
So you are the ideal refuter,
And the ideal partner for me,
As we shatter barriers and make our own way through the world.

Remember the day when you had a seizure
At a restaurant far, far away from home?
You slumped over and stopped breathing,
And I leapt up to support your head?

Do you remember the shock in everyone's eyes
When my actions opened your airway just enough
For your breathing to start up again?
I remember. One tends to, when a life is saved.

I lie quietly beside your wheelchair,
Grateful that I knew what to do then,
Grateful too that you probably don't remember that day:
I'll bear the terror for you on my own.

And I'll go on working for you, with you,
So we can slay the demons of disbelief and misjudgment.
It is my honor. It is my destiny.
I am content, for it is well with us.

Owner-Trained Dog

Young people are often better at expressing basic truths than adults, as shown in this essay by twelve-year-old Michael Schiavo who has Duchenne muscular dystrophy.

The Quiet Courage of Conan

by Michael Schiavo

"You gain strength, courage, and confidence by every experience in which you really stop to look fear in the face. You must do the thing which you think you cannot do."

-Eleanor Roosevelt

When most people think about courage, they think of someone risking their life by running into a burning building to save someone else, or of a pilot landing a plane in the Hudson River without one person getting hurt. People also think soldiers fighting in Iraq for our freedom are courageous. All of these things do show courage, and they get publicity for it. But there is another type of courage that doesn't get a lot of attention. You could call it a quiet courage. I've learned my greatest lessons in this quiet courage not from a human, but from my service dog, Conan:

Lesson of Courage #1: Have unconditional love for family and friends, even when they've made bad choices. When I yell at my mom and hurt her feelings and I'm afraid she might be mad at me, Conan still loves me wholeheartedly. He doesn't judge me for my bad choice. I've learned that love fixes everything.

Lesson of Courage #2: Show integrity no matter what. When I'm out in public with Conan, he's working for me, so he wears a patch on his vest that says, "Please don't pet me. I'm working." But evidently the dog is like a magnet for petters. Even though I ask them not to pet him and his patch emphasizes this, people ignore me and still do. I give my mom the evil eye and nearly lose my temper. Then I look at my dog and he's sitting politely, wagging his tail, taking it all in stride.

Lesson of Courage #3: Trust the path that God sets for you. Before I got Conan, he lived with a puppy raiser for a year and a half and spent six months at advanced training. His puppy raisers and trainers were like family to him. When he was paired with me, he had no fear of leaving his family behind. He knew his purpose was to help me. Even thinking about leaving my family is frightening. But Conan has showed me that you should have faith in God's plan for you, even if it's unclear or hard.

Lesson of Courage #4: Don't judge others for being different. Conan will do anything I ask him to because he is happy to serve and doesn't judge differences, like me being in a wheelchair. How could a silly dog that is happy chasing his tail in circles judge others? I've learned, no matter what differences people have, you can't judge them.

Lesson of Courage #5: Don't give in to peer pressure. Most dogs automatically eat any food they find on the floor, but Conan can only eat on command from my hand or his bowl. When I'm training him, I throw his kibble all over the kitchen floor and let our family dog in to eat it. Conan sits by my side and leans into my chair, never budging from the doggie peer pressure. I know how much he loves his food and really wants to eat it, but he never does. I've learned that even though it would be easier to do what everybody else is doing, I should lean onto the right thing like Conan leans onto my chair.

Lesson of Courage #6: Put other people before yourself. Whenever I ask Conan for help, he's happy to serve. He doesn't act tired or frustrated. He's happy to stop doing what he's doing to put me before him. I've learned that not only should I put others before me, but that I should also be *happy* to do so.

Lesson of Courage #7: Always forgive. When I get frustrated and vent on Conan and it would be easier for him to not bother with me, he still doesn't leave my side. I've learned that friends and family may say things they don't mean out of frustration, but I need to forgive and love them because no one is perfect.

Lesson of Courage #8: Always remain loyal to the most important people in your life. When family and friends visit, they give Conan a lot of attention by playing with and petting him. Although it would be easy for him to be distracted by all the attention, he is always most loyal to me. I'm the person he comes back to. I've learned that people may come and go, but your family and good friends don't, so stay most loyal to them.

Lesson of Courage #9: When the going gets tough, never quit. When Conan pushes heavy doors open for me with his precious pink nose, it would be easy for him to stop before the door is all the way open. With my encouragement, he never quits. I've learned that even when the world seems against you, you should still keep pushing through. When I first realized that my muscular dystrophy was getting worse, I didn't feel like doing anything. I wanted to quit school and youth group and stay in my house. But Conan pushed me to never give up.

Every day I feel more confident and act with more courage because Conan is by my side. I'm not afraid to do things I physically cannot do because of muscular dystrophy, because Conan can do it. Conan will probably never be famous or make the headlines of national newspapers for being my service dog, but in my eyes, he's the most courageous dog I know. Even if he did get a lot of publicity, he wouldn't notice. In his quiet courage, all he cares about is a pat on his head or a "Good job, buddy!" from me.

Canine Companions for Independence

Chapter 4

Even If

Confronting Challenges

Paw Prints of Wisdom

"Employees are required to complete one eight-hour day of training in a wheelchair. On a field trip to a local feed store with the class and the dogs, I was sitting out front waiting for the instructors in my wheelchair, dog by my side. A puppy raiser that I had known for over two years came up and asked if I was getting a dog and began to tell me how she puppy-raised for the organization, never once recognizing me in the chair. It struck me very deeply how much society tends to look away from those with disabilities. If not for that dog by my side, I know she would have never even taken the time to say hello to me. These dogs open up the social side of life for people with disabilities even more than the tasks they can do."

—Lorna O'Connor,
Northwest Puppy Program Manager,
Canine Companions for Independence

When eighty-one-year-old Bill Yates finds his diabetes spinning dangerously out of control, predictability is instantly gone.

Leading

by Kathy Nimmer

Eighty-one-year-old Bill staggered out the front door of the dentist office, unaware that an enormous test of the partnership with his guide dog Barnum was about to unfold. Having spent far longer with the dentist than anticipated, Bill knew his blood sugar was plunging, but he thought he could get home before the insulin shock would set in. He was wrong.

Barnum moved with quiet dignity down the hot streets that had been so repugnant to him at first. The grim California desert heat had amplified the thickness of the long golden fur that rippled in the dry wind, but he was used to it now. And, he knew where the bus stop was, three blocks away. Bill gave him no commands, seemingly disengaged and apparently disinterested. But, Barnum was good with repeated routes. He stopped at the normal corners, crossed the small streets, and sat down firmly at the bus stop which was marked by no shelter or bench. Even when Bill finally spoke up by telling Barnum to keep walking, the dog ignored him, knowing that they were in the place that would bring the pair closer to home.

The bus pulled up. Bill and Barnum boarded, unsteady shuffles blending with firmer, light clicks of toenails as they advanced into the air-conditioned rolling sanctuary. The familiar bus driver greeted them, directing them to a seat near the front of the bus. Forty minutes slid by with Bill falling deeper and deeper into a diabetic stupor. By the time the driver woke him to indicate their stop had come, Bill was nearly incoherent.

With careful, slow steps, Barnum led Bill down the sidewalk in the quiet community where they lived. Barnum knew by repeated routine that Bill's wife would be waiting at home for their return. He knew too that Bill's lunging, zigzag progress down the quiet streets was not the norm for this blind man who defied his age and would walk five miles or more a day when well. But, Barnum couldn't know that when Bill pulled them off the edge of a curb and nearly fell, time was getting dangerously short.

A scratching and whimpering alerted the woman inside the quaint little house that someone was at the door. She opened it to find a panting Barnum and a nearly unconscious Bill, speech slurred and body trembling with weakness. She darted toward the refrigerator and the nourishment that would pull Bill back to wellness, her own blood pumping with urgency. As she turned once more to admit Bill and Barnum into the house, her quick hand stroked Barnum's broad golden forehead before reaching for Bill's arm and drawing him forward, to safety.

Guide Dogs for the Blind

Debee Armstrong and Dutchess had learned to work well as a team, but neither could have anticipated how nature would create a life-threatening hurtle for both of them.

Trust

by Debee Armstrong

Since each guide dog born into their breeding program must have its very own name, Guide Dogs for the Blind had deliberately misspelled her name for their computerized database. Otherwise, Dutchess was a typical black and tan Shepherd. Low-slung and lanky, her tail at half-mast, she guided with precision and confidence in areas where she felt comfortable and safe. But like many of her breed, Dutchess was a bit nervous, trying sometimes a bit too hard to please. "Sensitive" was the euphemism my trainer used for "phobic."

Still, Dutchess was a good match for me. She was my second guide, and I was a high-energy young professional who absolutely loved dogs. I would take Dutchess on many explorations and was always there to build her confidence and make her happy to lead me. She needed a handler who was compassionate and never harsh, but she needed a handler who wasn't fearful either. It had taken Guide Dogs' trainers a long time to locate a confident handler for Dutchess, as many blind people themselves are pretty phobic after surviving the loss of their vision. But I had never seen, and as a toddler, I was the child who wandered off to fall down undetected stairs. I was the tomboy who climbed trees and rode my bicycle down the middle of the busy road. I loved to ski and raft rapids. I was the first blind person I knew to become a foreign exchange student after graduating high school, and in my twenties, when I decided to get my first furry guide, I took my adventures to a whole new level.

Dutchess, however, was the dog of my thirties. In choosing my second dog, I requested a calmer, more centered creature. I worked as a computer trainer for a company whose customers were lawyers, and I was expected to dress and behave accordingly. Unlike my first guide whose pranks were legendary, Dutchess fit perfectly into the corporate world: subtle, aloof, and predictable. Once, when a friend was guiding me to a meeting, with Dutchess heeling quietly at my side, I tripped on a curb and fell flat on my face. The fall was caused by my spiky high-heeled shoes, not by my lack of vision or my friend's incompetence. Even so, Dutchess lived in terror of that curb, giving it a wide berth whenever we were forced to pass it for the rest of her life, though she had not been in harness at the time of my fall.

We're always told to trust our guides, but in the back of my mind, I questioned Dutchess. Was I really safe with this Shepherd that spooked at blowing leaves and shook with fear on a loud subway? Once Dutchess got familiar with something, she was fine, but my first guide had loved the unpredictable and strange. Like many retrains, I mourned my first guide, still secretly wishing she could have just lived forever.

My most dramatic adventure with Dutchess happened on the way to yet another meeting, but since I was getting together with friends, I was wearing sensible Nikes and jeans. Dutchess had been guiding me for almost four years by that time, and everything about the route was routine. We were in downtown Berkeley, just passing the Hotel Shattuck, when for no reason I could determine, Dutchess rapidly walked off the sidewalk and took me directly to the center of the busy, six-lane Shattuck Avenue. She continued hauling me down the middle of the street, oblivious to honking horns and onlookers frantically shouting for me to get out of the traffic. Why would my uptight, rule-abiding guide suddenly go berserk in such a bizarre manner? Not normally given to panic, I myself became suddenly quite undone and began shouting and railing at my poor dog, calling her "stupid" and "bad" and many other unprintable names. And then suddenly, there was a rumbling everywhere, and I felt like I was on the deck of a floating ship. The traffic stopped, and from a construction site on the opposite side of the street, men came streaming down from high ladders. Everywhere I heard screams and running feet. Everywhere I heard glass breaking and the thunks and thuds of things falling. And suddenly a man was beside me, holding my arm, commanding that I stop scolding my dog. "That dog", he told me, "just saved your life." Above the sidewalk, where we had stood just a few seconds before, shattered window panes and a huge marble slab toppled from the façade of Hotel Shattuck. The marble slab lay where I had walked with Dutchess.

Somehow she had sensed the Loma Prieta earthquake a millisecond before it began. Somehow she had sensed that the slab was about to obliterate us.

Never again would I joke about my dog being phobic. Never again would I worry about my safety with her. That was October 17, 1989, and I was safer than the sighted because the unfathomable sixth sense was alive and well in my beloved Shepherd, Dutchess.

Guide Dogs for the Blind

What is the purpose of a service dog when human beings can assist with the same tasks? Deborah Wagner and Scarlet know.

Outdone by a Dog!

by Deborah Wagner

The sudden stop of a much-needed thunderstorm in the Midwest drew people out of their homes to chitchat with neighbors. Friends leisurely leaned against my modified van and debated whether a service dog is really necessary when people can perform the same task that the dog does and more.

As I drove my electric wheelchair onto the wheelchair ramp and into the van, I began the daunting task of moving my uncoordinated body from wheelchair to driver's seat. In a split second, my foot slipped on a floor mat dampened by the recent rain, my nearby friends completely unaware. The prospect of a slow slide off of the driver's seat to an inevitable and painful L-shaped position on the floor made my heart pound with terror as I shut my eyes and braced for what was coming.

Like a flash of lightning, the sliding stopped as my body wedged itself against something. I hadn't slid all the way into my dreaded contortionist's position as I'd anticipated. Dumbfounded, I opened my eyes to find my Golden Retriever service dog had instinctively jumped off the bench seat in the rear of the van, navigated past the obstacle of my wheelchair, and placed her left front paw against my foot to thwart the slide. Friends for a lifetime, still obliviously chatting outside, were outdone by the young service dog named Scarlet!

Assistance Dogs of America, Inc.

Dark streets in a bad part of town riddled with crime—a recipe for danger. Enter two men with a criminal history, Ron Milliman, and his guide dog.

Simba Saved My Life

by Ron Milliman

It was late on a very cold, wintry night in Ypsilanti when I set off with my trusty guide dog, Simba, from my little apartment near Eastern Michigan University to go to the post office. Simba and I made the trip almost every evening to go check on my post office box. I was in a small, mail-order business of my own, and every day I received sometimes just a few and sometimes several orders that came into my post office box.

The post office was a beautiful, new building constructed right in the middle of the very worst part of Ypsilanti. I guess the theory was that investing the millions of dollars in a new government building in that area of town would, somehow, miraculously turn that entire blight into some kind of Mecca with streets of gold. Whatever the theory, it didn't work in practice, because the area remained a very dangerous, crime-ridden area of Ypsilanti.

Especially on cold nights, the post office lobby filled with homeless people who slept on the floor and drank wine and whatever else of the alcohol variety they could get their hands on, and of course, there were drugs of all types too. I absolutely hated to have to walk through that area, but I simply didn't have any other choice. However, I felt relatively safe with Simba at my side. Simba was a small German Shepherd, but she looked vicious, like she would enthusiastically rip someone's arm off at the slightest provocation. Actually, nothing could be further from the truth. Simba was more of a pussycat than a vicious dog. Fortunately, the people congregating in the post office lobby at night didn't know Simba like I did.

It was a Tuesday night in late February, as I recall, and very cold. The post office's lobby was filled with the usual vagrants and winos, and yes, smelt very unwelcoming. Simba and I walked into the lobby and over to my postal box. I was quite proficient at manipulating the combination lock, and it took me only a very few seconds to get it open and remove the contents. As a part of my routine, I took the envelopes—some yellow, some blue, some green—over to a large table so I could organize them and put them in my briefcase that I carried with its shoulder carrying strap. Little did I know on that particular Tuesday night two guys, two very bad guys, were watching my every move. I suspect they had seen me go through my routine on previous nights and figured out that most, if not all, of those little colored envelopes contained cash and checks. These guys followed me out of the post office and down the street.

Like many people, for some strange reason totally beyond my ability to understand, these two bad guys evidently thought since I was blind that I must also not be able to hear. So, as they followed about ten or twelve feet behind me, I could actually hear them discussing their diabolical plan to attack me and mug me. One block up from the post office was an area that was very dark, a large vacant lot on one side of me and several parked cars on the other side.

I heard them boasting about how their knives wouldn't have any trouble slicing through my coat and up under my rib cage, and that it should be fast and easy. However, there was one big problem: Simba. They were afraid of Simba. They started arguing about who was going to jump me from the street side, coming from around the parked cars, and who was going to attack from the other side, the vacant lot side, the side that Simba was on. They were afraid that unless they were able to kill Simba instantly, she might be able to launch a counterattack and seriously bite one or both of them.

As soon as I realized the dastardly plot they were trying to engage in, I urged Simba to speed up. Usually Simba pretty much did as she pleased regarding our pace of travel, but I honestly suspect Simba sensed the danger that lurked behind us. Simba started walking very rapidly, almost at a trot. I felt that if we could get past the vacant lot and into the next block and up the next major intersection, we would be okay. That would get Simba and me up to one of the busier intersections that was well lit, with other people on the street. As Simba and I rushed up the block and past the vacant lot as fast as we could, I heard the bad guys start to call each other names, not nice names. One of the guys told the other one that he felt like sticking his knife up... well, that wasn't a nice place either.

Anyway, Simba and I made it to the main intersection, where we crossed over into the much better part of town. I was so happy to get back to my little apartment and see my wife again. I gave Simba a big hug and as many doggie treats as she wanted, the really special ones that were her favorites. When I told my wife what happened, we both cried, knowing just how close Simba and I came to not making it back home that cold, wintry night in Ypsilanti. I am absolutely convinced that if it were not for Simba, if I had been just using my cane that night, well, I would not be here writing the scenario for you to read.

Two guys were arrested two days later for mugging and stabbing an old lady to death in that same area. Her body was found in that vacant lot. Fortunately, not only were the guys very bad guys, but they were also very stupid. One of them was bragging about how much the old lady was carrying when they jumped her, and their bragging was overheard by an undercover cop in the lobby of the post office. I was never called to testify, but I am pretty certain I could have identified one of the two bad guys from his rather unique speech pattern.

Simba died several years ago, but the memory of how she saved my life will be with me until my death—hopefully, not at the hands of any bad guys, but perhaps fighting that record-winning bass out on Lake Barkley, Kentucky.

Guiding Eyes for the Blind

Robert Routten and Cocoa thrive together. Then comes the crisis that threatens Robert's life.

Priceless

by Robert Routten

I am a family man with muscular dystrophy and have been confined to a wheelchair for the past fifteen years. The disease has left me with little strength in my arms and absolutely none in my legs. Having longed to own a dog again, my wife and I decided to purchase a lightweight breed that we could love and care for.

I researched different breeds to find one that would blend well with our family in both size and manner; that is when I found Roxanna at weeaussies.com, a reputable toy Australian Shepherd breeder in Kentucky. After numerous phone conversations, Roxanna agreed to part with a puppy that she had been saving to show (the puppy's father was an international champion). That is when Cocoa (aka "A Touch of Magic") came into my life. She was an untrained puppy that we took to obedience class to learn basic sit and stay commands. She quickly adjusted to living around a wheelchair and my medical equipment.

One day as I was adjusting in bed my elbow slipped and I rolled over, landing face-first on a pillow, practically suffocating. My pleading screams were muffled by the pillow, so no one came to my rescue. Fortunately, Cocoa sensed the emergency. I cried for Cocoa to "get Blake" (my daughter). Cocoa's normally quiet nature amplified to the loudest and strongest barks I'd ever heard her make as she frantically scraped at the bedroom door. My daughter's husband heard the commotion, and they raced in to find me face-down, drenched in a pool of sweat and bright red in color. Had it not been for Cocoa, I cannot say that I would have lived to tell about it, as I had another hour of naptime before anyone was to come and wake me up.

As a result of Cocoa's heroic actions that day, I enrolled her in service dog training at the Oaks Veterinary Clinic in Smithfield, Virginia, with trainer Michelle. Today, at three years old, Cocoa is a proud, fully qualified service dog. Her skills have progressed far beyond alerting my family of an emergency. She closes the exterior house door for me, a task that used to cause me great pain. The weakness in my arms causes me to drop everyday items such as pens, gloves, and napkins; now Cocoa retrieves them all for me.

Her best quality, however, is recognizing that something is wrong with me—she knows before I do. She even wakes me up when I am unknowingly choking in my sleep.

In her off time, when Cocoa isn't chasing squirrels, she loves to swim in our pool and has been dubbed the "Pool Girl." There isn't a ball she won't fetch or a belly rub she won't accept. But when her service vest is put on, Cocoa is all business.

As a puppy she added love and laughter to my life; now, she also adds the sense of security and independence that most handicapped people long for...priceless.

Oaks Veterinary Clinic

Debbie Morgan, her guide dog Tinker, and Debbie's toddler walk down the street, oblivious to the danger ahead.

Spoken

by Kathy Nimmer

Said the toddler to his mom, in looks instead of words, "I would go with you forever, to the ends of the earth. I trust you with my life, my glowing, vibrant mom. I care not for the fact that you can't see, that your eyes do not lock with mine when I have learned something new and wish to show you. You see me with your heart, and that is enough. I trust you, Mom. I love you, Mom. Let's go out today, together."

Said the mom to her guide dog, in hugs instead of words, "I would go with you forever, to the ends of the earth. I put this harness upon your shoulders and follow where you lead me. I trust your judgment when I cannot understand the complexity of what lies in front of me. You show me in your strides and hesitations when it is safe to go and when I should wait. I trust you even with the life of my small son. We are going out today, together."

Said the guide dog to the toddler, in steps instead of words, "I would go with you forever, to the ends of the earth. I see you walking beside your mom, a plastic cord joining your small wrist to hers. I know her steps follow after me, but I know too that you are mine to protect. As you scamper down this sidewalk and sense not the dangers around you, I guide you too, in a different way, knowing two lives are in my care. So proud we're out today, together."

Said the toddler to his mom, in smiles instead of words, "I would go with you forever, to the ends of the earth. I know we are walking now to the restaurant where we often go, but it seems a grand adventure to me. I feel this way because you are with me, and your guide dog leads us both. I see your guide dog stop at the edge of a road, then start walking again at your command. I smile. I'm thrilled we're out today, together."

Said the mom to her guide dog, in gasps instead of words, "I would go with you forever, to the ends of the earth. But now, I hear a hiss of tires, pressing in close to my right. I feel you turn sharply, pulling me back from the curb just feet away, opening an alley of pavement for a careless car to traverse. He hardly hesitates on his brutal journey to something apparently more important than our safety. Because of you, we are all still alive today, together."

Said the guide dog to the toddler, in kisses instead of words, "I would go with you forever, to the ends of the earth. Don't worry now. You are safe. The car that had no regard for your wellbeing has gone far, far away. I watched and saw him coming, protecting your mom who couldn't see and you who couldn't know. I am trained to do this job, but love motivates me more than training, and I love you very much. We can do all things today and always, together."

Leader Dogs for the Blind

It can happen to all of us, but Barbara Currin didn't have a solution for the problem. However, Comet did.

Comet, Our Wonder Dog

by Barbara Currin

For the last thirty years I have owned and trained one of the most misunderstood breeds: the American Pit Bull Terrier. I presently own two: a male that is already a therapy dog with Therapy Dogs International (TDI) that I am now training to assist my handicapped husband, and a female that previously was my husband's little helper but due to advancing age and an ACL tear last year, we have retired. But this story is about my very first APBT.

Her name was Comet. Her intelligence and loyalty is what endeared me to the breed. At the time, I always trained my dogs to do tricks in order to entertain the neighborhood children. When my husband's condition worsened, I decided to turn the "tricks" into something that could assist him. This occurred in the early stages of her training, so she was not yet ready to accompany him on an out-of-town trip he had to make. I was home alone with the three dogs I had at the time: Comet and two males.

I went out the backyard door to check on my two boys. Comet had been in the house with me. Our entire property was fenced with a six foot chain link atop two feet of cement. The dogs were in their kennel runs. The front door of the house was locked (and on the other side of the fence). Suddenly I realized I had locked myself out. The only way in would have been to break the window on that back door, and I still may not have been able to reach the lock. I yelled out to one of my neighbors. They put a ladder over the fence. I figured I would be able to climb in the partially opened bedroom window. Unfortunately, because the cement grading was on a rather steep slope, the ladder was not very steady. I was afraid to go up high enough to reach the window.

I thought of calling for Comet to get my keys, one of the things I trained her to do. But I knew I had hung them up on a rounded door knob and it would be impossible for a dog to know enough to lift the ring up over the knob to remove them. I don't know why—it must have been desperation—but I took the chance anyway and yelled to Comet, "Get my keys."

I could tell she was attempting to do it by the jingling of all the keys. I suffered pangs of guilt as I thought I was giving her an impossible job and she would never be able to remove them. True to her breed, she wouldn't give up on her assigned task. I couldn't believe my eyes when I saw her stick her head out the window with the keys in her mouth. Even though I was afraid to climb the ladder, I went up as far as I felt was reasonably safe and reached for them.

She came through for me and placed them in my outstretched hand. But the questions remained: how did she get the keys off the door knob, and where was the large ring, the one that held the smaller ring that the keys were on? When I let myself inside, there was the larger key ring, spread open on the floor. It was next to the door they had been hanging on. This was no skinny little key ring; it had to be at least one-quarter inch thick and four inches in circumference. It was also soldered closed. Let me tell you, a grown man would have had trouble opening up that ring. My little sixty pound girl must have yanked on that ring so hard. I checked her teeth, and thank goodness none were broken.

Our girl is gone now, but I'll never forget her, especially the time she saved the day for me. I still have the open key ring. It was because of Comet that we still love and defend the American Pit Bull Terrier every chance we get.

Owner-Trained Dog

A thriving veterinary career had led D. E. Brown into contact with the assistance dog community, but one split second redefines everything for her.

Coming Full Circle

by D.E. Brown

My first recollections tell me dogs have always been important in my life. So much so I decided to become a veterinarian. Early in my career, I encountered service dogs through providing veterinary medical care to guide dogs in training, contributing my small part to support families so crucial to the ultimate success of working dog/disabled partner relationships. Helping to keep these carefully bred puppies healthy during their socialization and basic training was a fruitful endeavor, and I came to understand how loving families open their homes and lives to these pups only to selflessly send them on to a higher goal. Progressively through my veterinary career, I learned the far-reaching effects and utility of dogs working alongside disabled partners, not once considering the possibility that I would ever need the service of a dog in return.

Then, at age thirty-eight, I suffered a stroke as a result of injuries sustained in a car accident caused by a distracted driver. According to the Centers for Disease Control, stroke is the third leading cause of death in the United States and the leading cause of disability among adults. Three-fourths of strokes occur in people aged sixty-five and older. I became part of a small group—six out of 100,000 people between the ages of thirty-five and forty-four—who experience a stroke. The effects of stroke are devastating. My son was a young child, and I was at a peak in my career as a veterinary specialist. Not unlike numerous others, my life was abruptly changed. In the blink of an eye I lost the function of my right side and what would ultimately be the most long-lasting and significant loss: the verbal and visual-spatial skills attributable to the left side of my brain. My independence was suddenly gone.

Full days of neuro-rehabilitation including speech, occupational, and physical therapy alongside intensive medical therapy and surgery allowed me to regain major motor function and an ability to walk with assistance. Still I would trip, fall, and readily lose balance. Bright lights, loud noises, crowds, steps, curbs, patterned floors, and uneven sidewalks all contributed to my continued functional impairment and inability to be independent. Unable to return to work I lost my sense of self. My thought processes were fractured; language came and went in bits and pieces. My existence was a fragmented one.

When my accident occurred, I was working in a company with a progressive policy of advocating service dog training on site. Almost daily I interacted with a puppy-in-training in my area. This access, as I learned, was invaluable to the ultimate success of a service dog. After the stroke, a colleague integrally involved with service dog organizations suggested I consider a service dog. Me? I argued that as an ambulatory, visual person, I would not qualify. She educated me about the wide expanse of skills for which service dogs are trained, including partnering with ambulatory individuals. I was introduced to a longtime service dog trainer and to my training companion for the next six months, a remarkable Golden Retriever named Weiss.

Weiss's job was to train disabled trainees, preparing them for the arrival of their own service dogs. With Weiss I realized the opportunities for increasing independence. Through his patient, wise manner, I learned voice and hand signals and general handling skills that allowed me to maneuver through my day. Remarkably, despite my extensive background with dogs, my mistakes were many. Weiss knew dozens of commands which I needed to learn and remember. Directional confusion was part of my functional impairment, and Weiss would gaze up at me, waiting for me to succeed. With his assistance, I re-learned what were once simple tasks of maneuvering stairs, curbs, surfaces, and crowds. He allowed me to get back out into the world, preparing me to handle my own dog.

Kenya arrived from across the country: a beautiful, calm black Labrador Retriever who had been puppy-trained in the offices of my former company! Kenya and I became a team, and with my newfound independence and confidence, we also became educators. Having experienced the world as a relatively young person suffering a stroke, I found resources were limited and directed to an older population. Kenya, Weiss, and I met the task of teaching others what I had learned from my stroke and disabilities by providing pet therapy with Weiss to inpatient stroke victims and taking both Kenya and Weiss to schools and youth groups as "citizen teachers." I found a challenging world more receptive to me with one of these well-trained, gentle dogs by my side.

Through volunteerism and veterinary work and as a disabled partner, I became closely involved with numerous dog/partner teams. Dogs placed during and after the time Kenya and I were brought together have now passed from this world. Having worked closely with pet loss and its resulting grief during my veterinary career, I can tell you the loss of a service dog is truly an incomparable loss. Your eyes, ears, legs and arms are suddenly not there, again. Your closest companion is gone.

While my opportunities to provide care for service dogs have been especially meaningful, Kenya has given back to me much more than I could ever have expected, leading me through the rehabilitative and healing processes. As I now lift Kenya during particularly disabling episodes of her own illness, I remember the many times she held me up. As she slows down, looking to me with deep brown eyes that seem to express her desire to still try where she cannot succeed, I must reassure her so she can relax. Now Weiss has survived cancer, and two of Kenya's fellow trainees—Wally, the bouncy Golden Retriever, and Eli, the determined yellow Labrador Retriever—are failing, too. And in the end we will hold them up, support them and guide them through their final days as they did for us each hour of each day of their cherished, extraordinary working lives.

Colorado Assistance Dog Education & Training

Judith Vido and Tiki square off against a blizzard as they struggle to find safety.

The Blizzard of '96

by Judith E. Vido

As any recovering adult child of an alcoholic knows, trust and control are always character flaws to be addressed. The blizzard that hit Richmond, Virginia, in January of 1996 tested me on both of these fronts. I'm glad I passed the test when it presented itself, for I have learned that tests come in threes. The first two are when the Higher power just sort of taps one on the shoulder. If one doesn't learn the lesson on those two occasions, He/She really slaps you upside the head next time.

Tiki, my second dog guide, was a lovely black and tan German Shepherd. Where Mary, my first dog, had been my grand Duchess, Tiki was my princess. Three short weeks from the Seeing Eye to the classroom of my last year of graduate studies in social work, Tiki and I learned to trust one another on the go. Tiki boldly took me where many blind persons with dog guides had never dared to go before. Some of those trips were the result of a diagonal street crossing or a wrong turn…so we had no idea where the hell we were most of the time. But we survived! And that's what's important. If the dog gets you home without killing you, I was once told, that was a successful trip. I believe it.

The blizzard of ninety-six nearly purloined my sanity. I am a southern girl, and ice with snow up to my hips is not for me. Cabin fever was closing in, and I had to get out. At last the temperatures rose above thirty, nearing sixty degrees for one day. Surely, I thought, the sidewalks would be clear. I harnessed Tiki and headed up the sun-soaked side of Hanover Avenue.

Icy patches dotted the one-mile route to the vet; Tiki needed a manicure, having nails Dolly Parton would envy. Fearless from boredom and three weeks of being homebound, we forged ahead to the vet's office. What exhilaration! We made it and only a few places had been troublesome. Now for the trek home. Forward, hup-up!

The side street on which the vet's office was located I expected to be a bit rough, but we were only three blocks from Monument Avenue, one of the city's major thoroughfares. After only a half block, I began to wonder if I had not made a horrendous mistake. Piles of snow were blocking the intersections. Ice covered the sidewalks, and Tiki and I slipped and slid along the entire three blocks. It took nearly thirty minutes to access Monument Avenue.

Hurrah, I thought as I at last heard the traffic denoting our objective. Tiki stopped short of the street, and I reached out to see what the obstacle might be. Before me was a wall of freshly plowed snow! We turned heading east and found nothing but ice along the entire block. I began to silently curse then exclaimed out loud the stupidity of these people who had not shoveled their sidewalks. Block after block Tiki and I moved with tedious fear until yet another wall of snow and ice obstructed our way.

Evidently someone had a small home plow, for a five-foot wide, waist-high icy barrier blocked the entire sidewalk. Not a soul was to be heard—much less seen, and I stood wondering what to do with no way around or through the frozen mound.

My anger toward the people who had been so careless and my own helplessness to just see turned to panic when I realized the time. Sunset wasn't far off, and I had only gone less than a third of the way to get safely home. I had to do…something, but what?

As I stood stupefied by the dilemma before me, I realized this was a test. Now here I was with no control—and only one solid thing I could trust: Tiki and her training.

I took a deep breath, let it out slowly, and then stepped back from the wall of ice. I gave Tiki the command "hup-up," literally meaning "get to business." In this circumstance it would mean "take over girl and find a way out of here." With only a moment's hesitation, she turned toward the street and stopped at the curb, not too badly covered with ice. I found the step and followed her into the street. Again I told her, "Right, hup-up." She moved slowly, veering around the plowed mess and keeping me away from the rushing traffic at our left. After about ten feet, she pulled me back to the curbing, or as close as she could get to it. I stepped back up on to ice, but the wall was now behind us.

Tiki had done it! We had done it together. My arms went around her neck, and I dropped to my knees on the ice. I held her till she decided it was time to get moving and shook me off.

Cocky now, with tears of joy, pride, and fear, we started home. The trip usually took us about twenty minutes. On this day, however, it was an hour and a half. Light was still evident in the sky though as we stepped onto our back stoop.

Tiki had been nine years old on that trip, and only one more year was afforded us with such long travel. Afterwards, she retired with a kitten to play with for the last two years of her life. And, as I recall, she never much cared for snow after that, nor did I ever become a fan!

The Seeing Eye, Inc.

Canadian Mich Verrier didn't hear it coming, nor did he know how deadly the very next step could be for him and his guide dog.

Crossing

by Kathy Nimmer

The man and the black Lab guide dog move steadily down the sidewalk, approaching the corner across from the bank that is their destination. The dog passes a barber shop and an alley. He shifts left to avoid the crack that the man's white cane always used to spear, without fail. No spearing today, nor ever again, now that Dale is his guide. The team slows as the corner nears, then stops smoothly as one. The man feels the edge of the sidewalk with his foot, praising the dog who stands still, waiting. The man listens for cars, trusting the mobility techniques that daily keep him and his dog safe. He hears no sounds to indicate that he should delay his crossing. "Dale, forward," he commands with confidence. The Lab takes one step down onto the road. The man follows with his own first step.

Abruptly, Dale stops, angling himself in front of his partner, an insurmountable brick wall barricading the man against the open road. The man hears no sound, senses no obstacle, understands no reason for the dog to have interrupted their journey with such bravado. Then, a voice speaks from behind the man and dog, explaining.

The man's blood turns to ice as he begins to realize how close they have come to ending their teamwork with a hideous, deadly exclamation point. A quiet car, a hybrid, priding itself in transport without sound, had sped past them just feet away, paying no regard to the blind pedestrian who had been within seconds of becoming a brutalized statistic. The man had never heard the engine, a sputter, a whisper. He trembles. He doubts. He feels the firmness of Dale beside him. He knows he must try crossing this street again. He knows he must, but …

The Seeing Eye, Inc.

Her sugar level had been fine just ten minutes ago, so what was causing Dena Feller's diabetic alert dog to behave so strangely?

My Watchdog

by Dena Feller

My dog Bailey is a German Shepherd who I have scent-trained to recognize both high and low blood sugars. I have been a Type 1 diabetic for twenty-eight years and have always had what doctors consider "brittle," or hard to control, blood sugars. My sugar level can go from a great reading of 120 to a dangerously low level of 24 within a matter of mere minutes.

It had been one of my doctors who told me that there were people who were training dogs to hunt for the blood sugar scent. I had once owned a dog who had instinctively alerted to low blood sugars, so it was incredible to hear about efforts to train dogs for this specific task. At the point of being told about this form of service dog training, my children were five and two years old, and I had had multiple severe reactions around them and while driving my car. That was my worst fear: having an accident due to low blood sugar with my children in the car, endangering them and others. I knew I wanted a dog that could help prevent that kind of disaster.

About three months after Bailey was placed with me I was driving my daughter to preschool. Bailey was sitting beside me in the front seat, where she normally rests quietly, while I drove. All of the sudden, she sat straight up in the seat, looked right at me, whined and leaned over to lick my arm as if it were a piece of choice meat. I was confused. She had never alerted to a blood sugar problem in the car before, and never in this way. Her normal alerts had been to jump up on my chest and lick my jaw furiously. That kind of overt action gets my undivided attention and is so necessary, since when my blood sugar is dropping, I can pretty much ignore anything. However, the arm licking persisted.

I had tested my blood sugar before getting in the car to take my daughter to school. It had been 138. It was only a ten minute drive to our destination.

Since Bailey wouldn't stop licking my arm, I decided something must be very wrong. I pulled into a local parking lot, stopped the car, and tested. My blood sugar was down to 91. It had dropped forty-seven points in about five minutes. If you, as a diabetic, drop more than two points per minute, you are "crashing"—your blood sugar is dropping really, really fast.

Without her brilliant and unusual alert, getting my attention safely while I was driving, that outing to preschool could have easily turned into a disaster. With her help, I was able to turn off my insulin pump, drink an apple juice, and arrive at school on time without any problems. When I got to the school my blood sugar level was 77. It was still dropping, and without the dramatic alert, it is very possible that I may not have made it to my daughter's school that day.

Bailey watches over my life twenty-four hours a day, seven days a week. She allows me the ability to control my blood glucose levels better. That prevents complications down the line for someone like me. Bailey is amazing and I am incredibly proud of her. She is my hero.

Owner-Trained Dog

Cancer was sweeping away the mother Kim Shepherd loved. Could training with a new dog ease the pain, or would it all be just too much?

Scooby's Gift

by Kathy Nimmer

Loving her.
Holding her.
My mother.
Cancer winning.
Shattering me.
Frozen still.
Can't think.
Becoming alone.
Unable, unwilling.
Can't refocus.
Trainer encourages.

New dog.
Won't work.
Mother declining.
Mustn't stray.
Trainer reassures.
Will help.
Will heal.
I agree.

Meet dog.
Sweet, spirited.
Mother reaches.
Strokes head.
Dog knows.
Moves closer.

She's dying.
I'm disintegrating.
Keep training.
Good worker.
Excellent guide.
Wheelchair fearlessness.

Mother dies.
I disintegrate.
So alone.
I reach.
Stroke head.
Dog knows.
Moves closer.
Not alone.
Not alone.

ProTrain Dogs

Modern conveniences make daily life more livable, until they backfire hideously as they did for Katherine Hevener.

An Adventure to Remember

by Katherine Hevener

We were Toronto bound. I was excited! It was the first time Sunstar, my beautiful yellow Lab guide dog, and I had ever traveled outside the country alone. That's right, just the two of us. With her help, I just knew we would be fine. After all, I completely trust my dog to guide me around people and obstacles in our path, stop at changes in terrain, such as curbs and flights of stairs, and to disobey me if doing what I asked her to do would jeopardize our safety. I had also heard that Toronto was safe, people were quite friendly, and that public transportation was excellent. Besides all this, I am quite comfortable asking for assistance when I need it.

Sure enough, when we got to Toronto, everything was as I had expected. People were willing to give me directions. In fact, some even walked with us to our destination. Despite the crowds, the train stations felt and smelled clean. Had you been in the downtown train station with me and Sunstar, you would have seen my broad smile and noticed how we were weaving through the crowds as though we were dancing. You would have also heard the horrible sound that brought our movements to a screeching halt.

That sound is something I'll never forget. I can still hear it today. It was the gut-wrenching, blood-curdling sound of an animal in pain. That animal was Sunstar. She screamed just as we were getting off an escalator. I yelled, "Help! Help! Somebody push the emergency button! Stop the escalator! Help!" Finally, it stopped. I stepped off and froze right there in my tracks. I was afraid to move. I didn't know what was in front of me, and Sunstar was in no position to help. I reached down to see what had caused her to scream. Much to my horror, I discovered that she was standing on only three legs; she was holding the fourth one in the air. I barely touched her paw and was covered in blood. I thought she was going to bleed to death right there in front of me and there was absolutely nothing I could do about it. I was going to lose my best friend, my partner, and my eyes. I felt sick, helpless, and terrified. But worse yet, I couldn't think. It was as if my mind was paralyzed.

I recall some ladies trying to comfort me and others insisting I take their Canadian currency. Amidst the ensuing chaos, I heard an angel-like voice say, "Excuse me, ma'am. I know of a really good emergency vet who is close by if you need one." I thought, *Great. How am I going to get there?* As if reading my mind, she said, "I'll be glad to help you get there if you want me to." "I definitely need your help," I said.

She went in search of a taxi. While she was gone, a train station employee managed to stop the bleeding and bandaged Sunstar's foot. Then I heard the lady with the angel-like voice say, "Okay, I have a cab waiting. How can I best help you get to it?"

"Just let me take your arm and stay about a half step in front of me. If we come to a curb or uneven terrain, stop, tell me what is there, and I will tell you what to do," I told her.

A few minutes later, we were in the vet's office. It suddenly occurred to me that I did not even know this lady's name. "Oh my gosh! I'm sorry. I didn't even introduce myself to you! My name is Kitty, and this is my guide dog, Sunstar. What's your name?"

"I'm Sandra."

"Sandra, I can't begin to thank you enough for all your help tonight. I'm curious—how did you know what to do?"

"I didn't until I asked you. Finding out what help is needed rather than assuming you know what to do is just common sense."

I thought, *Wow, she really gets it. If only everyone else would ask if assistance is needed rather than assuming they know what to do. Thank goodness she was there for me!*

I said, "Sandra, I know it's a Friday night and I have already taken up so much of your time. I've no doubt messed up your evening plans. I'll be okay from here."

"Kitty, my plan is to stay with you until everything is taken care of and you are safe."

My thoughts flashed to Sunstar. *Will she ever be able to walk again? If she can, will she want to guide, or will I have to retire her?*

My thoughts were interrupted by the veterinarian. After examining Sunstar's foot, he said, "I don't care how much training dogs have had, they should never ever be traveling on escalators. I can't even begin to count the number of dogs I have treated that have been injured by escalators. Many never walk again. I think Sunstar will be one of the lucky ones. I can clearly see the tendons, but they didn't get cut." He stitched her foot, gave her a strict antibiotic regimen, and told me to limit her activity so the injury would have a better chance of healing. My enthusiasm for exploring Toronto with Sunstar had vanished. For that matter, all I cared about was getting home as quickly as possible so Sunstar could get any further medical care she needed.

The day she finally got her stitches out I was ecstatic. There had been no complications; she was as good as new! And, best of all, she is still guiding!

One day we will go back to Toronto. Only this time, we will steer clear of anything that remotely resembles an escalator! And, I will be better equipped to handle any emergencies.

Guiding Eyes for the Blind

A perpetual struggle for those with disabilities is acceptance from nondisabled individuals. Leigh Ann Shingler must figure out how to help a youngster in her own family get beyond this barrier.

The Sweetest Valentine I've Ever Received

by Leigh Ann Shingler

My service dog Candy has made my life sweeter in countless ways. As a team we have accomplished many things that would have been very difficult if not impossible individually. One such accomplishment happened on February 14, 2008. My youngest niece, Lily, who will be four later this year, used to be afraid of my wheelchair. As an infant she would cry if I held her. As a toddler she would not allow me to touch or hug her. Because of this, she would not even come near me without another adult whom she trusted present.

Family members began to really take notice of this fact when Lily started to walk, particularly on Sundays when we'd gather for dinner. If I came into the room and Lily was there, she'd immediately move to hide behind a family member.

Sometimes well-meaning family members would try to make Lily talk to me or hug me. Mama and I took turns telling people not to force the issue, that Lily couldn't help the fact that she was afraid, and that she would come to me in her own time.

I gave Lily her space and waited. While waiting for her to find her moment, I got extra hugs from other family who wanted to show Lily that it really was okay to touch me. Occasionally, I'd talk to Lily or ask her for a hug just to see if she was ready yet. When she declined, I'd say, "That's okay, honey, maybe next time." It was during this waiting period that Candy and I were partnered.

Prior to their first encounter, In November of 2007, I talked to Lily and her older sister and brother about Candy and about the things she does for me. Naturally all the kids were eager to meet Candy. The first time Lily's siblings saw Candy, they came running to the door to greet us screaming, "Candy!" We stopped and sat in the foyer of my parents' house, blocking the front door while Candy, Chris, and Heaven all got acquainted. While this was happening, I saw Lily peek into the foyer from behind the dining room doorway. Her eyes went wide, and she turned and ran farther into the dining room and out of sight. For a moment I thought she'd been frightened until I heard her exclaim, "Papaw, c'mere!" I heard my dad telling her to wait just a

minute, but Lily objected. "No, Papaw, c'mere NOW!" The next thing I saw was my then two-year-old niece leading, or rather, dragging my dad out into the hall, her small fist wrapped around his finger. Once he was out in the hall, she shoved him between herself and me so that she could have her feeling of security and pet Candy at the same time.

Over the next three months, Lily gradually started to warm to me. She even stopped hiding behind adults when in my presence as long as she could keep Candy between the two of us. She'd say, "Candy, c'mere," then take hold of Candy's collar and drag her to a spot between the two of us, as if Candy was her new protector. Then, she'd talk to me for as long as she had Candy there to pet.

Finally, on my way home from work on Valentine's Day, I stopped by my parents' house to visit for a moment. A short time later I was on the front porch hugging Heaven and Christopher goodbye. We agreed they could come and visit Candy and me soon, and I set out across the front lawn, headed for the street. I didn't get two feet from the porch before I heard Lily run down the ramp. I turned, intending to tell her to go back into the house with her brother and sister, but before I could she turned her palms up in the air, shrugged her shoulders, and asked, "Hey, what 'bout me?" I opened my arms to her and she came running, climbed up on my lap, and threw her arms around me. I sat there on the front lawn on that cloudy overcast day, holding my niece for the first time since she was a newborn, trying desperately not to cry. After a few seconds she scampered down, hugged Candy, and ran for the front door waving good-bye.

It took nearly two and a half years to get that first hug, but it was worth every minute of the wait. There have been many more hugs since, and I wonder sometimes how long it would have taken if Candy hadn't come along and helped comfort Lily's fears.

Texas Hearing and Service Dogs

Chapter 5

Though Sometimes

Appreciating the Humor

Paw Prints of Wisdom

POST-PUPPY RECOVERY PLAN FOR PUPPY RAISERS: A TEN STEP PROGRAM!

1. *Spend the whole day vacuuming dog hair from the car.*
2. *Clean nose smudge marks from the car windows.*
3. *Get out unused fashion shoes purchased just before puppy arrived, and throw sensible walking shoes to the back of the wardrobe.*
4. *Try to remove training treats from pockets after they have been through the washing machine and dryer.*
5. *Clean the front door and wonder how paw prints got that high up.*
6. *Remove dog hair from the patio door track and marvel at the way the door slides now.*
7. *Inform cats that life will now be very dull.*
8. *Repair or throw out everything with teeth marks on it.*
9. *Ring up former non-doggy friends.*
10. *Donate sticky 'dog-hair removal' roller to another puppy raiser, until the urge to love another puppy comes again!*

—Marilyn Valder,
volunteer puppy raiser for Guide Dog Services New Zealand

Kathy Zolo depended on Pasha to guide her to her university classes. Pasha did that well, most of the time.

A Learning Experience

by Kathy Nimmer

Bowling Green State University had a space crunch: too much growth in too short a time and facilities not expanding quickly enough to accommodate the high number of students. The temporary solution? Every available space was used for classes. Where there was room to squeeze in a cluster of desks, there was room for a class to meet.

Kathy and her guide dog Pasha moved quickly through the halls of the athletic building toward Kathy's Spanish class that met in the men's gym. Pasha was confident in her work. A beautiful Boxer, she was loyal and smart. She and Kathy had bonded quickly and worked well together as a team.

Pasha was so confident with her work that Kathy didn't need to give her commands on familiar routes. Patterned to certain destinations, Pasha took the initiative and repeated what was ingrained in her memory. Kathy enjoyed Pasha's independence and drive.

This day, as they wove up and down the hallways of the athletic building, Kathy's mind was consumed with the upcoming Spanish quiz. She'd studied, but she didn't know if it would be enough. This professor was tough. Kathy mentally surveyed the chapter as she moved, paying little attention to Pasha's maneuvers.

Finally, Pasha stopped. Kathy reached out her hand to locate the doorknob. "Good girl," Kathy murmured, conjugating the verb "trabajar" under her breath. She pulled open the door, let Pasha step in before her, and briskly entered the room. Within about two seconds, all conversation inside the room halted completely. So did Pasha. The sudden cessation of sound and movement jarred Kathy out of her mental review session. She wrinkled her forehead in confusion, trying to figure out what was wrong.

"Uh, Miss?" A hesitant male voice drew Kathy's attention to the right.

"Yes?"

"Uh, did you know you are...well...kind of...like...in the men's locker room?"

Kathy didn't need vision to know that a crimson stain was spreading like salsa across her burning cheeks. She fumbled for the door, apologized, and dragged Pasha out into the hall behind her.

"Pasha the peeper," Kathy muttered, turning and hurrying to her Spanish class. "Men's gym, not men's locker room! You should be the one taking a quiz on the difference between those two locations," she guffawed, "with extra credit for whatever you saw in there just now!"

Pilot Dogs, Inc.

Judy Brangwin's career-changed dog presents her version of the old saying, "Put your money where your mouth is."

Kasia...Show Me the Money

by Judy Brangwin

My name is Kasia. I'm a career-change four-year-old Golden Retriever who is employed by Shred Dogs, Inc., a company formed by some of my four-footed internet friends and me. I was just nominated for Employee of the Year. Why did I receive this nomination? Well, let me tell you. Mom and Dad have always thought the United States government should be hiring me for shredding classified documents. To keep up with my skills, last week I practiced shredding in my crate. Since I am known for my good shredding, I'm crated when Mom and Dad are not home. I just put in a roll of toilet paper when they were not looking. I ran into my crate like every morning at seven and stood there waiting for Mom to give me my treat and close the door. She never saw the toilet paper. I had a super duper time till Dad discovered it when he came home for lunch.

As I mentioned, Mom and Dad are aware of my shredding abilities and take precautions when they leave. But my most recent escapade occurred when they were home sleeping. Dad had just been to the bank to get some money for an upcoming business trip. He got lots because he wanted to be prepared. Mom was planning to go shopping the next day, and instead of just handing her some money, he laid ALL of it on the coffee table for her to take the small amount she needed. They never gave that money another thought, and off they went to bed. This money was twenty one-hundred German mark bills. That amount is valued at approximately one thousand American dollars. The bills were nicely rolled and secured with a rubber band. Well, you can imagine what I did next. I removed that rubber band and never even broke it. And then I started shredding all those bills. Oh, what a fun time I was having! Then I left my "handiwork" on the couch and went to bed. When Mom and Dad got up, Mom saw shredded paper. She thought I had shredded an envelope, but then she took a closer look. Oh, no! She couldn't believe that I had shredded ALL that money. She started picking up pieces and tried to put them together. When many pieces were missing she knew just where they went. Now I do have a sister, a yellow Lab, so I hoped maybe she would get the blame. But Dad said, "The proof is in the pooping!" Sure enough, the next day there was no doubt who the guilty one was! Then Dad jokingly said that I was like the goose that laid the golden egg, only I "laid" hundred mark bills.

Well, my Mom decided she was NOT above "money laundering" when it came to that amount of money, so she waited a day or two and poop scooped. Dad stayed way, way away. He wanted absolutely no part of the "money laundering" scheme. But Mom said it wasn't all that bad as she was laundering all those tiny pieces of bills. The next task was putting the pieces together. It took her several days before the job was completed. She was able to find all the serial numbers for all the bills I chewed up. Three of the twenty bills I left untouched. She taped the pieces together and then taped them to sheets of paper and put them in a plastic bag. Then off to the bank she went. The bank took the money, but told Mom she would have to wait. Well, Mom and Dad waited and waited and kept checking their bank account. Finally, the deposit was there—after making its way through the system.

Guide Dogs for the Blind

Jennifer Holladay did well in college, but Rainy did even better!

Top of the Class

by Kathy Nimmer

Jennifer succeeded well in college, but it was Rainy who lit up the campus! The yellow Lab guide dog tallied amazing marks, the highlights of which are something to behold!

Class: Abnormal Psychology. Grade: A+. The subject matter was serious. The studying was intense. The professor led the students through discussions of complex and profound mental disturbances that surely didn't paint happy dreams in the students' minds as they drifted off to sleep at night with textbooks splayed open in front of them. But, when the professor announced that they would have an "abnormal Christmas party" during their last class before exams, everyone cheered. College students never turn down free food, so the anticipation level was high.

Before the party began, the professor stood up in front of the students. "I have two awards to present," she said. Everyone stilled, anticipating academic honors to be given to those who had earned the highest grades in the class. "The award for the sanest member of the class goes to Rainy!" The class laughed and clapped. Rainy's ears perked up, but she remained lying quietly by Jennifer's side. "The second award is for being the best behaved member of the class, and that goes to Rainy!" The class roared. Rainy's tail thumped as the professor squatted down to present her with two certificates and a bag of treats. Jennifer removed Rainy's harness and rewarded everyone with petting time and belly rubs for Rainy.

Class: World Civilization. Grade: A+. Rainy was a vocal dog, while sleeping anyway. The bevy of moans, groans, whimpers, and whines she emitted while leaping through doggy la-la land was amusing to many folks, especially college students who appreciate any interruption to the normal routine.

One morning when the lecture was particularly long and tedious, the students shifted and wriggled in their seats, hiding yawns behind their strategically-placed palms and trying to stay focused on the material. Rainy awoke from a refreshing nap, looked around, and decided that it was indeed time for the class to end. She opened her mouth and released a belly-deep, screechy yawn that would have registered quite respectably on the decibel scale! The professor stopped in mid sentence, walked over to Jennifer who blushed in embarrassment, and knelt down in front of Rainy, placing his hands on the sharp creases of his dress pants, his suit jacket brushing the less-than-pristine floor of the classroom.

"Excuse me, young lady. I didn't ask for your opinion!" Hesitant snickers sputtered like movie theater popcorn throughout the room, followed by vibrant cheers as the professor smiled and waved his hands toward the door, signaling the release of class.

Class: Biology. Grade: A+. It was a true blue love affair. Rainy couldn't be close enough to the biology professor. He shared the same sentiments. On the numerous outings to zoos and nature centers, Rainy insisted on following right behind him, whether Jennifer felt up to walking quickly that day or not! Rainy's eyes, ears, and nose were always pointed in his direction as she aspired to be as close as possible to the man of her dreams!

As class wound down in April, the professor decided to treat his students to Easter eggs hidden around the science wing, filled with the sugary goodies that are staples for college students. As Jennifer and a classmate hunted together for the eggs with Rainy inquisitively walking beside them, they discovered a special one with Rainy's name on it. Inside, the professor had placed a luscious variety of dog treats! Needless to say, Rainy's attachment to the professor continued, long after the class ended.

Yes, Jennifer did the work, but Rainy did the charming. Upon Jennifer's graduation, the dean made a special presentation. "Throughout her academic career at Thomas More College, Jennifer has been accompanied by a faithful companion, Rainy. This four-footed friend has attended every class, listened to all the lectures without barking out any comments on the subject or the quality of the lecture. It must be recognized, however, that Rainy did occasionally catch a short nap during a lecture, not unlike an occasional student. Nevertheless, it seems appropriate that we award Rainy a diploma to accompany the diploma that Jennifer receives. It is for perfect attendance and Human Communications. Congratulations, Jennifer and Rainy."

The Seeing Eye, Inc.

Disney World offers amusement for people of all ages, but Lynda Enders didn't expect Cash to join in the entertainment.

One Magical Kingdom Day

by Kathy Nimmer

Ah, Disney World! The place where dreams are reality, where the beauty of magic is all around, where everyone is a child. Lynda and Cash had enjoyed every minute of it. Now primarily using an electric scooter following a stroke thirty years before, Lynda depended on Cash to support her when she walked short distances. At 125 pounds and measuring twenty-nine inches at the shoulder, the black Lab/Chesapeake Bay Retriever was a strong, loyal companion who traveled everywhere with Lynda. Thus, this little kingdom of Disney World had been a piece of cake, child's play.

It was now time to head out of the park, back to the real world. Waiting near the shuttle that was equipped with a wheelchair lift, Lynda knew that her previous method of loading both her and Cash onto the bus was the best option. Not fond of riding the lift with her, Cash was always uneasy with the mechanics of that procedure. His immense size, coupled with Lynda's electric scooter, made it rather unsafe as well. So, Lynda left Cash in line with other passengers waiting to board the bus through the main door, planning to meet him inside once she had ridden the lift.

All was well that humid Florida afternoon, until it happened. A rabbit appeared suddenly in a patch of landscaped ground not far from the loading area. No, this wasn't Bugs Bunny, just an innocent little rabbit whose mission was to nibble manicured grass and leaves, not to torment a usually obedient service dog. After all, Disney didn't see many non-Pluto dogs in the big scheme of things, so the rabbit was blissfully unaware that it had caught Cash's attention.

With little hesitation, Cash decided that all work and no play in the land of childhood dreams was just not right. He sprang to his feet and was off!

Bounding across the pavement and thrusting his way into the landscaping, Cash had but one focus: the bumbling bunny who now realized that his life was in distinct peril. Tucking in his tufted little tail, the bunny broke away. Not daunted, Cash employed his thick, rippling muscles to propel him across the pristine grounds and after the fast fluff ball!

Back at the shuttle, Lynda cringed in embarrassment. She was in no position to run after her dog, who almost never had a meltdown like this. But Cash was now acting as if he had acquired his own disability of profound deafness, ignoring her quite thoroughly, all of his senses turned toward the racing rabbit.

Lynda maneuvered herself toward the large parking lot that bordered the site of the chase and called to Cash again. By this time, quite a crowd of onlookers had gathered to enjoy this one last unexpected attraction. A few of them tried to help bring Cash back, but Disney World doesn't necessarily inspire the taking of initiative. Instead, this little drama was like "It's a Small World" versus "Big Thunder Mountain," and it was anyone's guess as to which one would win!

Cash, meanwhile, lost sight of the rabbit, who apparently used his home amusement park advantage to extend his life a little longer. Perhaps diving down a rabbit hole and straight into his therapist's office, the breathless bunny was just plain gone. With his quarry now invisible, Cash remembered his training and bounded back toward Lynda. Panting with excitement and exhaustion, Cash nudged Lynda's hand and assumed his normal position beside her scooter. They turned back toward the shuttle to try boarding again.

Owner-Trained Dog

Belinda Simpson from New Zealand appreciates sweet treats as much as the next person…or dog.

Thief

by Kathy Nimmer

She strides, confident and secure,
Through the mall filled with chaotic lives,
All spinning toward their own destinations.
She is unconcerned about where those destinations are,
For her own is steady and definite today.

He strolls, regal and serene,
Beside his special lady friend,
His tail wagging gently
As he collects bouquets of admiration
And remains unfailingly aware of his lady's needs.

Gasp!
Gulp!
Pause!
Stop!
Inquire!

She turns with a concerned query
To a child whose lip trembles
In unison with his clutching right hand
Now holding a solitary ice cream cone,
Newly bereft of its crowning, icy, gloppy goo.

And now a fluffy tail makes a trio
Of the lip and hand quiver duet,
While a stealthy tongue removes
One last incriminating smear
From the short fur encircling a so satisfied doggy mouth.

She frowns, then snorts with laughter,
Not so regal and serene as all of that,
But she buys the boy a new ice cream cone,
And his smile now mirrors that
Of the canine ice cream connoisseur!

Service Canines of Montana

Confidence comes from safe and independent travel as Alena Roberts knows well. Sometimes, a little something extra can accompany that confidence.

Carry On

by Kathy Nimmer

They were poetry in motion, Alena and Rico. Noble, confident, the team of all teams, the shatterers of myths that trumpet disability as a shameful limitation. On that autumn day on the campus of the University of Oregon, nothing was more exquisite than that young blind woman, loaded with potential, and that big black Lab who could move mountains with his broad, muscular shoulders. Striding, weaving, slicing through the crowds of students who noticed their dignity. Murmurs a-plenty were heard as they passed. "Ah, we're good," the young blind woman murmured to herself. "Fast and fabulous, and Rico isn't even panting. We're making a great impression."

They powered onward, carving a path to the bus stop on the far side of campus after leaving the disability office. If anyone could do anything, it was this pair. Dignified, noble, confident.

A chuckle? *Hmmm*, she thought to herself. *I wonder why they're chuckling. Probably has nothing to do with us. We chuckle. I chuckle at them, they of lesser dignity, nobility, confidence. Carry onward.*

The bus stop loomed ahead. Ah, the destination reached with success. "Rico, sit. Good boy. I will pat your head. What? Why are you breathing so oddly? Rico? What? You have something in your mouth? Rico!" A startling and humbling epiphany. Perhaps dignity, nobility, and confidence were not the first words that came to the minds and lips of onlookers who saw the powerful team as they strode across the campus. A more apt trio of descriptors might have been sly, slippery, and ridiculous. What had Rico chosen for his mouth's companion on the march across campus? A big, ripe, slimy banana peel! It was Alena's turn to chuckle.

Guide Dogs for the Blind

DeAnna Quietwater Noriega lets us in on a rather illuminating chat with her guide dog.

Conversations with My Guide Dog

by DeAnna Quietwater Noriega

Let me begin by saying that my dog's portion of this conversation is expressed in grunts, squeaks, snorts of disbelief, tail thumps, and let us not forget, various positions of those lovely German Shepherd ears. So this record of my half of our dialogue is not simply the ramblings of a disordered mind. Then again, perhaps you might not agree if you don't get into conversations with the nonhuman members of your own family!

"Good morning to you, too. I am sure it will be a wonderful day, and I know you need to run outside—as this house doesn't provide indoor plumbing for dogs—but I think it's raining and I need shoes and a raincoat. So please stop dancing around until I get myself together."

"You could wipe your own feet before coming in all muddy, you know."

"I know you are highly intelligent. You did graduate from one of the best guide dog training programs in the country. So how come you always manage to get your front paws tangled in your leash like this? No, I don't believe you were trying to play cat's cradle."

"You must know that eating grass or kitty excreta will give you gas, so why do you always look offended when you are the one fumigating the room?"

"I love you, but I don't like being used as your napkin when you have just dunked your muzzle in your drinking bowl."

"No, I don't think water tastes better when imbibed from a toilet! I just know so and don't have to try it!"

"Shaking fur all over a restaurant isn't funny. It isn't another way to say I'll be seeing you again."

"I don't own the whole sidewalk or every place we go into to conduct business, so don't think we have a right to be first."

"Now, I know that putting your cold nose on people makes them move and allows us to get to the front of the line, but we can wait our turn."

"Yes, I understand that he said something rude to you, but it's his yard and you are a professional, so just walk past and ignore him."

"No, you can't take your toys with us; you are working! Behave yourself or I'll put this harness on the cat!"

"Yes, we are shopping again, and the object isn't to go in one door and find the exit as fast as we can, and no, you can't just pick up things and expect me to pay for them."

"I brushed you this morning and you don't have fleas, so stop scratching and jangling your tags like that! You are interrupting the meeting!"

"Wake up; I know the sermon was extra long, but snoring is impolite."

"Yes, that's your dinner and I know mine looks better, but yours is well balanced and nutritious. Besides, it costs more than a dollar a pound, so it must be good."

"You are very smart to remember this place, but we aren't going there today. Don't huff at me, I am not being ridiculous. And yes, I do too know where we are going and it isn't back the other way!"

"It isn't alright to chase the neighbor's cat out of your yard just because it isn't our cat."

"Because it is on the floor doesn't make it yours. So give it back right now!"

"Yes, I know where the dog biscuits are, but you are not getting another one. Your harness is getting tight."

"I know everyone says you are beautiful and clever, but you don't need to thank them all for the compliments. Let's get going!"

"Dog biscuits aren't free; you have to work for a living!"

"Hey, you! Yes, you in the dog suit! We've got a bus to catch, so put down the ball and get your harness on!"

"You can too fit under an airline seat!...Okay, you win. Being half in my lap is reasonable when you get scared."

"Yes, you are the bestest dog in the whole world."

The Seeing Eye, Inc.

Griffen wouldn't have ever expected that his handler, Kristie Baker, would command him to "get the bunny!"

Griffen and the Bunny

by Kristie Baker

While Griffen, my first Canine Companions for Independence Service Dog, provided me with a tremendous amount of independence and did many things for me, I think the thing I will most remember is the day he saved the bunny.

I must preface the story with a little about the household Griffen joined. I was the only *human* occupant of a very crowded home; I had six cats as well, all strays that had been sick or injured when they adopted me.

The lone male, Frodo, was a year-old unneutered male when he ran afoul of a more territorial tom. Frodo came away much the worse for wear and with several wounds that had become infected. He found my house, and being the soft hearted, soft headed chump I was, I fed, coaxed, and finally captured him. After a trip to the vet for emergency medical treatment and an appointment with the neutering clinic, he fit right in to my menagerie.

But Frodo was a hunter. He would capture beetles and lizards and bring them to me proudly, using the cat door. Most often they were still alive and kicking when he would drop them in the middle of the floor. All the cats would have a field day chasing the prey around the house with me in hot pursuit in my wheelchair, trying to rescue the lizards or capture the bugs. Alas, I was usually too slow and clumsy to succeed, and usually all I rescued were the corpses.

It was during this time that I was matched with Griffen. He adjusted well to being the only dog in a house full of cats, ignoring them mostly and being very tolerant of their antics.

One afternoon about a year after Griff came to me, Frodo struck again. He captured a very tiny baby bunny, probably about weaning age but certainly not yet able to run or escape. That rascal Frodo brought the rabbit into the middle of the living room floor and dropped it. It didn't take long for a circle of six cats to start closing in. It looked like certain slaughter. I was on the outside of the ring of cats, and every time I moved closer to attempt to reach the bunny, the cats would tighten their circle and the bunny would act like it was going to try to make a run for it (which surely would have been a fatal mistake).

I despaired that I would not be able to reach the bunny before tragedy occurred. Suddenly, Griffen was at my side. He was *very* interested in what was occurring in the middle of that circle of cats. The bunny had zero chance of survival as the situation stood, so I told Griffen to "get the bunny." (As a Golden Retriever, he possessed a "soft mouth," an attribute that has allowed the breed to work well with hunters, retrieving downed game without biting down on the object in their mouths). I felt confident that he would not hurt the rabbit.

He walked calmly into the ring of cats, picked up the bunny, and brought it to me, gently placing it in my lap. Aside from a racing heart and some dog drool, that furry creature was unharmed. I put it back outside. I was so proud of Griffen. I reveled in knowing I now lived with a "knight in *golden* armor."

In the overall scheme of things, saving a baby bunny may not be what would define a service dog to the general public, but to me, what Griffen did that day is the core and essence, and indeed the very definition, of what a good service dog is all about.

Canine Companions for Independence

Air travel sometimes can be a tad complicated when an assistance dog is involved. Robin Smith and Chauncey encountered this first-hand when nature's call became an outright shout!

How Does a Service Dog Spell Relief

by Robin Smith

Chauncey, my service dog, and I traveled to Independence, Oregon, last summer to visit some good friends. Independence is about an hour from Portland in western Oregon and is a beautiful little old town of only about 7,000 people. While there we had a chance to experience a real small town Americana Fourth of July with a carnival, pancake breakfast at the firehouse, parade, and of course, fireworks. I'm a born and raised big city kid, so this was really a special treat for me.

Chauncey and I enjoyed our stay and were sad to leave, but when the time finally came we made sure that we left for the airport in plenty of time. What we didn't count on was the highway construction on I-5 near Portland and the subsequent traffic snarl that came along with it. Four lanes narrowed into one at rush hour and what started out to be a leisurely drive to the airport turned into a frantic bumper-to-bumper fiasco as time grew slim before our flight.

We finally arrived at the airport about twenty-five minutes before our scheduled departure time. I still had to pick up our boarding pass, check our bags, go through security, and most importantly for Chauncey, find a place for him to toilet. I asked everyone that I could find along the way if they knew of a place where Chauncey could go but to no avail. Nevertheless, there we were, getting on the airplane, and poor Chauncey's eyes were swimming. We found our seats onboard and took off for the first one hour and twenty minute leg of our flight toward San Diego with a stop in San Jose. During the flight, I could tell that my poor boy was really uncomfortable.

The plane finally landed in San Jose. Chauncey and I remained in our seat near the door and listened as the seemingly endless line of de-planing passengers filed past the flight attendants who recited their obligatory, "Buh-bye, buh-bye, enjoy your stay, buh-bye." This seemed to take forever, and I knew that somehow I had to find a way for Chauncey to get his business done, and soon. Not the least of our problems, however, was that my wheelchair had been stowed and I couldn't get out of my seat.

After all of the departing passengers were off the plane and before I could ask, one of the flight attendants asked me if Chauncey might need to relieve himself. I said, "Yes, he sure does!" She offered to take him off the plane for me. I told her the command for toileting ("Better go now!"),and off they went.

Several minutes later, the flight attendant and Chauncey returned, but the flight attendant looked very flushed and out of breath. She said (huffing and puffing), “I have a story to tell you.” This is what she told me: “I took Chauncey down the causeway onto the tarmac under the plane. I did as you said and commanded him, ‘better go now’ several times, but all he did was look at me and finally just lay down. I petted him, I said it again, but he just lay there. Chauncey began to attract attention from others. A baggage handler came over and tried to help. Then an airplane mechanic and a Transportation Safety Administration official joined in. We were all trying to figure out what to do so poor Chauncey would toilet. Someone then suggested that maybe Chauncey didn’t like to go on the concrete. The TSA official said excitedly, ‘FOLLOW ME!’ So we hurried up the restricted tunnels, gaining an entourage like a downhill snowball along the way. We were all running behind the TSA agent who was frantically swiping his security card past each of the many secured doors so that Chauncey could find sweet relief. Now far away from the airplane, Chauncey was finally shown a patch of grass in front of the terminal where he closed his eyes, lifted his leg and really let it flow. When we saw this, the mechanic, the TSA official, the baggage worker, myself, and by now several more of Chauncey’s new best friends burst into celebratory cheers, high fives and jumping up and down. And Chauncey seemed pretty happy too.”

Afterward, I sent a special thank you email to the airline citing the very thoughtful flight attendant who went out of her way to make Chauncey’s day.

Oh yeah, one more thing; how does Chauncey spell relief? S-O-U-T-H-W-E-S-T.

Paws’itive Teams

Donna Burke's dog Haley obeyed eagerly, until...

Golden Game

by Kathy Nimmer

Ah, what a wonderful meal! Thick, sweet carrots. Luscious, slightly crunchy green beans. Crisp, fragrant lettuce with an array of tasty toppings. And, juicy as can be, a grilled chicken breast, oozing with flavor! Heaven! At least that is what Haley assumes anyway, based on the exclamations of appreciation coming from the humans at the table above Haley's head. Selfish creatures, these humans, but she is strong enough as a service dog to ignore the temptations, so she sighs and closes her eyes for a nap.

Clatter! Clink! Splat! Donna's fork slips out of her fingers and falls to the floor. Her power wheelchair is too bulky and her arms too weakened by muscular dystrophy for her to reach down and pick up the fork. But, yes, that is what Haley is for, the lovely Golden Retriever who can retrieve dropped items, turn on lights, and open doors. So, surely picking up a fork is within her job description.

"Haley." An inquisitive gaze from warm brown eyes. "Get it," pointing toward the fork.

Haley pauses and looks at the fork. Not a large object, not an awkward shape, and not as bland and uninteresting as the remote control Donna dropped the other day or the countless other objects Haley has retrieved in recent weeks. She takes a step toward the fork, sniffs it, and walks away with a prideful raising of her nose as she demonstrates her self control. Surely this is a trick, meant to enforce the no-human-food rule that service dogs must abide by so they will behave while people are eating at restaurants or at home, as Donna is now. But, there is the "get it" command, so maybe it isn't a trick.

Haley returns and daintily picks up the fork, only to drop it in two seconds. "Must not must not must not taste human food, and there is definitely the yummy taste of human food on that fork, plus an icky metallic flavor that is ... just ... icky!" But Donna is watching, and she repeats the command once more. Perhaps if Haley just engages with the evil, irresistible object that would be enough.

So the game begins! Have you heard of the new Olympic sport, fork soccer, played between the right front foot and the left front foot of a large Golden Retriever, with the assistance of the large Golden Retriever mouth to pick up and drop the designated object, just for added style points? Bat it this way! No, now that way! Mouth grabs and drops to create a mega clatter! Let the nose bop it in for a goal! Woohoo!

Ah, but now Donna is laughing and repeating the command again. What to do, what to do? Haley wrinkles her forehead and reaches forward. Fork is in mouth, and Donna is smiling broadly. This must be the right thing! But, oh, the whammy of that juicy, succulent chicken, and the wallop of the icky, metallic flavor! Haley's taste buds are massively over-stimulated, so she wriggles in all six doggy directions at once (including up and down), finally leaping across the room and flinging the possessed utensil under Donna's computer desk, far enough away to keep Donna and Haley safe from its demonic devices! With the flying fur and rippling muscles of a gorgeous leaping Golden, Haley is poetry in motion as she twirls and almost bows following the final fling!

But, Donna is calling Haley back, chuckles still permeating the command. "I guess she just wants me to retrieve it and give it back to her after all. How boring!" Then, Haley obeys.

East Coast Assistance Dogs

As a minister, Bob Norris had handled many diverse reactions to religious ceremonies, but Carmen's was unique.

Prayer, Anyone?

by Bob Norris

I lost most usable vision after I retired from full-time ministry as a United Methodist pastor. Still, I have continued part-time by conducting weddings, funerals, and guest sermons while others vacationed, with the help of my guide dog Carmen.

In one such instance, after I had conducted a funeral, I noticed my wife and the mortician were standing and laughing together. When we got to the car I asked my wife what had been so funny. She said that the mortician had poked her during the service and told her to watch Carmen. My wife told me that every time I prayed, the dog sat, as though in respect. The mortician and my wife were both very amused.

I knew that Carmen was exceptional, and I thought that she might even be saintly, but I knew that Guiding Eyes had not taught her to pray. Her puppy raisers, however, were very religious and had told me that she had gone to church all her life. Still, I pondered her spiritual sensitivity but could not really explain her most appropriate behavior. Then I suddenly realized that every time I invoke the congregation to pray, I turn my palms upward and say, "Let us pray." Carmen was reading my hand single as a "sit" command!

I chose not to let anyone know my secret so all the church folk will think that Carmen is super spiritual. So far, it's working!

Guiding Eyes for the Blind

Chapter 6

But Still

Perseverance and Teamwork Win the Prize

Paw Prints of Wisdom

"There comes a day when the bond between a service dog and his human is complete. On that day, in that moment, they become partners."

—Dee Bogetti,
Canine Consultant, Author and Co-host, Bark Radio

"Animals, for some, afford increased opportunities to meet people, while for others they permit people to be alone without being lonely. All indications are that companion animals play the role of a family member, often, a member with the most desired attributes."

—Alan M. Beck,
School of Veterinary Medicine, Purdue University

When it works, a partnership can be magic, like Tracey Frost and Cheri, complete with heartwarming surprises.

I Love to Shop

by Tracey Frost

My second dog, Cheri, a Golden Retriever, adored shopping—to the point that she insisted on choosing her own things and carrying them home or to my office. Cheri oozed personality and lived and loved her work to the fullest. Regrettably, her life was cut short at six-and-a-half years from hemangiosarcoma of the spleen. The people she touched with her antics, love, courage, and intelligence I cannot even begin to count.

Our lives were busy, commuting thirty miles a day and working in a fast-paced medical group with upwards of forty doctors of every specialty. I shared an office with approximately five or six other women, my desk being the closest to the door so that Cheri had a lot of room and could stretch out, which she always did. We commuted by railroad and Cheri embraced commuting as much as she did shopping. Conductors were quick to remember her name and another commuter always made sure she had an open seat for me with enough floor area for Cheri.

As was customary, we did errands on my lunch hour, and anything we couldn't finish I finished on the way to the train station, sometimes picking up dinner to take home at many of the restaurants in my work town of Summit, New Jersey.

We frequented a lovely gourmet supermarket not far from my office where the fresh fruit and vegetables, as well as various prepared meals, were scrumptious. Being the salad lover that I am, I adored the salad bar located in the back of the store. Not far from the salad bar, there was also a bin of varying sized rawhide bones. Needless to say, it was very easy to teach Cheri where the salad bar was and no problem to motivate her to get there when time was of the essence to make up a salad and walk back to my office during my lunch hour. After selecting my salad fixings and loading them in a container with dressing and all the other condiments, I would head up to the front of the store to the cashier. When checking out, the clerk would say, "Oh, Tracey, that will be your salad and the rawhide bone, right?" I would always say, "I don't remember the bone," and would reach down to my faithful dog's head and there would be dangling a packaged rawhide bone. The store employees would insist that she could have it, despite my apologies and pleas to disengage it from her mouth. Needless to say, we had a running tab with the market, and invariably, Cheri made sure she had some amusement for the rest of the afternoon. No amount of discipline would discharge my little Golden from "shopping," and store employees thought it was just wonderful, which didn't help either. At her death, they sent me an oversized bone for my next dog.

At a restaurant near the railroad station, the manager always had baskets of beautifully polished apples outside the door as well as another basket of cherry and plum tomatoes. These did not escape Cheri's favor either; when leaving, she invariably helped herself to an apple or cherry tomato—or both—to carry back to the office. Her work never faltered when leaving the place, and it would be too late when I would discover the fact, as when standing at the intersection waiting to cross I would notice her tail wagging and people snickering as they passed. She had a vice grip on her treasures and would carry them the four blocks back to my office. Again, the store owners insisted that Cheri could have whatever she wanted, despite my pleas to the contrary.

Bad weather didn't stifle her shopping either. There were times when she really was working hard, jumping over snow banks at the curbs, slowly traversing over icy spots, and yet she would carry her "packages" just as proudly to our destination.

When people heard about her death, many sent me flowers, candy, and heartfelt sympathy notes. Some would approach me and burst into tears, saying, "That wonderful dog, I will miss her so." This was particularly true with the physicians for whom I worked, especially the ones who were dog lovers and even some who were not but admired Cheri's faithful work, love, and courage that she demonstrated every day, whether she was shopping for her favorite things or simply being her loving and wonderful self.

The Seeing Eye, Inc.

So much changes when handler and dog unite, as Donna Burke knows well.

Then and Now

by Kathy Nimmer

I had myself always,
A body not perfect, not even close,
Weakened by a vicious disease,
Holding me captive from motion,
Stamping "unhealthy" upon the forehead
Of a me who could always be counted on
To elicit a furtive stare,
A shifty, uncomfortable gaze
That shouted, "Pity."

I had the wheelchair as well,
Returning some of the motion
That others never were without,
But holding me down as well,
Making me lesser somehow,
Lower than everyone else,
Beneath their line of sight or interest,
Not fully "okay."

Now I have you too,
Your ripples of golden fur,
Your chocolate brown, all-seeing eyes
That look past my inabilities
To find what it is that I can do
And magnify that by four paws
So that we surmount reality, obliterate it,
Together.

And when you came into my world,
I found the will to change.
Cast off extra pounds
And extra insecurities.
Face the day with a lighter spirit,
Golden in color,
The ultimate prize.
Dependence on independence,
Addiction to possibility,
Wholeheartedly selling out to the formula
That proves beyond reason
How you and I together
Are more than I ever could have been without you.

East Coast Assistance Dogs

Caitlin Lynch finds her priorities shifting once Laser comes into her life.

Break Time

by Caitlin Lynch

My fingers fly across the keyboard as the clock races against me. I have two hours to finish a paper about the politics and economy of Britain in the eighteenth century. The only problem is that I know very little about the past of the Great Empire. I know about Jude Law, King Henry, and Jane Eyre; however, these sundry bits of information will not be enough to finish a six-page paper. I am a college freshman, and I have not yet mastered the art of skimming books looking for pertinent facts, or consuming copious amounts of raspberry tea at two A.M. that can help one stave off the chains of sleep. As a matter of fact, I haven't really mastered any study tactics yet, which is why I find myself in such a quandary.

I am jolted back to reality by the cold nose pushing against my arm.

"Come on, Laser," I say, exasperated. "Do you really have to go out, now?"

I check my watch and notice that yes, the large cream-colored dog probably does need to go outside. I sigh dramatically and attempt to find a pair of shoes amongst yesterday's jeans, empty water bottles, and discarded papers that litter the area around my desk.

Laser runs around me in tight circles, squeaking a toy delightedly. I grab his leather leash off the back of my door, clip it to his collar, and remind him gently that his plaything must stay in the room. The soft thud I hear confirms that he has complied with my desire. Before we exit my room, I have him sit by the door so that I can find my I.D. card, which will grant us access back into the building.

Laser trots down our long hallway. His long tail curls up over his back, and I effortlessly match the long strides he takes.

"Good …door," I say as he stops directly in front of the door that will take us outside.

As I swing the door open, the chilly October air greets me. My arms are bare, and they prickle almost immediately. My thoughts are not on my dog or the autumn sun that I vaguely notice warming my face. If I weren't so distracted by the looming deadline, I would notice that this is one of my favorite types of days; my college campus is never more beautiful than in autumn. As it is, my mind runs through names of long-deceased kings and queens and thoughts of trade routes.

Laser and I walk gingerly down the steps of the back porch of my dorm building and to the square of grass where he relieves himself. On bright days, I sit with him on the porch and brush out his thick coat or talk to a friend on the phone. Today, despite its brightness, will yield none of those ventures. I lengthen Laser's leash, remind him of the task at hand, and am glad when I hear a trickle. In minutes, I tell myself, I will be back to work.

"Good boy," I murmur as he guides me back to our door. I remove his leash, distractedly pat him on the head, and resume my place in front of my computer.

Laser lies beside my chair, completely content with the scratch I deliver every minute or so to his ample side. I am at work for no more than five minutes when a knock disrupts my typing.

"What now?" I mutter to myself as I save my document and hurry towards the door.

Laser is happily galloping around the room. He loves when people come to visit. I open the door a crack, Laser's gigantic body waiting patiently beside mine for the visitor to come in and play.

"Hello?" I ask to the hallway.

"Hi, um, I think you left this outside," a boy says from in front of me. I reach out a hand to him and take what he's offering.

"Wh-what is this?" I ask, not recognizing the soft, cylindrical object he offers me.

"It's your dog's, I think," he says.

I am horrified. In my hand, I hold Laser's stuffed pink salmon. It doesn't squeak, but it is one of Laser's favorite toys nonetheless. I'm not sure how Laser got the salmon out of my room, but decide I was so distracted I must not have noticed something in his mouth after I retrieved my I.D. card.

"Well, thanks," I say to the boy.

I close the door and sink to my knees. I don't know that guy: what if he thinks I'm a bad dog owner for letting my dog take his toy outside? What if he thinks my dog is attention-starved and never petted? I shake my head, hard, and tell myself that I am being ridiculous. In front of me, I can hear Laser's happy panting. I am certain he is eyeing the dirty stuffed salmon I still hold in my right hand.

"We can't play, bud," I tell him sadly. "Mommy has work…"

Then, I stop. Laser's licking the side of my hand that clutches the salmon. I am overcome by love for this dog, and decide, instantly, the he is more important than my paper ever will be. What will it matter in ten years if my paper gets turned in late? What are a few points off a paper, anyway? What's truly important right now? And, aren't college kids notorious for playing harder than they work?

I kiss the side of Laser's head, get to my feet, swing my arm back, and release the grungy salmon into the air. I hear my dog take off after his toy and decide that the sound of his tags jingling and his tail smacking the side of my bureau in utter glee are the best sounds I have heard all day. King Henry can wait; I have a game of catch to play.

Guide Dog Foundation for the Blind, Inc.

The holidays became even brighter for Debbie Morgan with Shasta by her side.

December

by Kathy Nimmer

The wind outside is whipping.
The skaters are sliding and slipping.
The hot chocolate drinkers are sipping.
It is December indeed.

The shoppers are pushing and shoving.
The couples are ogling and loving.
The snowball throwers are mittening and gloving.
It is December indeed.

The stores are discounting and selling.
The cookies are delectably smelling.
The songs are rising and swelling.
It is December indeed.

The guide dog is bobbing and weaving
Through crowds that are arriving and leaving,
Leading her handler who has no problem believing
That it is December indeed.

The aisles are emptying and filling
And the guide dog is constantly willing
To face chaos or spots that are stilling.
It is December indeed.

While shoppers heft bags they are toting,
An odd sound is suddenly floating
In the air, and the guide dog is noting
That it is December indeed.

Her ears are listening and cocking
As she passes the wreaths and stockings,
And the reindeer and the horses rocking.
It is December indeed.

Toward the sound she is quietly advancing,
Walking quickly, practically prancing,
While the odd sound becomes subtly entrancing.
It is December indeed.

Around a corner, the guide dog goes flying,
Her handler huffing and sighing,
Upon a discovery they are both relying.
It is December indeed.

Revelation! The guide dog is peeping
At a mechanical Santa who is sleeping
With snores the reward he is reaping.
It is December indeed.

The guide dog, the answer no longer missing,
Investigates the Santa's breathy hissing
And graces him with slobbery kissing.
It is December indeed.

Leader Dogs for the Blind

Not only did Yulea make Detra Bannister's life more manageable, she gave it real purpose.

Threading the Eye of the Needle

by Detra Bannister

At age twelve, living in rural West Virginia, I had never seen or even heard of a guide dog or any other service animal. All of the animals I knew were either pets or farm animals. Something else I had never heard of was juvenile diabetes. But it hatefully caught up with me one Thanksgiving, in 1967, and since then it has been incessant checking, recording, monitoring, balancing, juggling, and correcting glucose levels, all the while keeping up with and learning new management methods, techniques, and technologies as treatments advance. In spite of my diligence, I still developed severe retinopathy in both eyes, and years later I became legally blind.

Out of all the blindness compensatory skills I needed to learn, orientation and mobility was probably the most needful. While out on a mobility lesson during my stay at a residential blindness rehabilitation center, I commented on how much I disliked the white cane. While it certainly has its usefulness, I disliked it because it frequently got hung up in the cracks on the sidewalk, slowing me down, and it was something I had to hold which constantly tied up one hand. The instructor commented, "You can always get a dog guide, but first you have to be cane mobile." Having admired the work of the dog guides I had witnessed before losing my vision—thinking as they weaved in and out of pedestrian traffic and crossed busy intersections that it was like threading the eye of a needle without hitting either side—this new information gave me a choice about how to be an independent traveler again.

Throughout the year after leaving the rehab center I kept thinking about those four-footed helpers. Then one day a friend gave me a book about the travels and adventures of a dog guide and his owner and, the day I finished it I got online and researched the different schools around the country. Settling on The Seeing Eye, I filled out an application; nine months later I met what would become the love of my life for the next ten years.

Yulea, my trusty guide, travel mate, and daily companion, was a true gift. Understanding how important this relationship would be and believing that God knew far better than I did what was in store, I trusted Him to provide the perfect match. I received above and beyond what I had asked for. I knew Yulea could do the work, but I didn't expect her to change my life to the extent that I could say with all honesty that through her, God took the thing in life I hated dealing with most (the restrictions blindness can impose) and turned it into my source of greatest blessing.

Now that I had this marvelous creature, I wanted to expand my opportunities and attended a meeting at a local organization for the blind to learn about what jobs people who are visually impaired really do. (I had lost my nursing license after vision loss and had worked hard to get the license reinstated, despite the disability. However, it seemed my options within the field of nursing were limited.) But two people from the American Foundation for the Blind were there presenting a resource they had: a database of people with varying degrees of vision loss who worked in more than 300 occupational fields. These volunteers mentored other people with vision loss on how to handle the obstacles and challenges of getting and performing a job as a visually impaired employee, including in nursing.

Later, through my connection to a local foundation, I learned that that same national foundation planned to open an office in my hometown of Huntington, West Virginia. I felt this would be a tremendous opportunity to affect the lives of more people than would be possible otherwise, so I applied for one of the positions. That was nine years ago. Today I work with the same two people who came to show their database resource and am now privileged to be a part of developing new online programs, which incorporates this database, for career education and exploration. It is now a robust, interactive website where many thousands of people learn about the transition process from school to work and have peers with like disability mentoring them.

Yulea was with me throughout this entire process, and we traveled frequently across the U.S. and Canada on business for AFB. These trips introduced me to hundreds of memorable people; some I'm still in touch with to this day.

Church is yet another place where, because of Yulea, I've met hundreds of people I would not have known otherwise. People considered Yulea a part of the congregation, and always made her welcome. Her excellent work and amiable demeanor were transparent, capturing frequent media attention, especially locally. I admired my dog so much that I used to say, "I want to be just like Yulea when I grow up!" I actually used her as a role model for developing character.

At age eleven, her health began to decline, and I started thinking about her retirement. We had one more trip to make that year, and I decided this would be her last service of duty. However, while she and I slowly threaded the eye of the needle in NYC as we walked through Penn Plaza to Broadway on our second day there, she crashed and could not catch her breath. We flew home on an emergency flight and went straight to the vet where bilateral interstitial lung cancer was diagnosed just a few days before her twelfth birthday. Her vet did everything he could to make her comfortable, and I took her home to love her and brace myself for the decision I knew lay ahead. On December 18th her vet came to the house. She was happy to see him, wagging her tail in greeting. When he put the needle in, she gently went to sleep leaving all suffering behind. That was one of the hardest days of my life.

Around 3,000 attend my church, and for months afterwards those who had not learned about her death would burst into tears when they heard. For weeks I received hundreds of cards, calls, letters, email, and even flowers from people all over the country saying how much they enjoyed knowing her. Throughout the years of constant discovery since Yulea joined my life, the real discovery, I think, was coming to realize how much of an impact she had had on the lives of others, not just my own.

Nine and a half months later I returned to The Seeing Eye. Getting another Seeing Eye dog to thread the eyes of those needles with me throughout the years ahead is the best tribute I can think of to thank her for all the joy she gave to so many.

The Seeing Eye, Inc.

All hope seemed gone when a terrible accident altered Ariana Solimando's life, but Nexus was yet to have his say.

The Gift of Nexus

by Kathy Nimmer

Silent as a lurking sea monster, the sand bar hid beneath the tossing Atlantic waves. Ariana turned toward her friend who beckoned her to come into the water and join her. Wearing her favorite swimsuit and positive that the world was hers to enjoy at the invincible age of seventeen, Ariana leapt lightly off of the shifting sand to complete a skim dive in the direction of her friend. But the sand bar had other ideas. With the angry firmness of something more solid than mounded, wet sand, it halted Ariana's dive without mercy and halted the unfolding of the life that she had always believed would be hers.

The C4 and C5 vertebrae in Ariana's neck were shattered, causing immediate paralysis from the chest down. In a swirl of memories that ebb in and out like the tide, Ariana recalls the realization that she couldn't move while she was still in the water. She was floating face down, as if she were dead. She remembers the panicked crowds surrounding her on the beach, the frantic expressions of nurses in the nearby hospital trauma room, and the cutting off of her favorite bathing suit. That last was devastating then, seemingly a horrible tragedy, seemingly a life-changer for the young woman who had much to realize about the new life she was just beginning.

Surgery followed to stabilize the spinal column, then one month on a ventilator, followed by the terrifying weaning process to get her off of the breathing machine. She retained limited use of her shoulders and arms and some random sensations in other parts of her body, but no other movement returned. Many friends didn't return either. Intimidated by the drastic alteration in Ariana's life, they felt more secure running from the situation than staying nearby and becoming part of the new reality that Ariana had to face.

Time passed. Tears passed. Anger passed. But everything that passed left an imprint on Ariana, who had to figure out new ways to exist. Many things were beyond her ability to master on her own, but she fought for as much independence as she could find. Not much seemed possible. Discouragement came, but it didn't pass. It lingered quietly, powerfully.

Ariana's brother went on the internet and researched. He knew of guide dogs and hearing dogs, but surely, there were dogs that could help his sister. Surely there was something that could send that discouragement into remission.

He was right. He found Canine Companions for Independence, a large nonprofit organization that trained a variety of dogs to help with numerous disabilities. Ariana applied and was accepted. In 2006, Ariana and her mom headed off for two weeks that would be as significant in her life as that lurking, menacing sand bar had been.

The first dog chosen for Ariana didn't work out, but, on the exact date of Ariana's birthday, she met the perfect match! Nexus, a seventy-five pound black Lab, leapt to Ariana's side in one graceful bound. Laying his head on her lap and looking into her face with his deep brown eyes, Nexus seemed to be promising his devotion. Ariana beamed, delighted with this birthday gift who seemed perfectly charming and already so memorable. The commands he knew were many: "get" to pick up something from the floor, "lap" to gently place his long front legs across her lap, "give" to drop the retrieved object, and "tug" to pull on ropes placed strategically on doors for opening. The command that he wasn't taught but executed better than any other was even more important: "love" this young woman who needed it so much.

At graduation, Ariana and her classmates watched as the puppy raisers, who had been so important in the dogs' early lives, led each dog to its new owner and symbolically handed over the leash. When Ariana's turn came, she watched the approach of her beautiful black Lab, who was holding a red rose in his mouth. Nexus lay the rose on Ariana's lap, resting his chin there for a moment. Tears filled Ariana's eyes as she looked into the furry face of her new companion. They were now a team.

More time passed. More tears passed. More anger passed. But now, discouragement passed too. With Nexus as a constant companion, Ariana's world didn't have room for a permanent resident like that anymore. She has not returned to the shore where the sand bar probably still lurks, deciding that she doesn't need the reminder of what used to be. What she has now is enough—two brown eyes, one black head, one red rose—definitely enough.

Canine Companions for Independence

Those moments of absolute synthesis are unspeakably precious as Megan Kelly shows in this poem.

Our Pattern

by Megan Kelly

Together,
we weave a fluid pattern,
stitched together with trust,
with love,
with willingness to learn.
Threaded with respect.

Together,
we discovered our true textures.
We started out as separate strings:
I commanded,
you didn't readily obey.
You guided, I hesitated.

Slowly,
we listened.
Sometimes, our strings snarled;
with work we smoothed them.
We continue to weave tighter,
as you guide me through city streets,
as we ride subways
and board buses,

the patter
of your four paws,
and my two feet,
becomes our unified tapestry.

Guide Dog Foundation for the Blind, Inc.

It is hard to say who is the luckier fellow: Rich Dixon or Monte.

Monte and Me

by Rich Dixon

The woman watched Monte and me climb the ramp. As we reached the top she called, "You've got a mighty handsome companion!"

In a futile effort to salvage my fragile self-concept, I shouted back, "Are you talking to me or the dog?" We chuckled and exchanged dog stories while my charming sidekick accepted affectionate scratches. She assured me that I was every bit as handsome as Monte. I found her affirmation oddly comforting. Something's wrong when comparison to a Labrador Retriever improves your self image, but that's just one revelation I've encountered in my adventure with a service dog.

I thought Monte would do stuff for me. I imagined a combination butler/maid with a cold nose. Instead I got a floor littered with toys, a constantly wagging tail threatening anything in its path, and a tireless Retriever who returns a tennis ball until it's too slobbery to hold. I got a devoted partner who greets me enthusiastically, instantly forgives impatience, and eagerly performs nearly any task in return for an occasional crunchy biscuit.

I anticipated a furry attendant, always on call, no appointment necessary. Monte fulfills these expectations with a comical twist. When I drop something his head snaps upright. He's instantly prepared to retrieve—after he stretches, shakes his head, then pounces to subdue the lost item before he can safely return it.

As he transforms the frustration of an unreachable object into an entertaining pursuit, Monte reminds me that everyday calamities aren't the disasters I often perceive. I expected a service dog. I received a constant reminder that life can be calm and peaceful—as long as nobody utters the word "Frisbee."

A wheelchair creates invisible interpersonal barriers. Others shuffle aside and try not to stare. Children are shushed when they point and ask innocent questions. I'm embarrassed, smiling like nothing's wrong while I seek the quickest possible escape. But the awkward silliness disappears when Monte's around. Dogs forge instant relationships; service dogs amplify that effect because they appear in unexpected places. Anywhere we go, Monte elicits excited grins from kids and warm smiles from adults. Most folks ask permission to pet him, but many simply cannot resist. The most reserved individuals become puddles of mush as they share the life stories of their own dogs. Complete strangers become Monte's instant pals, and I'm an automatic member of his social network.

At our favorite hangout he's welcomed warmly with a doggie veggie plate. If the server's new, one of the veterans introduces her—to Monte. Usually they greet me as well, but he's the guest of honor. Other diners giggle as I violate service dog protocol by tossing an occasional carrot to the star of the show.

The harried check-in clerk at an upscale resort apologetically reported that I'd have to sign a damage waiver to allow Monte in the hotel. She relaxed when I assured her that I posed a much greater risk of unacceptable behavior. Soon the clerk, manager, and a couple of weary guests were chatting, smiling, and admiring Monte. Each time I saw those folks during my visit, I felt like I was encountering old friends.

Monte even impacts the normally reserved atmosphere in church. He usually lies quietly, garnering jealous glances from those who wish they were sleeping so soundly. A guest musician once halted her performance when she saw Monte. She stopped singing, ran down from the stage, and knelt on the floor to rub his tummy. Laughter filled the auditorium as he rolled onto his back in the immodest pose we've dubbed "The Full Monte."

I love my hand cycle, but cranking with Monte in tow redefines the experience. It's impossible not to share the joy as his ears flap in the wind and his tongue lolls playfully. Monte doesn't care where we're going, but he loves the experience of getting there; I'd swear he smiles as he romps along.

Monte brings life and connection to an isolated culture. In a strange paradox, he makes things a bit more human for people immersed in iPods and cell phones. He's a catalyst for interaction, breaking down walls of seclusion for an owner who's frequently preoccupied with disability. Monte invites people to relax. He's totally here and now, and his presence promotes a quieter, calmer atmosphere. The effect is especially evident at school. I teach junior high math, which isn't every kid's favorite subject. But many kids gravitate to Monte. Some get on the floor and hug him. During a test, if I sense that kids are unusually anxious, I simply move around the room with Monte. His simple, calm aura, along with an occasional lick on the face, helps them relax and concentrate.

Before Monte arrived, I feared that a service dog's presence might create disruptions and distractions. I was right: Monte disrupts my efforts to hide. Life in a wheelchair tempts me to withdraw or blend into the scenery, but blending is no longer in the script. "Inconspicuous" disappears in the company of an eighty-pound people magnet. He distracts from my tendency to miss the blessings that surround me. His jovial eyes and constantly sniffing nose lovingly mock my incessant need to accomplish a task. Monte transforms the simplest excursion into an adventure. From the reactions of the people we encounter to his intense interest in every sight and sound, there's always an element of unanticipated magic in Monte's world. Life's less serious when you always have to keep a doggie treat handy.

I'm sure that the lady who called to me on the ramp meant well, but my informal public opinion survey contradicts her affirmation. My floppy-eared friend headlines this partnership. It's a joy to be part of his supporting cast.

Canine Partners of the Rockies, Inc.

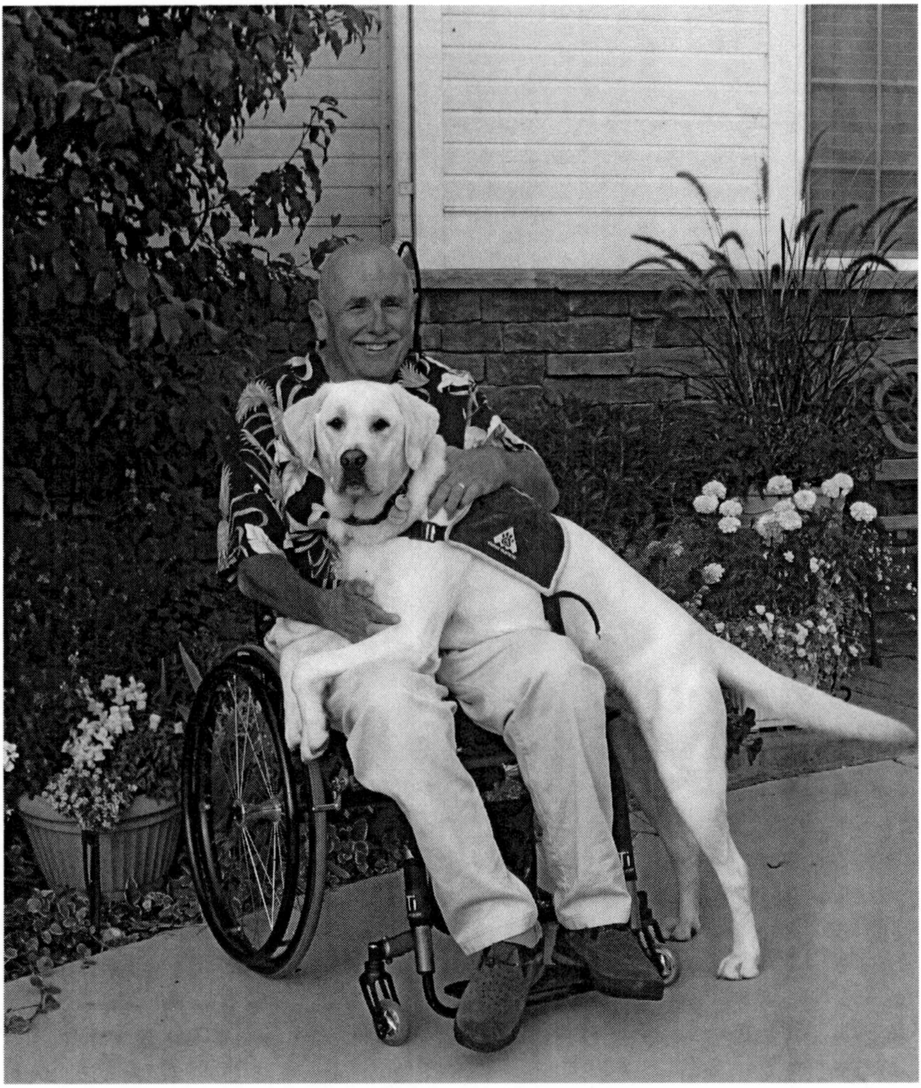

When the two front paws creep onto the edge of the bed each morning to wake Joe Mauk, they add yet another page to an incredible story.

Here I Am

by Kathy Nimmer

It starts with one paw placed gently and quietly on the edge of the bed. Soon after, a nose follows. Then, a second paw joins the first paw and the nose. If this trio of gestures hasn't been successful, one slightly indelicate snort joins the brigade, saying in canine nostril language, "Here I am." By that time, if Joe hasn't awoken, all bets are off for the preservation of decorum and tranquility!

Joe's journey to meet his first guide dog did not proceed in a straight line. Years back, he didn't even have a vision problem or a clue about what guide dogs did, let alone a sense that he would ever have one himself. It took him lifting something slightly too heavy in the factory where he worked to start the movement from Point A to Point B on his journey to meet Roxanne. The retina in one eye detached, and instantly, the vision there was gone. Within a couple of years of that incident, his other retina had degraded, and Joe was firmly implanted in the world of the visually impaired.

Accompanying and accelerating the deterioration of his vision was diabetes, vicious and dynamically out of control for Joe. It gnawed at his body and spirit, eating away at what Joe considered "normal life." His kidneys took the brunt of the attack, failing profoundly, sending Joe to the dialysis machine. For five years, Joe had dialysis treatments three times a week, relying on them to stay alive until a kidney transplant could occur. And, if the kidneys were going to be replaced, the pancreas needed replacement too. Joe's body was failing, but all he could do was wait.

The call came when Joe was out. He had to call back in an hour or the kidney and pancreas would go to another patient. He didn't get the message until several hours later, but he called anyway. The organs were gone, assigned to someone else. This was the sixth time that a potential match had not worked out. He was still waiting.

Just one week later, the phone rang again. A drunk driver in West Virginia had t-boned a car, killing the thirteen-year-old boy riding in the passenger seat. The grieving parents honored their son's wishes and donated his organs. It was a match, and Joe would receive the transplant. How shocked he was to learn, after the surgery, that the first set of organs from the week before had gone to a friend of his! Two lives changed and saved in a one-week span! Joe marched on, toward a yet unknown yellow Lab named Roxanne and toward their future together.

Roxanne was born three years after Joe's successful double transplant. She too, of course, didn't know that her destiny was to walk by Joe's side. She burst into the world with the spirit of a fiery yellow Lab pup who loved to play, particularly when someone was focused on her. She responded to firmness when obedience was taught to her, matching intensity with intensity, displaying a concentrated focus when she knew the pressure was on. Still, as she bounded through her puppyhood, Roxanne didn't know that a gentle, intelligent man was hoping for a partnership with a special dog. He'd gained independence from the dialysis machine, and now he wanted independence of even greater dimensions.

When they met at the guide dog school, Joe was shocked by how soft Roxanne's fur was. He also noted her flirtation with the other dogs in class, her attachment to the trainer, and the early promise of her connection with him, displayed by her graceful, long front legs stretching across his feet while he sat in his bedroom at the school, thinking about the journey that had led him to that place. In the next days, he marveled at the freedom he felt without the white cane. He was in awe of how many people said a friendly "hello" to him when he walked with Roxanne, whereas most people had ignored him when he used the cane. He grew more and more confident as he and Roxanne progressed from block-long walks with the trainer's leash still attached, all the way to an excursion through Manhattan while a rainstorm surged around them.

Joe always wakes when that first paw touches the corner of his bed. He wakes, but he doesn't give any sign of his wakefulness, except for an anticipatory half smile that Roxanne can't see. He feels the heavier thump of the nose settling on the bed beside the first paw, his smile widening. When the second paw slides into place, Joe's sightless eyes crinkle at the corners as a grin suffuses his entire face. He remains unmoving, like a sprinter waiting for the starter's pistol. It comes: the snort! Joe rolls over in one strong, smooth motion, his hands reaching for Roxanne's satiny fur.

"Here I am," says Roxanne's snort.

"And here I am," says Joe. "Here we are."

Guiding Eyes for the Blind

Deborah Wagner was undertaking a responsibility she knew she could fulfill, but she didn't expect Scarlet to be so instrumental.

The Therapeutic Foster Parent

by Deborah Wagner

It was a sunny, brisk late afternoon in March that carried with it the hope of increasing warmth of the spring and summer seasons to come. I opened the door after hearing a knock. There stood my first foster parent experience: two girls who were ten and fourteen years old.

As a first time foster parent, I of course wanted to do everything right. My purpose was two-fold. First, I simply wanted to carry on my desire to change the community in which I lived for the better by positively influencing its youth. And by being a foster parent, I would also no longer wonder what it was like to be a parent, thereby gaining a deeper appreciation for all single parents.

The caseworker for the children knew that I had a service dog from reading my history. She explained to the girls, "This dog is a working animal that Deborah depends on to accomplish daily tasks such as picking up dropped items, changing clothes, doing laundry, opening and closing doors, and many more tasks." The girls listened closely. As days turned into weeks, they learned that my need for Scarlet superseded their need to play with her at any particular moment.

But perhaps I was mistaken in thinking that my need for Scarlet was always much greater than the need for the girls to interact with her. Could it be that allowing Scarlet to serve these children was equally important? Was Scarlet the unassuming, easy-going, non-disciplinarian counterpart of me to them? Scarlet seemed to be the bridge between my tenacious human spirit to model a stable home environment and the relaxed, non-judgmental, unconditional love these children also needed. Scarlet ended up being a benefit to both children by providing what they needed when they needed it.

The older girl, a teenager, dealt with various mental and emotional challenges that left her unable to label a feeling and communicate that emotion appropriately. As a means of coping, the teen would often bottle these intense emotions until they would erupt into a public sit-in of protest to gain attention.

Scarlet proved to be uniquely engaging with the older girl during one particular crisis. After the children returned from their daycare provider, the teen was unusually withdrawn and notably bothered by something. Based on past similar experiences, I knew this meant the girls needed to be engaged in physical activity that evening, so we went to the mall to walk and find something to eat.

Not long after entering the mall, rather typical sibling chatter began between the girls. One seemingly harmless comment incensed the older girl to the point of sitting on the floor with knees to chest and hands shielding the ears and head. My repeated attempts to intervene in her self-defeating thinking and behaviors with methods that had worked in the past were unsuccessful, so I called my supervisor who tried a few more interventions to no avail. As a last resort, he suggested that I call the police and have the teen admitted to a local mental health clinic. I pleaded with him to let me try one more time and he agreed.

The teen loved animals, so I decided to use Scarlet as the intervention. I purposefully gave Scarlet commands that would back her into the girl from various directions. My thinking was that the more times the troubled teen would make physical contact with Scarlet, the more relaxed and willing to negotiate she would become. Scarlet gently touched her back end to the teen's side several times, resulting in a push from the teen that said, "Get away from me!" With each touch from Scarlet, the girl's demeanor became more relaxed. As she began to uncoil, Scarlet licked an arm and squished her feathered golden tail across the girl's cheek. A sheepish smile soon crept back to the girl's face followed by a willingness to stand and resume our plans at the mall.

Scarlet was not trained to intervene in crisis situations such as with this teen. Some well-intentioned passers-by even claimed that they had seen a television documentary on service dogs and knew that my use of Scarlet in this situation was not how service dogs were intended to be used. However, I could see the bigger picture.

Even though Scarlet will never receive her state license to provide therapeutic foster care, she was the team member she is trained to be for me that evening in the mall. She provided me assistance in daily living, which included on this particular day, helping me care for my foster children in ways that at times, such as this one, no other human being could.

Assistance Dogs of America, Inc.

Odete Delice Moreira calls Brazil home and calls her relationship with her guide dog transforming.

Brazilian Butterfly

by Odete Delice Moreira
Translated by Ines Almeida

I was born in the Town of Florianópolis, located on Ribeirão Coast of the Island State of Santa Catarina. Always motivated and dedicated with big thoughts of great accomplishments, I started working at a very young age with the intent of helping my parents. Still very young, at fifteen years of age, I married and with a lot of love and affection, I started helping my husband in the routine running of a beauty salon, where I greeted the clientele.

When I was thirty-five years old, I lost my vision due to an illness called diabetic retinopathy, which made it impossible for me to keep doing the work that I loved so much at the beauty salon. Even with this big change in my daily life, my personality did not change, and I started using a cane to get around. I confess that I felt lonely, insecure, and many times I would bump into things that were impossible to be detected by the cane.

Having daily contact with people who moved around much better using a guide dog, I came to find out about Guiding Eyes for the Blind located in New York. In January of 2003 they presented me with a black Labrador Guide Dog named J.K. and all the training necessary.

The time that marked most my memory during my training was when J.K. and I got into the car and after a while, at a certain distance from the school, the instructor asked me to leave the car and try to get back to Guiding Eyes using J.K. I confess that at the moment I had a feeling of desperation, having recently arrived from a country where it was summer at a thirty-five degree Celsius heat, and now being in New York where it was winter and there had been a big snow storm. But I remained calm. I had a talk with J.K. and went for it. Though I could hear the sound of a lot of cars hitting their brakes while I crossed the streets, and though I also came across blocks of ice or snow on the sidewalks (which to me was very new since I had never seen snow in my entire life), we kept going. To everyone's surprise, especially my interpreter's who couldn't stop crying in the car the whole time, we arrived at the school where we were received with a round of applause.

Since that day, I can say that he has given me back my eyes, giving me total confidence, more than a cane or even another person could give me. Right now, I work doing alternative pain management treatments. I am also studying transpersonal psychology and take pottery and ceramic works classes at Oleiros School, in São José. Today I see much better than when I had vision, because I'm always much more aware of whatever I am experiencing in life and I appreciate each moment more. Today I trust J.K.'s eyes more than those of my own husband, because J.K. and I have become one. I am like a butterfly who has left its cocoon.

Guiding Eyes for the Blind

Autism steals so much from those who struggle with it daily, but Heidi Fernandez's son claims much of that right back with the help of Teddy.

Everyday Miracles with Teddy

by Heidi Fernandez

We have just welcomed a new addition to our family: Teddy. Teddy is an autism companion dog for our son Andrew.

On our first visit to the vet, Andrew was so excited and couldn't wait to meet Teddy's doctor. While I was filling out paperwork at the front desk, Andrew was sitting in the waiting area with Teddy. All of a sudden I heard a lady say to Andrew, "You have such a handsome dog."

By the time I turned around, I heard Andrew respond, "Yes, he is, and his name is Teddy and he is a Golden Retriever. He is a special dog, and I love him". Then in a completely spontaneous manner, Andrew said to the woman, "And your dog is beautiful too."

The lady said, "Thank you."

Right then and there we witnessed one of the many miracles that Teddy has brought to our family. Having a conversation with a stranger is very hard for Andrew, but Teddy took all the fears away. Now Andrew is so proud of Teddy and loves to talk and introduce Teddy to everyone.

That's just the start of how Teddy has touched our lives. He has also helped Andrew with motor planning, sensory issues, confidence, and responsibility. But most of all, Teddy is Andrew's best friend. Teddy never leaves Andrew's side and is always showing unconditional love.

Never underestimate the power that one dog may have. Every day we witness more of these simple but powerful miracles occur around us.

Georgia Canines for Independence

Witness the morning travel routine of Melanie Moore and Vaughn, from an unexpected point of view.

My Favorite Passenger

by Kathy Nimmer

The train slices through the dewy morning, rushing to the next stop. It wonders as it spins over the tracks who will get off and who will get on. Surely the elderly lady whose husband is in a nursing home a block away will depart with shaky steps, propelled by a love for the man who has shared her life for sixty years before sinking slowly into Alzheimer's. Probably the young teenaged couple would exit at the next stop, leaning into each other like crossed shadows, off to one of the new cafes where they would share one cup of a fancy coffee with a name that the train couldn't begin to pronounce. The man in the heavy work boots that scuff up the surface of the train's floor would not depart here. His newest work site is one stop further on, so the floor would be safe for now.

And who would get on? Lots of people. A crowded stop, the train recalls, with many starting their too busy days by pouring onto the train in impatient throngs. The train's engine warms with anticipation as it contemplates its favorite passenger, or passengers, to be technically correct, though especially one. Would they be here this day? Hopefully yes, and the day would be just fine if so, even with the heavy work boots still to make their mark.

Chug chug chug. Screech screech screech. Hiss hiss hiss. The train stops, not as silently as it used to in the past when it was young, but well enough still, and just where it needs to be. The elderly lady stands, stumbling a bit as the teenagers ooze past her without even noticing that the kerchief covering her sparse hair is now askew due to their infatuated carelessness. The work boots shift, but as predicted, do not assume the bulky weight of their owner. Others pass, and the train waits breathlessly to spot the passenger of choice, the four-legged one who would make this day just right.

Ah, there. Waiting for others to pass so the pushing and shoving is not so rough. Standing now precisely parallel to the edge of the platform, blocking his companion from an unforgiving plunge that would make this day a nightmare, even worse than when the train's old springy seats were replaced by efficient, easy-to-clean, sterile plastic benches. They move forward, he still serving as her guardrail, she still seemingly unaware. The train emits a puff of steam and leans downward, just a tad, to make the retractable stairs just tap the edge of the platform: anything to help his favorite passenger.

No need for that extra gesture after all, for everything goes as smoothly as the gleam of newly laid tracks, of course, just as it does every day that they step onto the train. She settles on a bench, forgiving of its lack of personality and comfort, and he settles on the floor. The train sounds its horn with delight, wriggling with the pleasure of transporting him, them. And, when the day is done, the train will ease into a contented sleep, a good day's work under its gears, as evidenced by the scuffs of heavy work boots and the remnants of wheat-colored fur from the guide dog.

Guiding Eyes for the Blind

Elaine Harris's life journey takes her over thousands of miles all the way to Tasmania, a faithful guide dog by her side for much of the way.

Another Country

by Elaine Harris

...and Ruth said, "Entreat me not to leave thee, or to return from following after thee: for whither thou goest, I will go; and where thou lodge, I will lodge: thy people shall be my people, and thy god my god." (The Book of Ruth, 1:16 King James Version)

I had been working in radio part-time for a little over a year when I was offered my first full-time job; news of my first guide dog came through on the same day. In Britain in the 1980s it was customary to receive a letter and a few weeks' notice confirming dates and arrangements for training with a dog; on this occasion, thanks to a late cancellation, I had a little over thirty-six hours to get myself ready. Kati and I formed a mutual adoration society from day one. Less than a month later we began our first full-time job together.

Our first fourteen months as a team were busy and productive. Although we were based at a radio station in South Yorkshire, we traveled the country with a tape-recorder, picking up interviews and learning the trade. Kati loved working through rush hour London and coped with everything I asked her to do. (Her impromptu plunge into the Earl of Snowdon's fish-pond in the snow when I interviewed him at his London home was an added extra.)

The end of that first frantic year saw me on holiday with family in Australia, a trip that changed my horizons, my world, my life when I met my future husband. We married in country Victoria a year to the day that we met, but not before I had been denied, then eventually granted immigration, and Kati had developed a life-altering medical condition that, mercifully, didn't affect her work.

Kati was unable to be at the wedding, as she was still in quarantine in Melbourne. Leaving her there after a journey of over ten thousand miles was not easy. But the staff was marvelous. We were granted unlimited visits instead of the standard one each month, and I was permitted to put her on harness to work her around the compound. Yet I always felt her eyes boring into my back every time we left. It was akin to having a child in the hospital.

Once released she adjusted incredibly quickly, learning new routes with miraculous speed and adjusting to her new, foreign life. Her first encounter with a kangaroo was worthy of *Funniest Home Videos*. A major department store in

Melbourne is famous for its annual Christmas displays and for some reason one year featured an open-air animal nursery on the roof. Kati saw the kangaroo and decided that imitation was the highest form of flattery; her bounces were rather impressive.

A few years later Kati missed another family wedding by rolling in something unspeakable in the bush a couple of hours before the ceremony. It took three baths to remove the essence of whatever it was. The drive home was certainly memorable.

Kati and I ran a community radio station, made our television debut together, and did extensive freelance work before moving to take a job in Canberra, the national capital. The city, surrounded by New South Wales and located some ninety-three miles from the Pacific Ocean, can have a forty-five degree temperature variation within six months: minus five or eight degrees Celsius overnight in August to forty or more degrees Celsius in January. She coped better than I did with Christmas in summer, enjoyed the air-conditioner as much as the wood-heater, and loved our occasional visits to the snow.

Lazing in the sun (before we knew better) is known in Britain as sun-bathing; in Australia it is more aptly called sun-baking. A healthy tan is now deemed an oxymoron, but Kati loved to stretch out on the grass when it wasn't too hot. The bare patch on her tummy was pink in spring and brown by autumn. The birds hopped around her knowing she would never give chase in this mood.

The toughest part of working with a guide dog is the shortness of their lifespan compared to ours. Yes, it means you get to love and work with more wonderful persons-with-paws, but that doesn't help when you lose your best friend. Kati died two years before we moved to Tasmania, the island state occasionally forgotten by mainland Australia. Kati would have loved it here; easy access to the beach with seagulls to chase—but never catch—was her idea of heaven. I miss the carrying calls of the currawongs, the caroling of the Australian magpies, the gossiping rosellas, and noisy friar birds and the flocks of cockatoos; but we still have many birds in the garden gorging on the banana passion-fruit, not to mention many rabbits busy with their own doings, bandicoots and myriad tiny lizards. The raucous laugh of the kookaburra is often heard outside our kitchen window. She would have loved all that too, and since racing up and down stairs was always a joy for her, our terraced garden would have been paradise.

Naturally, there are numerous pictures of Kati on the walls, but one of the first things I did on moving here was mentally to place her bark in my garden. Only then could it feel like home.

The Guide Dogs for the Blind Association, UK

Chapter 7

Finally When

The Agony of Retirement and Loss

Paw Prints of Wisdom

"To tell a client that their dog needs to retire from service is agonizing. It is the hardest part of my job, feeling personally all the emotions that it brings a client when the end of a partnership draws near."

—Kim Ryan,
guide dog mobility instructor, Royal Guide Dogs, Tasmania

"It breaks my heart when I have to do grief counseling and someone has lost that special companion. Nothing can replace it. You have to move on and get past it, but get over it...never."

—Liz Norris,
Founder and Master Instructor, Pawsibilities Unleashed

In a reversal of roles, Kristeen Hughes takes her retired guide dog for a walk.

Sniff Walk

by Kristeen Hughes

The roles are reversed now. As I grab his leash in my left hand and a white cane in my right, he is excited, looking forward to the coming stroll. He's learned that when I get the cane and then his leash, fun is headed his way. He wags and jumps. It's the way he used to get about work; he's just changed the object of his joy from the harness to the cane. I would never have thought that would happen. He never liked it before when I chose the cane over him, which wasn't often.

These walks are a chance for him to sniff every piece of gravel and blade of grass along this alley down which he so courageously led me for over six years. Then he knew about every coming and going car, every crack in the sidewalk or uneven surface that might trip me up. He knew when the streets came even when there were no obvious curbs. Now, though he still knows these things, they are no longer in the forefront of his mind.

This is his time, and hopefully he will have many years of it. Now I lead him, or at least that's how it's supposed to work. He gets to learn where every flower blooms with its own special scent. He finds where dogs and cats and other little critters have passed by and left their unmistakable olfactory message, each one miraculously different from any other. He feels more freedom to leave his own mark on this, "his" alley.

He has waited all day for this late afternoon walk. I had things to do and he watched me do each one, hoping it was the last. He followed me throughout the house, building up great anticipation for this "sniff walk." There is always more sniffing than walking. I am often reminded of a song from the musical *The Music Man* as we walk:

"Sniff a little,
walk a little,
sniff a little,
walk a little.
Sniff sniff sniff,
walk a lot, sniff a little more."

For the most part, he feels no responsibility for me. He doesn't try to lead and he doesn't pause for curbs or obstacles. He is in his own world communing with nature as only a dog can. I do not ask much of him on these walks. He must heel when I ask him to. He mustn't cross in front of or behind me, and he must, above all, thoroughly enjoy himself. This is now his only job.

It's a wonderful gift for me to have this part of his life with him after all of the working years. The only part of his life I missed sharing was knowing him as a puppy. Oh, how cute he must have been!

And, just like other people walking their dogs, we stop and say hello and maybe pet and sniff the other dogs. Today, we met a father and his baby girl and she got to have a pet. I can do that kind of thing now because I'm not running to somewhere and I don't have to worry about the rules or fret about proper guide dog etiquette. Bower and I no longer need to be so focused on our travels that we are forced to block out the rest of the world around us. It's just regular dog-walking.

There are still rare moments when he will dust off his guide dog thinking cap and assist me. I was veering slightly across a street the other day, and he just jerked the leash a bit to the left and got us back on track. We stepped up on the sidewalk perfectly. Some things are second nature for him, I imagine. Since he doesn't have to do these things, they are all the more special.

On the off chance that I have made this transition sound easy, full of joy and warm fuzzies, it is definitely not that. Our new ways of being with each other have been an incredibly difficult adjustment and it is a process I am still working through. In the newness of Bower's retirement, I felt shattered into little bits and didn't believe I could ever manage the pain of losing him as my working partner. My grief at times was total and I knew nothing else. I was overwhelmed and I felt powerless to stop it.

As time went by, I realized I was grieving largely for myself, but Bower was teaching me something very important: he was showing me how to move on, if I would only pay attention.

I hope he is enjoying his life now and that the awful sadness and ache I still sometimes feel about him is just mine and not anything he is feeling. I can't bear to think he's sad or lonely or hurting in some way physically or emotionally. I think that's a human thing, not a dog thing, but I wish I could be sure. He doesn't seem troubled, but I sure hurt. I can't stop the hurting and I can't stop the tears that can, even now, come unbidden when I least expect them.

I can't imagine not having him and I can't imagine how I can ever convey to him how very much I love him. I have to hope he knows, because dogs are better than we are at knowing these things. He is so incredibly special and he has to know it. I'm so afraid that I haven't given him enough hugs, kisses, words, smiles, treats, walks, and even tears. Since we're both still here, I have a quota to fill. I'd best get to it!

Guide Dogs for the Blind

Love does not cease with the end of a partnership, as Sherry Gomes expresses in this poem about her guide dog Bianca.

Dancing: A Tribute to Bianca

by Sherry Gomes

You burst into my life, dancing,
giving new meaning to the words joy of Life.
If you could have done so, you would have been laughing;
if you could, you would always have been laughing.
You came into my life, bringing:
bringing me laughter, bringing me joy,
bringing me many reasons to smile,
bringing safety and freedom,
but mostly, you came bringing me love.
I always think of you dancing,
dancing in your own way,
body wiggling, tail wagging,
pure excitement for what came next shining in you.
You came into my life, giving,
giving me a reason to live,
giving a reason to laugh,
showing me I could keep going, no matter what.
When you left me, you were still dancing—
You were waiting for your next adventure,
never knowing you weren't coming home,
never knowing we would not be sharing that adventure.
I let you go, crying,
I cried for myself, missing you,
I cried from the emptiness,
my world so empty without your joy.
Every minute I think of you, aching,
I am aching, missing, remembering.
I hide it; I smile,
I tell the world I am better, healing,
but I'm aching, missing you,
the void without your joy in every minute,
knowing you are at peace,
knowing you need no longer fear,
you need no longer face your responsibility in the face of your fear,

knowing you are free at last,
free to dance your dance of joy, always.
I think of you, remembering,
all our journeys, all our steps from here to there,
all the games, all the mischief,
the warm feeling of you snuggling beside me.
Time helps, brings acceptance.
The gift of you was beyond my deserving,
I cherished the gift, thankful for the moments, the time to know you.
Accepting eases the ache though never completely buries it.
Be free from fear and anxiety, my precious friend,
my love reaches across the miles, wishing that you
spend your days with your own kind of laughter,
burst into your days, still dancing,
still radiating your absolute joy.
I will have peace, knowing you are still you.

Guide Dogs for the Blind

Crossing a street in Johannesburg, South Africa, never before had cost Marilyn Crouse Bland as much as it did that terrible day.

Another New Beginning

by Marilyn Crouse Bland

I hated coming into the busy part of Johannesburg, but this appointment was unavoidable. The sidewalks were so crowded that from time to time I had to wait for a space to occupy. At last we came to the curb. "Good girl, Pickles," I praised, stroking her head. "Only one more block." The light changed and I gave her the command to cross the street. She moved closer to me and pressed her head against my thigh. "What's wrong Pickles?" I hoped there wasn't some kind of obstruction ahead. "Come on. Forward!" I urged. "Come on, let's go!" The engine of the car in front of me revved impatiently. This meant the light was changing again; we were too late; we would have to wait for the next cycle.

"Come now. Get ready now," I urged again as I heard the engines of the parallel traffic revving. "Now! Forward!" She stood. "Come, Pickles, come!" I pulled at the lead, but she would not budge. The light changed a second time. My stomach was in a knot. Commissioner and Fox Street was the busiest intersection in the city, and there was no other way I could get to my appointment; the office was on the other side of the street she would not cross. My clammy palms gripped the harness handle and tightened on the lead. The light was about to change in our favor a third time.

"Now! Forward!" I nudged her head with my knee and pulled the lead. "Come on, Pickles! Forward!" My voice had become shrill and urgent. Then she moved. "Good girl. Come on, hup-hup, hup-hup." But instinctively I knew something was wrong. The street seemed as wide as eternity. We were walking, but far too slowly, and where was the up-curb? "Find the up-curb Pickles, find the up-curb." For a moment, I thought her leg had buckled. Then I realized that she was sitting down—right there in the middle of the intersection.

Suddenly, everything was magnified—the intense heat, the noise, the smell of the asphalt. I began to panic. No amount of pulling or coaxing would move her. Drivers began honking their horns. People began shouting—at each other and at me. I could not move. I wasn't going anywhere without Pickles.

I dumped my shoulder bag and sat down in the street with Pickles. Her head found my lap, and my streaming tears fell uncontrollably. I no longer heard the horns or the shouts. It felt as if we were in a soundproof bubble—just me and Pickles. We were together, though, and nothing else mattered. Everything was suspended.

"Ma'am, let me help you up," the traffic officer's voice intruded. His strong arms lifted me. "Here, I have your bag. Walk with me. I'll get the dog once you're out of the road."

Pickles pushed herself up with her forelegs but was unable to stand. She whined pitifully. I pulled away from the officer and crouched down beside her. "I'm not leaving you, Pickles. Never, see, never." The tears were streaming again. "She can't move," I sobbed. "Can you pick her up? I'll hold the lead and walk along with you. I'm not moving without her." Never had I felt so desolate, so helpless.

"Ma'am, I'm so sorry. Here, let's see how we can do this. Can you hold your bag?" He slung the strap over my shoulder and placed the lead in my hand. He bent down and gathered my precious Pickles up in his arms. "Okay. Ready? Here we go." He strode to the sidewalk, me alongside. At least Pickles was safe. Two other officers were trying to disperse the crowd forming around us. "Ma'am, we have radioed for help. They're sending a vehicle to come get you and take you to the traffic offices. You'll be able to call anyone you need to from there." Dazed and trembling, I stood there, crying, talking incoherently and fumbling for tissues in my bag. Pickles lay at my feet, shaking and whining intermittently. "She won't be working any more, will she?" the officer asked, but it was not a question he wanted an answer to. I heard his voice break off and he placed a comforting arm around my shoulders. I cried even harder.

I was a little more composed when we arrived at the traffic offices. The officer in charge dialed the guide dog school and soon had Brian on the line. Briefly the officer outlined what had happened. He cupped his hand around the receiver and turned away from me as he spoke as though that meant I couldn't hear him. Brian said he would come immediately.

* * *

"Marilyn, this is harder than anything you and Pickles have ever had to do." Brian sat on the opposite couch, talking softly but firmly. "We never know just how it's going to happen, but the two of you are still together. She's healthy and well for an old dog, but her concentration has snapped. I'm sure I don't have to tell you that she just cannot wear the harness again." He paused, I nodded. My eyes were closed and my head rested against the back of the couch. "There is no other way of saying this to you." A longer pause. "You will have to use a cane again—at least for now while you decide what you want to do. Do you still have a cane? If not, I'll get one for you."

"I've got one." My reply was barely audible.

"If you want a new dog, we'll put you in the very next class. As it happens, the next class starts four weeks from next Monday. There are two dogs that are good options for you, but I can't do anything about them until you decide if you want to join that class or not."

"What about Pickles?" I hardly dared to ask.

"You'll keep her, of course. You know that. She'll be waiting here at home for you when you get home with the new dog. One of us'll come home with you and introduce the dogs to each other just to make sure there's no trouble."

"But I'll be gone a whole month! Why can't she stay with me at—"

"Because you have to give her up as your guide before you can take on a new one. Pickles will be here for you when you get back."

I could not stop crying. Give up my dog. Give her up? Brian let me be, and I was grateful to him for that. "I'll call you tomorrow, okay?" I said, sniffing and dabbing my eyes for the umpteenth time.

"That's fine. I'll wait to hear from you then." Brian got up to go. "You've had many good years with Pickles. Treasure them." He hugged me, then patted my shoulder and left.

I rinsed my face and called Pickles. As always, she was never far from me. She followed me to the bedroom. I lifted her onto my bed and propped myself up on the pillows. Her silky head found the crook of my arm. I stroked her muzzle and traced around her eyes with my fingertip. Her ears twitched and she snuggled closer to me. Occasionally she would lick the tears that plopped onto my arm. The truth of Brian's words came back to me. And now...what now? I had learned to trust Pickles implicitly. I would walk anywhere with her, anywhere at all, and walk with confidence. No matter the time of day or night, whenever I picked up the lead, there she was, ready to be harnessed and guide. My heart ached at the thought of leaving her behind and getting another dog. Her whole life had centered around me. I felt ashamed—I was repaying her loyalty and devotion with abandonment. I could not bear to think of my life without Pickles at my side.

We lay there for a very long time, just drawing comfort from each other. Later, after the initial shock subsided, I would begin to realize that the sudden retirement of Pickles was a sad ending to a remarkable chapter in my life, but it also marked the beginning of a new one, for me and for Pickles too. At that moment, though, I just wanted to hold her close to me.

The South African Guide-Dogs Association for the Blind

When a dog leaves the working world, it is sometimes not so much about the end of something as the beginning, as Linda Elmore Teeple realizes.

Hope for the Holidays

by Linda Elmore Teeple

June 2006 through September 2007 was a difficult and discouraging time for my family as we experienced a series of significant losses. My husband's oldest brother, Mike, was diagnosed with terminal brain cancer in June 2006. Early in December he was admitted into a hospice care facility for his final days. That very same day, his other brother underwent emergency heart surgery. Within a day or two, I received the news that a friend had died of breast cancer after a courageous battle that began when she was only thirty-five.

In the midst of all of this, we were waiting on a much-anticipated call from Leader Dogs for the Blind. Our Leader Dog puppy, Hope, was due to be assigned to a blind person and graduate from the program as a full-fledged guide dog. However, the call we received was to inform us that Hope was being released from the program, due to being too timid. We were shocked and dumbfounded. How could this be? How disappointing!

As her puppy raisers, we were given first dibs on adopting her, and on December 26, 2006, my husband and I made the five-hour drive to Rochester Hills, Michigan, to retrieve our very own Golden Retriever. When Hope first saw us from a distance, we weren't sure if she knew who we were. But as soon as we were subjected to the sniff test, she immediately recognized us. Her re-entry into our home was as if she had never left. If she was miffed with us for subjecting her to the rigors of kennel life and Leader Dog training, she never let on. She was her affable self. Our newest Leader Dog puppy was delighted to have an energetic playmate.

Our Sunday school class had been praying for us through one stressful situation after another. On the Sunday after Christmas when we shared that Hope did not graduate and become a Leader Dog, we received a brilliant gift of words from a classmate. Following class, she wrapped her arm around my shoulders and said, almost prophetically, "God knew that you were the ones who needed HOPE this Christmas."

Prior to this, we'd only thought of Hope's dismissal as a failure on our part as puppy raisers. Our friend's insightful words flipped this perceived failure into a gift of God's grace for grief-filled days. Yes, we indeed needed an infusion of hope during a very dark time. And how ironic that "God" spelled backwards is "dog."

Hope, the Golden Retriever, and God's hope continued to be with us as we learned that my brother-in-law had succumbed to cancer. This providential ray of hope shone into 2007, offering support when my mother died in April, when our next-door-neighbor died of cancer in May, and in September when the home of our other next-door-neighbor was destroyed by fire.

Our beautiful, beguiling Hope is a vivid and tangible reminder that we need never lose hope, no matter what losses befall us. Grief is inevitable, a side effect of love. And HOPE is the Golden Retriever that sticks close to our side and gently and faithfully leads us on.

Hope is a gift that God intends for us to share with others. Thus, Hope and I are preparing to become an animal assisted therapy team. I have completed a course on animal assisted therapy, and once Hope and I pass the Delta Society Animal-Handler Evaluation, we plan to visit senior living communities and other facilities where interaction with canines is beneficial. Maybe we can be a reading buddy team in a classroom. I am a marriage and family therapist, and Hope can be a valuable co-therapist, especially when working with children. The possibilities are endless when infused with HOPE.

Leader Dogs for the Blind

Surely Pam Liles would have a long time with Emma, surely.

Emma's Impact

by Kathy Nimmer

Pam never realized when she brought Emma home as a pet that the little Pekingese/ Pomeranian mix would be her service dog, able to alert to Pam's frequent seizures before they happened. She never guessed that the little dog she would call her "baby" would provide such remarkable companionship and support. And, she never contemplated that Emma would not stay long in her life, tiptoeing into her heart quietly and, sadly, leaving almost the same way.

A car accident that threw Pam into a coma was the initiating event in their partnership, long before Emma was even born. Pam emerged with her life but also with chronic seizures, some brief in nature and others classified as grand mal with profound effects. Swelling of the brain from the accident had changed Pam forever, but so would the tiny dog who became Pam's gentle companion.

Jumping, barking, and licking. That was the indicator. Jumping, barking, and licking. With uncanny regularity, a seizure would follow. Pam's husband noticed the pattern. Pam's own recollections were often fuzzy after the seizures, but her husband noted Emma's consistent ability to pick up on whatever chemical changes were the precursor to Pam's seizures, and the alerting behavior followed. When she began to reward the jumping, barking, and licking, Pam discovered an unexpected avenue stretching out before her, a chance to medicate before seizures, a chance to reduce their intensity and live a safer, steadier life.

She had so much more too in the devoted little dog: companionship, support, confidence, security, happiness, and love. She had it all and expected to enjoy it for a long time.

It was not to be. Starting with refusal to drink, then refusal to eat, Emma began to shut down. None of the praise and treats and encouragements that had worked so beautifully to enforce Emma's abilities had an effect anymore. The little dog just lay in her basket and stared at Pam with forlorn eyes.

Diagnosis came quickly, taking Pam's breath away: a brain tumor. No chance for operating, no chance for survival. In the blink of an eye, Emma was gone.

Not everyone understands the bond between a person and a service dog, though many do understand the fundamental human/animal connection that adds such happiness to millions of lives worldwide. In this one little corner of the world, Pam was devastated. She couldn't bring herself to get rid of the basket where Emma had liked to sleep, nor could she throw away the tiny collar Emma had always worn. When her second service dog started carving out a place in

Pam's heart, there remained a question mark, a hesitation to trust the new relationship because it too could so swiftly end.

Even with the passing of time, Emma's entry into and departure from Pam's life has remained defining. Tears still reduce Pam's voice to a shaken whisper, as soft as Emma's footsteps that Pam still imagines she hears sometimes. After all, when Emma left Pam's side forever, the precious little dog who would jump, bark, and lick had only reached the age of two.

Owner-Trained Dog

Theo's life and death wove their way deep into the heart of Sarah Gales.

Theo: Song of My Independence

by Sarah L. Gales

I loved you from the moment I heard your name: Theo. It was like the music of water sliding over round rocks, the song of my independence. You were like a blanket insulating me from the world's troubles and dangers, your guide work flawless and dependable. Every day after high school we'd weave through the redwoods, exploring the forest where we lived. Sometimes we walked for miles, passing along the river where you would stop and look upon it as if with wonder.

Later, in Colorado, you plowed paths through the snow on our college campus; nothing stopped you from finding our way in life. We spent afternoons on the porch watching thunderstorms charge across the plains to touch the Rocky Mountains. At midnight, on that same porch, we heard the owls call to us from the few trees where they rested, under the round moon in the still air.

When you got cancer they cut away your leg, to keep the illness from spreading, to save you. You lived another year on the borrowed time they said you'd never have. I nursed you with fresh foods, supplements, and the knowledge of healing passed on from my ancestors. You waited for Ricky to come, watched him work, and mentored him in the language of the canine pack. He followed your lead in all things and slowly became an outstanding guide.

The cancer crept into your lungs, tendrils of the disease spreading and robbing you of your strength. The day before you took your last breath, we went on a picnic. You used your final hours on this earth to run free up the mountainside, where we both found peace in knowing you were ready for your next journey.

In the end, you lay down in soft grasses, and as the needle found your vein, you looked up to see my face for the last time. In that way, it was no different than other days, you looking upon me with love and devotion, my hand touching you lightly, returning the same sentiment. Then suddenly you were gone, my first companion swept away in the arms of our Creator.

Years later, my life still feels empty from the loss of your presence here, yet it is fuller for having shared so many days with you. As I move down streets, among trees and up mountains, I remember your step beside me. Others walk with me now, their names like new verses to my song of independence. Still you are all around me, in vivid memories, treasured lessons, and the music of flowing water.

Guide Dogs for the Blind

Karen Derx was forever changed by Shocker.

Shocker's Promise

by Kathy Nimmer

She was the perfect dog. Shocker, a gorgeous black Lab, was everything to Karen. From the moment they met in training, Shocker wanted nothing more in life than to please Karen. And, she did that for ten glorious years.

Karen was a teenager when she met Shocker. In a wheelchair with muscular dystrophy, Karen was hoping that a service dog could give her more independence, help her gain opportunities to accomplish more things without the assistance of other people. In Shocker, Karen found all of that and then some.

Trained to do many things to assist Karen, Shocker was particularly good at picking up dropped items and opening doors by jumping up to push the button. Able also to open drawers, tug on clothing or socks for removal, and brace Karen physically, Shocker had it all down pat.

And, she did everything with joy. Karen grew from a teen to a young adult with Shocker by her side, lending her confidence and support. The dog who loved kids seemed to grow richer and stronger as her beloved Karen grew from youth into adulthood. Loyal, dedicated, and ready, Shocker enriched Karen's life more than she could have imagined.

It was a normal Tuesday, or so it seemed. Shocker had aged, put in over ten years of service, and slowed down a bit. But she was still healthy and happy, and she still preferred being by Karen's side more than any place in the world.

As suddenly as the clock ticks by its seconds, everything changed. Shocker staggered. She lost control of her limbs. By the very next morning, Shocker could not walk. She was diagnosed with myasthenia gravis, a devastating disease of the nervous system. Shocker was dying.

Karen trembled, speechless and without real preparation for the goodbye that was coming far too quickly. She'd known retirement must be coming soon, but death? And the death of a dog that would be the standard to which she would hold all future service dogs! Even the highly-equipped veterinary school at a nearby university couldn't save Shocker. Her esophagus had swollen, causing her to aspirate, and pneumonia had settled in. The end was very, very near.

It is never easy saying goodbye to a service dog. When it is the first service dog and an excellent worker, it is even harder. More even than the incredibly profound bond with pets, this is a parting of abilities that were matched so well as to supplement for any inabilities on either side. It is the harmony of partnership, where you just can't imagine one without the other. It is agony, and Karen, like many other service dog users before and after her, had to find a way to say good-bye.

There was a sort of goodbye, inadequate and incomplete as it was. “I love you,” Karen whispered. “You have been a good girl.” She choked back tears. “If you have to go, you can. I promise I’ll be okay.”

That Sunday, just five days after the first stagger, Shocker was gone. Karen mourns for her with the bittersweet knowledge that her life is better for Shocker having been in it, but the absence is still profound. And, even today, she is still working on trying to fulfill that last tearful promise to Shocker.

Kansas Specialty Dog Service

Rona says goodbye to her handler, Marcie Wallace, in this poem.

Going Home, Mom

by Kathy Nimmer

"Not today, Mom."
The rain drums a gentle rhythm,
Perfect conditions for a morning nap.
But the click of the white cane wakes her, a plastic interloper,
And loyalty beckons her to rise.

"Once more, Mom."
The harness slides around her like always,
But the halting, unsteady steps
Speak of too many miles walked already
And the right time to step away from the job.

"Going home, Mom."
The footsteps accelerate like propeller blades
So that home and the plush, enveloping bed
Get closer faster, much better
Than trying to do what is beyond her now.

"You're leaving, Mom."
The wistful but wise canine eyes
Watch the tearful blind woman stagger away
Into the building where she works,
Where they worked together, until now.

"I'm happy, Mom."
Days, weeks, months, years,
Three full ones, of blissful peace
As retirement cloaks her aging body
With a superhero's cape, a just doggy reward.

"I'm leaving, Mom."
A chest fills up completely
Not just with the courageous heart of a willing guide
But with tumors, "From peanuts to softballs,"
Says the vet, her words whispered, breathy, bleak.

"Be strong, Mom."
Memories and tears cascade as one,
And every single shred of the blind woman's soul
Cries out in agony to change the truth,
And undo what is so very nearly done already.

"Always yours, Mom."
A golden head nestles into the blind woman's lap,
Content to be where she most belongs,
Guiding her mom down one more path,
This one ending with a gentle goodbye.

Guide Dog Foundation for the Blind, Inc.

The passing of a friend's guide dog leaves lasting impressions on Nancy Rumbolt-Trzcinski.

He Was Almost Like My Own

by Nancy Rumbolt-Trzcinski

Yesterday we said goodbye to Ricky. Ricky was not my dog, but he was a part of my family, just as Sarah, Fargo, and Alfalfa were.

In 2002, I met Sarah and a big yellow Labrador at the American Council for the Blind convention in Houston. At that time Sarah, two other friends, and I roomed together. It was a room full of laughter, dog fur, and snoring (both dog and human). Sarah and I shared one of the two beds in the room. In the middle of the night that big yellow Labrador stole my pillow and my heart.

In the over three years that Sarah has lived in the upstairs apartment in my house there has not been a day where I have not heard the sound of Ricky chewing his bone or Ricky running down the stairs to go out or to come into my part of the house to investigate what was for dinner, what boxes he could destroy, or what was in the toy box.

During dinner Ricky would sit at my right side, put his head in my lap, sharing his drool and his love. His pleading big brown eyes would implore me to give him a treat, whether it was from my plate or from the candy dish on the counter. Ricky helped me do the dishes, sitting in the dining room door. He was there till the last dish was rinsed and put in the drain-board to dry.

Every night before I would go to bed, I would climb the stairs to say goodnight to Sarah and give Ricky his good night hug and kiss, sometimes grabbing his muzzle. I was one of the only humans he would allow to do that.

After his retirement and since my husband Bruno had been working nights, Ricky would come to my place for what we affectionately called "day care." He would either sleep on the couch or, many times, with Bruno and my Golden Retriever, Phoebe. There are memories of coming home to Ricky's latest destruction project, boxes torn, food eaten. But if you knew Ricky you could not stay mad because he purely enjoyed his project and was proud.

I could go on with many memories, but it would take too long and too many tears would flow. But along with those tears are the smiles Ricky brought to our house.

Yesterday Sarah allowed me to share in Ricky's passing. As he slipped away from us, I laid my hand on his chest, wanting to feel every last heartbeat. I sang him his favorite song ("Oh, Ricky, you're so fine, you're so fine you blow my mind, Hey Ricky!"), wanting him to know I loved him as if he was my own dog. He passed peacefully and, hopefully, knowing he was loved as much as any dog possibly could be. He is now with my beloved guide, Baxter, and the other dogs, and I pray they are running free and happy.

It is too quiet. This will get easier, but for now the house is cavernous in its silence.

I love you, Ricky, and you have a piece of my heart. Rest in peace.

Guide Dogs for the Blind

She had no time to prepare, but Marla Johnson had to face this parting anyway.

Two Steps

by Kathy Nimmer

It only took two steps: that is all. Two steps ended the journey that had freed Marla from much of the agony of living with unpredictable seizures. Two steps to the place Marla never expected to be, not that quickly anyway.

The seizures were a result of a head injury inflicted through domestic violence years before. Marla found hope through her friend Angela in the form of a Shepherd/Greyhound cross named Hattrick. A poster child for the obedience school Angela owned, Hattrick was bored. Doing demonstrations for clients was not enough for this bright dog. He needed a challenge. He needed purpose. He needed Marla.

Teaching him commands such as retrieving medicine bottles and bracing Marla before a seizure, Angela stimulated the dog whose intelligence seemed boundless. Uniting his abilities and her needs together was fitting the last piece into an intricate puzzle.

Marla's confidence rose with Hattrick by her side, ready to respond to her needs when one of the grand mal seizures would threaten. So in tune was he that he began alerting her to the seizures before they happened, giving her a chance to find a safe place and even medicate herself enough to reduce their ferocity. The alerting is never a guarantee, but it was a solidly dependable alarm when Hattrick was around.

Years of teamwork followed. She, once isolated and mocked in public for wearing a helmet to protect against falls from sudden drop seizures, now engaged people in conversations about the tall, lean dog who carried himself with such authority. The go-getter nature that was Marla's innate inclination asserted itself again. Anything was possible with Hattrick by her side. Even dealing with rampant clusters of unpredictable drop seizures was not so hard when Hattrick was near.

But it only took two steps to change things. One. Two. The end. An undetected, fast-growing tumor on his heart swept Hattrick away. He collapsed by Marla's side, gone before he knew it; no pain, but also no goodbye.

Marla, the survivor, wept. She held his head in her hands, the light gone from his eyes. She mourned the loss of something so important that it felt as if her arm was severed, her leg, her own heart. But, in his honor, she would not abandon what he gave to her: hope.

By Your Side

It wasn't old age or illness that faced Tar that day but the preservation of Gail Selfridge's life.

Tar

by Gail Selfridge

After my first Leader Dog died at far too young an age, I returned to Leader Dogs for the Blind and was matched with a black Labrador Retriever named Tar. Two years after Tar came into my life, I received a job offer that meant moving to Denver, Colorado, far from Michigan where I had grown up and attended college. Tar and I made the trip, and over time, I moved to Colorado Springs and then back to Denver as a computer programmer.

In 1980, I was working for a bank in downtown Denver. I traveled to and from work by bus every day. The part of the route not covered by the bus ride was fairly easy, except for a bridge that crossed a creek. There, pedestrians walked on the shoulder of the road, a lane open to cars as well. A sign indicated the possible presence of pedestrians, but it wasn't easy for drivers to see anyone traversing the bridge on foot, so close calls happened occasionally. It wasn't ideal, but Tar and I managed it well enough.

One winter day, I had finished my work and caught the bus to go home. It was snowing lightly, a precursor to one of Colorado's notorious big snow storms. I stepped off the bus at our regular stop and began the walk home, about two-and-a-half long blocks.

It is foggy to me now, the details of that bridge crossing, but the physical and emotional scars of what happened next still emerge from that fog enough for me to know that my life changed in a fraction of a second that day thirty years ago. I was on the bridge, moving along close to the edge as usual. Then, I heard it. The motor of a speeding car coming toward me sent chills down my spine, to match the wintery air surrounding me. I had no place to go, no options at all.

The car hit me head-on. I have no memory of the impact. Perhaps that is a blessing. It left me unconscious. Broken bones, a week-long coma, and six weeks in the hospital were the physical residue of the impact, but much more than that was destined to linger with me forever from the collision on the bridge.

Tar, my beloved Tar. When the car was just feet from hitting me, he jumped up against me so that he would take the main brunt of the impact. No one could survive that direct hit, not even Tar. He was thrown violently aside, sustaining grave injuries. Somehow, as dogs often do, he must have known his time on this earth was ending, so he looked for a quiet place to rest. He crawled down the embankment near the creek and began to die. My husband's guide dog found him when they came to the scene of the accident. Tar died, a hero to me and responsible for me still being here these many years later to tell his story.

I've always felt that Tar knew he had to give his life to save me. In a fraction of a second, he defined loyalty. In a fraction of a second, he traded his life for mine.

Leader Dogs for the Blind

The last moments of life for Kathy Nimmer's own first guide dog live forever in her memory.

Raffles

by Kathy Nimmer

I will never forget that room. It was the library in the vet clinic where my first guide dog, Raffles, had been a patient for ten years. The furniture was wicker, not all that sturdy or comfortable. Perhaps they bought it knowing that few people would sit to read when they came in with their animals for routine or not so routine visits. Perhaps it was the last room to be furnished, so the budget was low, and wicker was more affordable. Regardless, the crunch of the stretching wood fibers, lightly muffled by the thin cushion covering the woven mat of the seat top, signaled for me a special situation, a talk that needed privacy.

We had been in that room only a few times before. When allergies became so controlling that Raffles needed to have twice-a-week shots, we met in the library. I learned to give the shots myself in there, under the guidance of a wise, seasoned vet who had given thousands of shots by that point in his career. I gave my first shot to Raffles in that room and felt the pride that a mother must feel when she successfully helps her child to take his first step.

We met in there, too, when my parents' dog tore a tendon and I made the special request for my own vet to do the surgery. Known to be an excellent surgeon, she would be able to care for the feisty terrier better than anyone else, and she said yes, of course.

But that day, I didn't hear the crunch of the wicker, nor the wise voice of the allergy vet, nor the French-Canadian accent of my vet chatting with my parents. What I heard was the pant of Raffles, the delicate footsteps that should not have been so delicate, coming from a dog who had been eighty strong and elegant pounds at his prime. Now, those footsteps eased forward a Golden who had shriveled into a skeleton covered with golden waves. The powerful steroid we'd used the last month to extend his life from the vicious, merciless lymphoma eating away at his body and spirit had eaten away at Raffles, too: two dueling monsters who would ultimately share a claim on my first guide dog, my first love.

It had been Thanksgiving when my mom put my right hand under Raffles' chin to feel the two marble-shaped balls that turned out to be enlarged lymph nodes. Raffles had retired in May and was living the life of luxury with my parents. My mom found the hard balls that dangled under his chin like a mockery of celebratory Christmas ornaments, but she didn't know what to make of them. I knew, as I touched them, that they signaled a change, a decimation of what I had cherished for so long.

Now, I sat on the cold floor of the library, my hands spasmodically clinching the folded comforter that the staff had spread out for Raffles. He lay in the middle of the comforter, not at ease. He was spacey, distracted, probably consumed with the inner sense that his body was betraying itself. He was not happy.

The two vets who were my favorite caretakers of Raffles knelt nearby, tears in their voices. My mom, so attached to Raffles when I worked him for ten years and so proudly his new mom following his retirement, cried bitterly. I sat silently, frozen in a grief tableau that I simply couldn't believe was playing out at the start of this new year, only a month from Raffles' twelfth birthday. He would not live to see that day.

Sometimes blindness is a blessing. I miss out on visual scenes that otherwise emblazon themselves on the minds of viewers who never forget them. That day, I never saw the needle. No, not even when I would later stroke the unmoving body of my precious Raffles, I never saw the needle. I didn't touch it either. I never had sensory contact of any kind with the mechanism that would end Raffles' suffering and take him away from me.

What I touched was that comforter, rippling it between my fingers. It was softer and more giving than the furniture pressed against the walls of the library, wicker soldiers stoically unwilling to become emotionally involved in the scene playing out on the floor at their feet.

Then I touched the silky hair of the dog who had changed my life. It was familiar and unfamiliar at the same time. Familiar in bringing me back to our first meeting, when he proved to be the largest dog I'd ever seen. Back to our first walk when he stopped on the dime at the first corner we came to, shocking me even though I knew training placed curb identification as a very basic skill. Taking me back to our long walks near my first apartment building, the first day of school when I returned no longer as the blind teacher but as the blind teacher who had a guide dog, our first plane flight when he trembled like a leaf in a spring storm, our first everything.

But, the silky fur was also unfamiliar, somehow different in texture already, changing substance as the cells that were shutting down his body seemed also to be shutting down my connection with him. This both was and was not the fur that I had combed every day, brushed off of my clothing in the morning, picked out of my mouth when I finished snuggling with him on our carpeted floor at home. This was my Raffles, and yet, he was already not mine.

The first injection went wrong, collapsing his fragile vein and causing the dog who almost never cried to yelp. I crumbled then, finding no reserves to accept that in the last moments of his time on this earth, pain would be one of his final sensations. So I reached for him, the real him. His long, noble body, as long and tall as they come, perfect for my lofty height, an ideal match. I massaged the tail that would wag with enthusiasm when he saw his best buddies at school, the teachers who meant the world to him. There was the man who offered Raffles bacon treats to launch each school day with style, and the woman who would line up in her designer clothes and fancy shoes to count 1, 2, 3 … and race Raffles down the English hallway to her room. She never once won, not once in ten years. I knew if she were here now, she would have her first victory. Raffles did not want to run anymore.

The second procedure did not cause pain. His veins remained open, hidden pipes that carried the sedating liquid contents toward their destination. I leaned over Raffles as the injection surged into his body. I held his head in mine as he began to still. I heard none of the sobs and last wishes of others swirling around me. I didn't hear the crunch of the wicker either. What I heard and still hear years later is the sigh, his last breath. He was silent, then took a deep, gusty breath, and was silent again. I still hear that breath and I still hear the silence. Sometimes, I wonder which one is louder.

Pilot Dogs, Inc.

Chapter 8

After That

Starting Over, Finding Hope, and Cherishing Inspiration

Paw Prints of Wisdom

"I began working with my dog when I realized that even though I had rescued him, he was ready to rescue me."

—Katherine Walters,
handler of an owner-trained psychiatric service dog

"The most rewarding part of working with dogs is seeing a relationship blossom and grow between the client and their dog. Two special beings can form a new, independent life together."

—Marilyn Lazarus,
Head Trainer, Assistance Dogs of America, Inc.

Sarah Gales knows what matters most to her in this world.

Life in Dog Years

by Sarah L. Gales

Most people measure their time on this earth in years or even decades, while some of us measure our time by the animals we spend it with. The horse I was riding when I was nine-years-old, the goat I was showing when I won my first championship ribbon, or the dog that accompanied me to my first job interview. Non-animal people have told me that the way I lay out my life by the animals in it is strange to them. I always reply that I know no other way to count the time and that my existence would be lonely without them in my life. Perhaps it is that I much prefer the company of animals to that of humans, that I fill my days with them and count the time by paw prints, hoof prints, and feathers. Sometimes we don't realize the ordinary, everyday things that happen with our faithful companions all around us, their presence emphasizing that it is the little things that make our lives complete.

This morning, as I crossed the street behind a noisy, parked bus, there was a car I couldn't hear. My guide dog, Fargo, crossed the first lanes of traffic, paused at the flat median, and turned his head to look at me. I stopped beside him, as simple as breathing, one body, one mind, moving together. We stood for just a few seconds as he judged the distance between us and the vehicle and continued on as the car passed. This is why I say it is the little things that make a life. They seem little, but in reality, they are not. Years ago, before dogs, I would have waited for that bus to move so that I could hear the traffic better. Maybe I should have waited. Maybe I should always do the safest thing. After all, shouldn't blind people be cautious and always on their toes? This morning though, I wanted coffee, and it was across the street. So off I went, maybe taking things for granted.

Later, after lunch, I went to a mattress store to look at new mattresses. The salesman in his crisp suit took me to the first bed.

"I want you to try this one first," he said, patting the mattress.

I reached out to touch the bed, and the next thing I knew Fargo had leaped onto it.

"Get off!" I said in surprise.

Luckily the salesman laughed. I think I'll always remember how Fargo tried to help pick out the new bed. The rest of my time in the store he waited patiently while I tried out various beds. Always wanting to please, he knew it wasn't the time or place to be on the bed. The humorous part of the story is that I did end up purchasing that first mattress he jumped on. I guess he has discerning tastes with regard to the one piece of furniture he is allowed to use. As I write this, he is sound asleep on my own bed, our bed.

As I stood in the vocational rehabilitation office today, planning the retirement party for my friend Nancy's guide dog, Waylon, with colleagues, I began to think about how many lives a dog can touch. We don't think about it as we go through our days, how their retirement or death is a loss for others. It might not be a big, life-changing loss, but it means something to them also. In the case of Waylon's retirement, it's even the talk of the town. After work I went into the local candy shop to get some hand-dipped Easter candy. The shop owner loves the dogs. (I need to convince her to make white chocolate dipped dog bones.) She had already heard about Waylon's retirement and asked me how he and Nancy were as soon as she saw me. It's funny how fast word spreads in a small town. Not only do people gossip about each other, they also talk about our dogs. I guess that's only fitting when you rarely see some of us without a four-legged companion working hard at our sides.

At the grocery store, just as I was leaving, one of the girls ran over to say goodbye to Fargo. She's moving away. It was not important for her to necessarily say goodbye to me, but she wanted to give Fargo a big hug and got all choked up when he licked her face. What Fargo means to her, I have no idea, but perhaps he'll live in her stories for years to come.

When the cab driver brought me home he asked if he could carry my groceries upstairs so he could say hi to my retired dog. I had to tell him that Ricky died suddenly last November, and my apartment never felt so empty as he carried the groceries up anyway and no one came to greet us.

"How could he just die?" he asked me.

"I don't know," I said. "He just went like that, one minute he seemed fine, the next he was bleeding from a ruptured cancer tumor."

I thought to myself: it was the end of an era, the era of Ricky. People who aren't animal people might not understand. I put away the groceries, and Fargo watched, as he has finally learned to stay out of my way. I sat in my recliner, and Fargo crawled into my lap. He doesn't know he weighs seventy-one pounds and has pokey elbows. What he does know is that he's not allowed on my chair, but he is allowed on my lap. So if my lap is in the chair, that's fair game. We sat there and he wagged and seemed to think that everything in his life was quite fine. I thought to myself that decades from now, dogs from now, I'll remember days like this, days where everything was measured in dogs. Dog days are the best days of all.

I want all of my seconds, minutes, hours, days, years, and decades to be measured by the animals I spend them with. All the days I do not walk alone are good days. Most animals are with us only for a short time. They pass in and out of our lives far too quickly. It's best that we count every moment with them and remember it.

Guide Dogs for the Blind

It would have been excusable for Mike Hambly to give up, but then, he would never have met Tucker.

A Gentleman

by Kathy Nimmer

Almost nothing that was true on July 31, 1994, was still true on August 1, 1994, at least for Mike. Yes, he was still young, still big and tall, still married, and still the father of a beautiful little girl and a handsome little boy, but the rest of his world was like a sleek silver train that had entered a long, dark tunnel cut through the center of a mountain, only to emerge on the other side as a hobbled, unsteady stage coach with peeling paint.

The root of the drastic metamorphosis? A terrible accident, inexplicable in its cause and voracity, that stole away both Mike's vision and ability to walk. The truck he had been driving down a secondary highway not far from his farm flipped, sending him crashing through the windshield face first to land on his head on the unforgiving ground. His eyes were destroyed as was his T9 vertebra. The vital young man who knew no bounds was suddenly unable to see and unable to feel anything from the waist down.

Tucker was not even alive yet. His Labrador ancestors were romping through the year 1994, unaware that one of their descendants would be just special enough to defy expectations and be able to help someone with one of the most difficult pairings of disabilities imaginable. After all, guide dogs can lead the blind, but they are not meant to pull. Dogs trained to give mobility assistance can help people in wheelchairs, but they are not taught to judge visual matters for their handlers. Could a dog be trained to work with someone both blind and in a wheelchair, particularly when that person chose to use a manual wheelchair instead of a power chair, to preserve the upper-body strength that suddenly seemed to be so precious?

Years later, when Mike was able and ready to find out if it could be done, he was met with the firm answer, "No." Hearing that single syllable enough times that discouragement had every right to take up sanctuary in Mike's heart, he discovered that something else had survived that crash in 1994: his determination. After having undergone years of surgeries, therapy, and repositioning of his life goals into new pathways through recovery, Mike was finally ready to see how a dog could add new dimensions to his life, restoring the freedom that had been lost in that farm field.

Finally, Mike located a school that was willing to give it a try. They pledged to find a large, strong guide dog among their string of trainees who would be able to cope with the added encumbrance of a manual wheelchair. That is when Tucker found his calling. Mellow enough to be nicknamed "a gentleman" by his trainer, this

110-pound black Lab had the strength and spirit to adapt to a special challenge.

They embarked upon three intense weeks of training in 2002, exhaustively practicing the guide work that was Tucker's primary focus. Using an angled harness that kept Tucker far enough away from the wheelchair to avoid being injured by the spinning wheels, Tucker was the guiding presence for Mike, who held the harness with his left hand while his right hand propelled the wheelchair forward. It took a while for the two to develop a rhythm that would keep them going in a straight line, but they persisted. It helped that Mike pledged to work Tucker only inside buildings, avoiding the risky edges of curbs that could send Mike into a dangerous plunge onto a street if Tucker was even a quarter of an inch off in judgment.

Mike and Tucker finished training and moved forward. Tucker instinctively developed a subtle pull to counterbalance Mike's right-handed propulsion of the manual wheelchair. He learned routes after only one try, defiantly sitting down with impatience when Mike would attempt to reiterate the directions that Tucker didn't need to hear again. When the bus they often rode would pull up, Tucker barked twice to let Mike know it was outside waiting for them; he did not bark for the approach of any other vehicle.

Mike flourished too, starting his own company that offered Braille embossing on business cards. He found his confidence and strength soaring with the teamwork that was so perfectly in sync. With Tucker's support, Mike's blindness and paralysis became less significant, only secondary descriptors of a man who claimed "successful," "productive," "independent," and "able" far more readily than "disabled."

So when the news came that lymphoma was beginning its quick and relentless trek through Tucker's body, Mike picked up the phone. The trainers needed to know. They needed to be looking for a large, strong dog who could handle the added encumbrance of a manual wheelchair. They needed to be searching their stock for "a gentleman" whose nature could handle extra challenges well. They needed to find a dog whose strength, stubbornness, and intelligence would be the perfect complement to his handler's like traits. They needed to start looking, right away.

As soon as Mike placed the phone back in the cradle, he reached out his calloused hand to find Tucker's large head and silky ears. It was 2009 now, not 1994 in the farm field, not 2002 when Tucker stepped into his world. It was 2009. The sleek silver train was no longer a hobbled, unsteady stage coach, but not really a sleek, silver train either. It was a brilliant tandem masterpiece of mobility, otherwise known as "partnership." As Mike's hand fingered Tucker's silky ears, it was impossible to know just exactly who needed whom more.

Dogs with Wings Assistance Dog Society

Italian Carmina Martire's journey found her overseas and overwhelmed with love for Darien.

Darien Found Me

by Carmina Martire
Translated by Gabriele Giuliani

I was born in Calabria, but in order to attend college, I moved to Rome. I was born with retinitis pigmentosa, a progressive eye condition, and I slowly lost my sight. As my sight inexorably dimmed, I graduated in psychology and specialized in psychotherapy. I then began to work in my profession.

One year ago, I first decided to acquire a guide dog. I discussed it only with very few people; all, knowing my doubts about dogs in general, tried to dissuade me, but all their attempts were for naught. A strange assurance pushed me to go ahead and look in Italy for a good guide dog school. Unfortunately, in Italy I found the discouraging reality that I would have to wait for two years before obtaining a guide dog. A friend mentioned someone who had attended an extraordinary guide dog school in America. The contact with the girl was immediate, as was visiting the website and filing an application online. All was done as on a whim, seemingly without much thought, as if I had done it for somebody else.

I began taking accelerated English lessons. English was a language I never had a desire to learn, but, given my motivation, I had no problems tackling this obstacle. While my English was improving, in October I received an email from the school's manager…the subject read "good news." I was accepted! On March 30 I landed at JF Kennedy airport. I thought, *I am in America to get a guide dog, alone, better yet only accompanied by my fears!*

I will never forget the day I actually met Darien. The previous night partly because of jet lag and partly because of my anxiety, I had not slept, weeping and being uncertain about my choice. But, just like magic, when Darien entered my room led by the instructor, all my worries disappeared; Darien at first seemed to me to be too small. Waving his tail he stole my heart, just like that. Yes, precisely him: a male, a black Labrador, had seduced me, and just like magic all my qualms and uncertainties had disappeared.

I immediately understood that he had a strong character, that I had to wait for his tempo. To gain his confidence, I then used my knowledge and expertise of psychology and set out to build an alliance, gradually, the way you do with the most difficult patients.

Thus we started our own adventure together on the streets of America. Day by day, I began to feel the new and different autonomy I was acquiring with my new guide; after about a month, I was ready to go back home!

I had a really beautiful experience in America, but in Rome my own life was waiting for me. While the aircraft took off, I felt an inner sympathy for my new friend for I thought I was taking him away from his land. I knew that he would find a lot of love but thought that the beginning of his new Italian life would be hard.

As they had told me at the school, the first six months of getting used to the changes were to be the most difficult for the puppy. In fact, upon his arrival in Rome, Darien was confused, stressed, and disoriented. Understanding this situation, I decided to proceed step by step since for him everything was new and different. This proved a winning choice, for today, five months after his arrival, he does not have signs of stress and confusion. He understands how to guide me through the disorderly traffic of Rome, how to allow me to negotiate illegally parked cars or use the pedestrian crossings.

Every day I dedicate to him my time with all the love one can give to a little being like him. I describe to him all we do and how we will spend our day together. He and I play a lot together, and when I focus on him to play or for other more serious activities, there are no phone calls that can distract me: for him everything can wait! Even when he guides me, I adopt the same method: there is only he and I! I am quite sure that the little American has realized that I respect him in everything. If I err with him, I apologize and thank him for all the beautiful things he does. I am more and more convinced that it is Darien who found me, to educate me and help me appreciate the marvelous experience of finding the heart of a dog.

What a strange blueprint is life patterned upon. To discover all of this I had to arrive all the way to America. With a smiling gaze to the future and joy in my heart, today I tell Darien, "Thank you for deciding to be part of my life and to have offered me your light, for having waited for me, and found me."

Guiding Eyes for the Blind

Marla Johnson and Brie converse together about their partnership in this poem.

You and I

by Kathy Nimmer

I wake to find you draped across my belly,
Protecting me from the world that can be so unkind.
You, a barrier against the evil
That led me by the hand to this place.
                    You wake to find me draped across your belly,
                    Pulled there during the hiding night
                    By a seizure you had but didn't know about
                    But I knew and protected you even then.
I rise to find you standing beside me,
Your youth a freshness I wish to drink in,
A loving, soothing burst of sunshine
I long to use to whitewash the past.
                    You rise to find me standing beside you,
                    A reminder of what is good in this world,
                    And we together are part of that good,
                    So trust in me and be my friend.
I turn to find you still with me,
Your subtle ways alerting me to the times
When consciousness will swiftly elude me
And bright turns from haze to gray to black.
                    You turn to find me still with you,
                    Ready to grab medicine, helmet, bag,
                    To carry the vest that says I am working,
                    All to warn you, caution you, give you a chance.
I sit to find you pressed against me,
So unaware of his rage that once created this whirlwind,
Battering fiercely against me long before you drew your first breath,
Wishing with fury to ease me into drawing my last one.

You sit to find me pressed beside you,
And I do know of his hand that struck the telling blow,
The same way I knew of the seizure
That had me drape across you last night.
I lie down to find you beside me,
And my spirit is once more whole
For the demons can't have dominion here
When goodness is made of a tail and fur.
You lie down to find me beside you,
So if it is acceptable, my friend,
I'll stay here, perhaps always,
And you and I will be free.

By Your Side

There is more to the job than guide work for Clara French's dog Landria.

True Worship

by Kathy Nimmer

Two figures stroll into the church, ready to participate in fellowship and worship: a woman and a guide dog. Landria moves forward with no commands, walking a direct path, not toward an open pew but toward a row of individuals who sit apart from everyone else for now. These people are different somehow, and either because of that or in spite of that, Landria seeks them out.

She places her soft yellow head in the lap of the woman in a wheelchair, wiggling with pleasure when a gnarled hand awkwardly strokes the silky ears. She moves next to the man with Down syndrome and nudges him until he too caresses her with jerky, uncoordinated hands. The oxygen tank by the next man is nothing too intimidating, nor is the woman who speaks with a loud voice, repeating every minute or so, "Is this your dog? May I pet her?" Landria doesn't care that the question is spoken so often, the answer not registered for more than a fleeting second in the mind of the elderly woman who used to take Landria and her blind person to the grocery store for goodies but now is being engulfed by Alzheimer's. After the service, Landria looks for the young boy with cerebral palsy, her presence diverting the child from his erratic exclamations and random, jarring noises. And what does the blind woman do while Landria completes her missions of mercy and joy? She smiles.

Leader Dogs for the Blind

Nazi guards at a concentration camp had taught Max Edelman to fear dogs, so how could he possibly trust one to become his eyes?

Overcoming the Fear of Dogs

by Max Edelman

After arriving in America in 1951, I envied my blind friends who had guide dogs. They had so much more freedom of mobility than I did with a white cane. My problem, although I was reluctant to admit it, was that I had a fear of even being close to dogs.

In spite of my feelings, the day I retired I decided to apply for a guide dog at the Guiding Eyes for the Blind guide dog school. I wanted the freedom of mobility a dog could give me so much that I had to make the attempt.

When I arrived at Guiding Eyes for training, Charlie, the training supervisor, had a few cheerful welcoming words for the twelve of us who arrived for the May 1990 class. After the welcoming ceremonies, I took Charlie aside and said, "I would like very much to have a guide dog. But because of my negative experiences with dogs, I'm not sure I can bond with one." Charlie, curious, asked me to explain. "I am a Holocaust survivor," I said. "In one of the Nazi concentration camps I was in, the commandant had a big, vicious German Shepherd. Sometimes when he entertained guests and wanted to show how cruel he could be or how vicious his dog was (or both), he told a guard to bring a group of inmates into his courtyard. Once, before I was blinded, I was in that group. I watched as he chose one of us to stand apart. Then he gave the dog the command, 'Fass!' meaning 'Fetch!' With one leap, the dog grabbed the victim by the throat, ripped it open, crushed his larynx, and pulled him to the ground. In a few minutes, that man was dead. The dog, his face bloody, returned to his master for his praise and reward, and the audience applauded the dog for a job well done. More than four decades later, nightmares about that and other similar cruelties still torment me," I confided to Charlie.

After a moment of reflection, Charlie said, "No human being is born evil; some become evil. No dog is born vicious; some are trained to be vicious. Give us a chance to prove to you that the dogs we train and the one you get will guide you safely, love you, and protect you."

His words strengthened my resolve. I was determined, I told Charlie, to give it a chance. Should I fail, it wouldn't be for lack of trying. Charlie and his staff decided Calvin, a two-year-old, eighty-pound chocolate Lab, would be the right match for me.

The four-week training at the school was difficult for all concerned: Calvin, the instructor, and me. Nevertheless, the training time passed too quickly. The real test was yet to begin.

Calvin and I were waiting for our flight to be called to go home. Jan, my instructor who drove us to the airport on that sunny day in May 1990, issued a gentle reminder: "It's obvious that Calvin loves you," she said, "but he doesn't respect you yet. That's something that will take much more time, and you'll have to have patience." It was a struggle to forge a bond with Calvin. I was in the process of learning to love him, and, although I understood the helpful role Calvin was to play in my life, I was still cautious around him, never fully relaxing and accepting him.

This struggle affected Calvin as well. During this period, Calvin ate but lost weight. He had a sad expression on his face, my wife said. The veterinarian told me it was because the dog could sense my emotional distance.

Often I recalled Charlie's words, "No human being is born evil, and no dog is born vicious…" My instructor Jan called me several times, offering advice and giving me encouragement.

Slowly but surely we began to break down the invisible barrier between us. One day we stood at a busy intersection, waiting to cross the street. As we had been trained, when I heard parallel traffic start to move, I waited three seconds, then gave the command, "Calvin, forward." When we stepped off the curb, a motorist suddenly and unexpectedly made a sharp right turn, directly in front of us. Calvin stopped on a dime. He had reacted exactly as he had been trained for such a situation. Realizing that he had saved us both, I stepped back onto the sidewalk, crouched down, gave Calvin a hug around the neck, and praised him for a job well done. It was the turning point in our life together. After that, the love between us flowed freely. It took six months, but any lingering doubts I had about Calvin were completely dispelled.

With time, Calvin seemed as happy to have me as his partner as I was to have him as my guide. Based upon mutual respect and admiration, and a lot of hard work, we formed an interdependent partnership to which I, lacking in sight, contributed the power of reason, and Calvin, lacking the power of reason, contributed the sense of sight. And so, with much affection and occasional correction, we became a dynamic duo.

Calvin also formed a loving relationship with my wife, Barbara. She was coping with several chronic physical conditions and was homebound, and they became inseparable pals and playmates. At one visit to the doctor, he noticed that her blood pressure was lower than it had been for a long time. Barbara asked the doctor if Calvin's companionship could have anything to do with this. "Most unlikely," he replied. "I'll change your prescription, though, since your blood pressure is better. Come back in two months." The blood pressure stayed down.

The doctor, although unconvinced, grudgingly accepted that Calvin's companionship might have had a favorable effect. Barbara and I had no doubt; the facts spoke for themselves.

After Calvin eventually developed arthritis and I regretfully had to retire him in 1999, I applied for a replacement at Guiding Eyes and was teamed with a yellow Lab named Silas. He turned out to be, in every respect, a mirror image of Calvin. We nicknamed Silas "Boychick" (a Jewish word of endearment meaning "a nice little boy"). Unfortunately, in December 2008, Silas was diagnosed with incurable cancer and was euthanized on January 5, 2009. On the same date, five years prior, my wife Barbara had passed away. What a coincidence.

The loss of Silas/Boychick, affected me more than the retirement of Calvin. But, life has to go on. At the age of 86, I applied to Guiding Eyes for a third guide dog.

Unlike some guide dog schools which set an arbitrary age limit, Guiding Eyes for the Blind approved my application. In July 2009, I was teamed up with a black Lab named Tobi. Tobi seems to have all the tools he needs to become a good guide. I am confident that, with time and patience, Tobi and I, as was the case with his predecessors, will forge a successful partnership.

Yes, Charlie, you were right, three times over: "Your dog will guide you, love you, and protect you."

Guiding Eyes for the Blind

Belinda Simpson wanted her service dogs to make a difference for others too.

Reaching Out

by Kathy Nimmer

Belinda knew that both her first and second service dogs were invaluable to her, alerting her to seizures before they happened and calming her when her PTSD threatened to overwhelm her. She knew too that their gifts were too precious to be kept from others, so she chose to have them certified as therapy dogs too. This decision has led to some incredible moments when Belinda saw young people's lives changed profoundly.

Brads provided an amazing breakthrough moment for a young child at a special school in Montana. After the other children had taken turns walking Brads, Belinda handed the leash to a seven-year-old boy. Though the boy moved forward, Brads didn't budge.

"You need to tell him to come with you," Belinda said.

"Oh, this boy doesn't have the ability to speak," the teacher said, stepping forward while reaching for the leash.

"My son can't talk," added the boy's mom, embarrassment in her eyes.

"Come on, Brads."

Stunned silence.

The dog stepped forward, walking proudly beside the boy who had just spoken for the first time in his life, his first words said to a Golden Retriever who somehow knew he could do it.

Belinda also took Brads to a facility for young offenders, where the dogs served as companions and support for the teen inmates. One day when a young girl was petting Brads, she flung her arms around the Golden and began to cry.

"I just want to be normal, Brads."

"Tell Brads what 'normal' is," Belinda whispered. Thus began a conversation with the girl pouring out her heart to the dog who seemed to be listening intently, while Belinda sat quietly beside them.

Theo shared similar incredible moments with young people. Once as they visited an eleven-year-old autistic boy who had refused to speak for several days, Belinda recalled how Brads had bridged the communication barrier with youngsters, so she decided to see how it would work with Theo.

"If you need anything, you can tell Theo, and he'll tell me." Belinda waited.

"Theo, tell your mommy that my tummy hurts."

"Theo, ask S*** what would make it better."

"Theo, tell your mommy that I am thirsty."

"Theo, ask S*** what he wants to drink."

"Theo, tell your mommy that I want a drink of water."

So began the longest conversation that the boy had carried on with anyone for some time, facilitated by a happily accepting dog named Theo.

When Theo visited the same facility for young offenders where Brads had helped the young girl, Theo enchanted the inmates with his silly puppy ways. Once, as a young man scratched Theo behind the ears, another inmate came running up to Belinda.

"You shouldn't let him touch that dog. You don't know what he did that got him in here."

Belinda smiled. "It doesn't matter what he did, or what any of you did. Dogs love unconditionally." She glanced down at Theo whose tail wagged like a hyperactive windshield wiper. "Tails don't lie. You are all perfect in Theo's eyes."

Belinda sees the therapy work as a natural extension of what her service dogs have done for her. She is certainly not alone. Many handlers choose to extend their dogs' gifts to the world beyond them, a no-lose gesture of love.

Service Canines of Montana; Perfect Partners Assistance Dogs Trust

Elaine Jordan shows Destry her soul in this poem.

Shadows

by Kathy Nimmer

I was a shadow dweller,
Insulated from the world around me,
Hiding from all of my fears,
Then amazingly you found me.

Once a go-getter and dreamer,
Soaring with eagles on high,
But pain forced me into those shadows
Where I began to wither and die.

No confidence to speak for myself,
No ability to trust anyone,
No safety except in the shadows,
No happiness at all, just none.

I looked into your eyes that day,
Asking if you'd be my friend.
I stroked your midnight black fur
And knew on you I could depend.

Your strength and your sure security
Gave me hope to step ahead,
The warmth of your comforting presence
Replaced fear with belief instead.

Once needing many medications
To even breathe the air each day,
I now need only you
And your silent, stable way.

I was a shadow dweller,
Hiding from all that might destroy my soul,
But now you…you are my shadow,
And I am once again whole.

Owner-Trained Dog

Teaching students with severe disabilities led Susan Smith to an unforgettable realization.

A Lesson

by Susan Smith

I had just completed my teaching degree and was searching for a job working with students who had severe disabilities. I knew the job search wouldn't be easy. I had to find a place open-minded enough to see the potential of a teacher of severely disabled students who, herself, was almost totally blind.

The job search wasn't the only challenge I faced that spring and summer. Soon after completing the requirements to obtain my teaching degree I returned to the campus of Leader Dogs for the Blind to train with my second Leader Dog. Aster was a beautiful seventeen-month-old yellow Lab who faced life with a lot of energy and enthusiasm.

I often wondered how my yellow bundle of furry energy would manage to remain quietly on tie-down in the corner of a bustling classroom for an entire school day. I wondered how she would react to the sometimes unpredictable atmosphere of the type of classroom I hoped to call my own within a few short months after she and I became partners. I had faith in my instructor, Judy Campbell, and knew that she had chosen Aster for me with this type of environment in mind. But when Aster let out her pent up energy in a "disaster run" in my home, I wondered. A "disaster run" usually lasted up to ten minutes during which Aster would run as fast as she could, low to the ground, skidding past tables and chairs, barely missing walls and anything else that happened to be in her way. Her "disaster runs" couldn't be stopped. They had to be endured until she wore herself out and flopped exhaustedly to the floor. Aster was amazing in harness, a good worker, careful and on task. Sometimes she pulled too hard, but I knew we'd work that out. It was her high energy that concerned me.

I did finally find a job, and Aster and I relocated to a new city. My job was teaching young adults ages eighteen to twenty-two. I had a variety of different students with differing abilities and disabilities in my classroom and two to three classroom assistants to help. I placed Aster's tie-down in a remote corner of the classroom away from the majority of the activities but close enough so that she could see me and I could keep an eye and ear on her during my busy days of teaching.

I had one particular student who was in a wheelchair and was uncomfortable a majority of the time. We often took her from her chair and positioned her on the floor to relieve her discomfort. This student was not very mobile due to her physical limitations, so it surprised me one day when I went to lift her back into her chair and she was facing the opposite direction from where we had originally positioned her. She was on her belly facing Aster's tie-down. I asked if anyone had moved the student, but no one had. The student was not able to speak, so I could not ask her how she had changed positions. We decided she must have scooted herself around to face Aster, but none of us thought any more about it.

However, it kept happening. We'd place the student on her stomach facing away from Aster and toward the activity in the classroom, and when we would go back to help her into her chair, she would have scooted herself around so she was facing Aster.

Soon we noticed that when we returned to put the student back into her chair, she no longer was in the center of the positioning mat where we'd left her. She began inching closer to the edge of the mat nearest Aster. Before long she was drag-crawling off the mat entirely, but always toward Aster. She made daily progress in how far she was able to drag herself on her stomach toward her goal, which was obviously Aster.

I began to get concerned that in Aster's excitement, my dog would accidentally injure the student if she should ever make it all the way to Aster's corner, so we began positioning the student farther away. That didn't stop her. She continued to pursue her goal. She worked harder and made progress toward reaching my bundle of excitable yellow fur.

Finally, I realized that if Aster was a draw for this student, I should use that and encourage her to continue working on reaching the dog. We began to closely monitor the two. Finally, the student reached her goal and made it all the way to Aster. We all watched their interactions closely. Aster sniffed the student gently and lay quietly as the student patted the now serenely calm yellow dog. What a great sensory experience for a student who normally viewed the world from the confines of a wheelchair.

The two became fast friends and spent a lot of time together. The student remained in my classroom for three years, and not once was there a problem between her and Aster until the student's mother pulled me aside one day with an uncomfortable, hesitant chuckle sliding through her words. "Aster has taken on the role of teacher," she said. "She has taught my daughter to kiss, like a dog, with her tongue!" The family had to re-teach her to kiss like a person, not a dog! Fortunately, the family had dogs and understood. We all got a big laugh out of it.

I never would have believed that the incredibly high-energy dog that did nightly "disaster runs" in my apartment was the same dog who would lie quietly and be so gentle with a young woman with the physical challenges my student faced. Aster taught me in a very tangible way never to assume there is only one aspect to a dog or a human's personality. Both she and my student benefited from giving one another a chance, and it was beautiful to watch.

Leader Dogs for the Blind

Big joy comes in small packages, as Dennis Wright's dog Sparkle exemplifies.

In Small Packages

by Kathy Nimmer

It isn't easy being a Chihuahua, not a service dog who is a Chihuahua, anyway. They are always underestimated by people who think only of Labradors or Golden Retrievers or German Shepherds. But, within the tiny exterior of one Chihuahua can be a mighty big heart, as big and bright as the sun.

Sparkle is her name, and helping Dennis is her game! He needs her and loves her; she needs him and loves him. From the moment Dennis and his wife picked her out of a litter being sold in the parking lot of a local Walmart, she proved to be more than a pet. Now, she is a helper and companion who demonstrates that size is insignificant when it comes to service.

Sparkle's person has had a rough time of it. Dennis has hearing, vision, and heart problems, as well as diabetes, and he uses a wheelchair to get around. None of this has dampened his love for life, and Sparkle keeps that love alive.

Where would Sparkle rather be than anywhere else on earth? In Dennis's lap as he moves out into the world, his wheelchair carrying both of them through laughing highs and devastating lows. She wags to say, "Let's go, Daddy!" And then they are off!

And their journeys are not without roadblocks. The workers and business owners who question Sparkle's role as a service dog because of her size pale in comparison to the adversities they both have faced. There was the time when a car hit Dennis's wheelchair while they were crossing a street, seriously injuring Dennis and violently flinging Sparkle into the air. Somehow, amazingly, she landed on her feet and was unhurt, concerned only for the wellbeing of Dennis as the ambulance attendants bustled around him.

Then there were the nine months when Dennis was without a job, homeless on the streets of California. It was a tough test of survival and character, and Sparkle lived through it with him, eating dog food purchased with spare change, curling up beside him in shelters that weren't always eager to accept a dog, staying close when another homeless man wanted to borrow Sparkle to increase his intake when panhandling.

But they stuck it out, together. And along the way, Sparkle didn't stop doing the job she seemed destined to do, watching out for Dennis as a medical alert dog. If his blood sugar goes low, Sparkle will lick him frantically. If his heart begins to flutter, Sparkle jumps on him and barks. After he had a stroke, there was Sparkle, kissing his face and yapping wildly while the medical people did their thing. Even when Dennis is in another room, Sparkle somehow senses his needs, and presto! There she is. Yes, in the chest of one of the tiniest dogs beats a heart that is enormous. “To meet Sparkle is to love Sparkle,” says Dennis. And behind his words is a glow that makes you believe it.

SARA

Bill Yates, a World War II veteran, knew nothing seventy years ago of what lay beyond the exploding grenades.

The War

by Kathy Nimmer

World War II, the German/Belgian border.
He crouches with his six men,
Nineteen years of age,
Reconnaissance for the building of a bridge,
A combat engineer and his squad,
Scoping the safety of the proposed endeavor,
Doing what he must, what they must, doing it well.

Shells begin to fly,
Mortars tossed by targeting hands
Of Germans who had been hiding
In a barn across the whispering river,
And who now seek to kill
And do so with proficient gall.

Three solemn visits from Army personnel
To tear-shocked families,
But not to his,
Though the needle-like pain, shrapnel,
That seers his shrieking eye
Shouts cruelly of grief, loss, change.
He will not see the bridge
Being built on this river before him,
Nor see anything much again, forever.

He will not see, fifty plus years ahead,
The wagging tail of a Golden Retriever,
Trained to guide him across other bridges,
Through the whispering streets of life,
Pocked with other mortars that lie waiting,
Careless drivers, broken sidewalks, overhanging branches,
Those who target disability
As deserving a crimson "caution" sign.

He will not see a partnership,
So absorbing and profound
That when a tumor carries away the guide dog,
The elderly man will murmur with tear-choked dignity,
"When I die, his ashes will be buried with me,"

Two soldiers, two survivors,
Two stories, two victories,
One peaceful and fitting and just right…"the end."

Guide Dogs for the Blind

Count it all joy for Michelle Massie, her son Cole, and his dog Ilia.

The Best is Yet to Come

by Michelle Massie

"Mom, I want a dog."

My son Cole was a six-and-a-half year old boy who loved pirates and firemen and Gilbert and Sullivan and history. He also had cerebral palsy and used a wheelchair.

Having lost my Golden Retriever to cancer a few years prior, I was resolute in my non-dog household status. I couldn't handle a disabled child *and* a dog, I reasoned. But Cole would not be deterred. So in November of 2004, we found ourselves training in Oceanside. On graduation day, our dog's puppy raisers flew in from Texas to present us with the leash, showing us the most concrete lesson in unconditional giving I have ever witnessed. I sobbed from a place I did not know existed.

We came home and embarked on the quiet life of a boy and his dog.

Which lasted about a week.

That's when we went to a play date at Shane's Inspiration, a universally accessible park. During their "Good News Time," Cole told the crowd about getting his new dog. Tears flowed, noses honked. A representative from Shane's recruited Cole on the spot. With Ilia at his side, Cole narrated the presentation for their website.

And then they sent us an e-mail: Would we please share Cole's and Ilia's story with The Learning Channel? Not wanting to turn down a request from the people who'd built the only park where my son could play, I agreed. It took about half an hour to get a response. Cole and Ilia were featured on TLC's "My Life as a Child," which aired in February of 2007.

After doing some volunteer work with the Pasadena Ronald McDonald House, my phone rang again: Would Cole and Ilia like to ride on the Ronald McDonald House float in the 2007 Rose Parade?

Then Canine Companions for Independence phoned: Would Cole and Ilia mind doing a public service announcement? It's a national ad campaign, they said. The two will be on TV, billboards, and buses.

But amid all the flurry and excitement, real life continued unfolding. Cole soldiered on gamely through endless therapies, Ilia always by his side to encourage, soothe, and inspire. But we soon realized that Cole was going to need surgery. He was not keen on this at first. But when we explained that it would allow him to someday walk Ilia on his own, he cradled his dog's head every night and whispered: "I will walk you Ilia, I will walk you."

Immediately following surgery, Cole's painful screams tore at my heart. The agony came in waves. I was holding him and trying to will it all away but an odd, distant sound kept needling at my occluded consciousness. I finally looked up, and there was Ilia. In an extraordinary act of defiance, he had popped up out of his "down" command and was standing there, tail spinning, ears perked and eyes wide. When my gaze met his, he grunted his irritation at what was clearly my impenetrable obtuseness. I moved aside. In a flash, he bounded up and began licking Cole furiously. The pain vaporized.

The following day, Cole took his first steps with his heels touching the ground, Ilia by his side. Afterward, we laid Cole back on the bed to ease the intense pain behind his knees. We put Ilia on the bed too, but instead of going up near Cole's shoulders, he stopped and put his head on Cole's knees. Terrified, I asked Cole if I should move him. "No, Mom," he said with stunning calmness. "It actually feels really good." Ilia kept his head there for two days, something he had not done before nor since.

While Cole recovered at the Ronald McDonald House in New Jersey, Ilia continued to spread the love. There was one little boy with a spastic arm and hand who would reach out completely, just to get his hands on that glossy black fur. There were half a dozen autistic children who at first were terrified of Ilia but then became hypnotized by his gentleness. Soon, they were gathering around him…ten little hands at once…so excited that they began using their words: "Ear!" "Tail!" "Nose!" "Paw!" Teary-eyed parents stood watching.

In all, Ilia had travelled a total of 7,000 miles on six different planes to be by Cole's side for the surgery.

After we arrived home, we received yet another call: the ASPCA. I was about to tell the nice lady that we couldn't donate at this time when she asked if we owned Ilia. She then told me they'd been contacted by the Ronald McDonald House. From their story, she said, they'd decided to make Ilia their 2008 Dog of the Year. Could they fly us back to New York for the awards ceremony? At the Rockefeller Center, the elevator whisked us to the Rainbow Room on the 65th floor. After being humbled by the other honorees, we tearfully accepted our award and flew home, dizzy with gratitude and puffed with love for all who had been so gracious to us.

And that was that.

Until the phone rang.

It was the nice people at Southern California Honda, calling to tell us that we were finalists for the Honda Helpful Awards. (Each year they give a car to three people who work actively to support their community.) Because we'd done so much volunteering for Canine Companions, Shane's Inspiration, and the Ronald McDonald House, a friend had secretly submitted us for a Honda Element. Cameras came back to the house. After watching the resulting video, the Honda people decided that what we *actually* needed was a fully-adapted Honda Odyssey van.

So they gave us one.

Now how could this journey possibly get any better? One day, Cole will walk Ilia by himself. No walker, no parents. No cameras, no press. Just a boy and his dog. Because Ilia has made Cole want that more than anything.

And that's how I know the best is yet to come.

Canine Companions for Independence

Here lies a poetic victory celebration for Ricky Jones and for everyone who perseveres and overcomes anything in this world.

Second Chances

by Kathy Nimmer

Tears.
Tears fall.
Tears fall like raindrops,
Cascading in a torrent of pain.
Wholeness swept away by the rushing deluge.
A careless driver didn't see him,
White cane, traffic light, and all.
Rush, thud, impact, scream,
Flinging him high like tormented leaves,
Fracturing his body and spirit in one blow,
Neither to be quite the same ever again.

Doubts.
Doubts form.
Doubts form like the eye of a hurricane,
Glaring at his soul with menace.
Confidence obliterated by the lurking terror.
A street crossed many times before
Has become the royal throne of unending questions.
Screech, skid, honk, whoosh,
Haunting sounds that send him to retreat,
Cutting off potential with closed doors.
One step would bring risk: too much, too much.

Hope.
Hope descends.
Hope descends like winter's first snow,
Softly, slowly, gently settling on his bent shoulders.
Possibility slips into his consciousness.
A school stands ready to help with the healing,
Their first bandage a nuzzle from a willing black Lab.
Sniff, snuffle, pant, whine,
Reminding him of companionship,

Awakening his dormant zest for adventure,
A rebirth initiated by one wag of a tail.

Tears.
Tears swell.
Tears swell again, now like spring's chorus of birds,
Filling his blind eyes with resurrecting joy.
He who once quaked when cars zoomed by
Strides through the universe, harness in hand.
Command, walk, stop, continue,
Washing away nightmares with synchronized steps,
Replacing defeat with bellowing victory,
A life, saturated by trust. Freedom reclaimed.

Guiding Eyes for the Blind

Biographies of Contributors

Moto Arima is the president and director of Japan Hearing Dogs for Deaf People and the trainer of Mikan, the first certified hearing assistance dog in Japan. Mikan is now partnered with Yoshiko Kishimoto. All three are advocates for the acceptance and awareness of service (especially hearing) dogs in Japan.

Debee (pronounced Debby) **Armstrong** is the resident computer nerd for Disability Support Services at Deanza College, in Cupertino, California. In her spare time, she geeks out with her home computers, travels with her husband Bob, cooks, and reads voraciously. She's currently working Bev, a Golden Retriever, as her fifth guide dog and has enjoyed the partnership with guide dogs for over three decades.

Born and raised in Chicago, **Kristie Baker** contracted polio at age four. A resident of central Florida since 1979, she is currently working with her third service dog from Canine Companions for Independence. A member of the Church of Jesus Christ of Latter Day Saints, she loves to do genealogy (including volunteering at the Family History Center), and cans and dehydrates many of her own foods.

Detra Bannister, CareerConnect program specialist for the American Foundation for the Blind, enjoys helping the mentors and users of AFB's career development and exploration program, designed to expand employment possibilities for people with vision loss. Teamed with her second Seeing Eye dog, Brook, Detra enjoys flower and vegetable gardening, home improvement projects, hiking, and being involved at church.

After twenty years in the airline industry, **Kay Bennett** retired, thinking her independence was gone once she had been diagnosed with MS. Then she met Rufus, her service dog, who helped her regain her life. Actively involved with The Friendship Club, a group she started from dogchannel.com, she and about fifty other ladies and their dogs go on walks, travel, and help each other out however they can.

Marilyn Crouse Bland teaches English at a high school and for a local community college in Dallas, Texas. She is a PhD candidate at UT Dallas where she is working on a translation project as her thesis. Teamed with her third guide dog, Poko, Marilyn enjoys music and the outdoors and has traveled extensively throughout the world.

A graduate of Indiana University, **Sidney Bolam** is an aspiring artist and illustrator living in Brown County, Indiana. She lives with her husband, son, two dogs, and other pets on their hobby farm where she enjoys amateur homesteading, doing various arts and crafts, and exploring the great outdoors.

Judy Brangwin is a retired elementary school teacher who lives in Germany with her husband and three career-change guide/service dogs. Her dogs, now therapy certified, volunteer at the library where children read to the dogs. Judy enjoys walking with her dogs, speaking about guide/service dogs, and attending the annual conventions of the American Council of the Blind and Guide Dog Users Association.

Rebecca Bridges lives in the Washington, D.C. metropolitan area with her husband and their two guide dogs. She is currently working as a project manager for a nonprofit government contractor and recently obtained her Master of Science in organization development and knowledge management from George Mason University. In her spare time, Rebecca enjoys cooking, traveling, and attending sporting events.

Sarah Broderick and her service dog Luna live in a small town in northwestern Washington state where Sarah has been training service dogs for people with disabilities for the last nine years. She and Luna visit nursing homes and elementary schools where they are in a number of programs such as reading to dogs programs, physical therapy, and counseling. She also enjoys traveling, hiking, camping, and reading.

D. E. Brown is a veterinary clinical pathologist, earning her DVM and PhD degrees from Colorado State University. She has published articles in scientific journals including the *American Journal of Pathology* and the *Journal of Inherited Metabolic Disease*, while her poems have appeared in such journals as *Kaleidoscope*, *Kalliope*, and *Earth's Daughters*. Her story is meant to honor all service dogs, especially her own dog Kenya.

Born in Cobleskill, New York, **Lori Buffington** moved to southern Pennsylvania at age five. After retiring her blue Standard Poodle Fennec, she is now partnered with her second service dog, Tinker, a black Labrador Retriever. She enjoys working as an administrative assistant, riding a side car motorcycle, spending time with her seven grandchildren, and volunteering for Canine Partners for Life.

Judy Burch is employed by the state of Missouri as a rehabilitation teacher for the blind. She is working with her sixth guide dog, Indy, and is active in the blindness community. Some of her favorite pastimes include bowling, reading, cooking, and spending time with her grandchildren.

Donna Burke was born with muscular dystrophy over forty years ago and is adept at using a power wheelchair to get around independently. She lives with her husband of seventeen years and service dog Haley, who came from East Coast Assistance Dogs in Dobbs Ferry, New York, nearly six years ago. She delights in music, many TV shows, and good friends.

Alysa Chadow teaches the blind and visually impaired in the San Francisco Bay area, where she lives with her second guide dog Ellen. She is active in the blindness community and is currently working on her third children's book, as well as other short creative nonfiction pieces about her dogs. One of her poems was published in the summer of 2010 by *Kaleidoscope* magazine.

Chris Chapman lives in South Carolina and is a wife and mother of two adult children and a fifteen-year-old step son. She is working with her first guide dog Fellow, co-leads a local support group for visually impaired adults in her community, volunteers at church, leads a Life Group for Women, and works a part-time job. Chris enjoys exercising, yoga, yard work, cooking, and most of all being an encourager and inspiration to others.

Barbara Currin was raised in Brooklyn, New York. After her retirement from the NYPD, where she met her disabled husband, she attended the NY School of Dog Grooming. To better assist her husband when his condition worsened, she turned to her own dog training expertise; she and her husband now travel with their two American Pit Bulls to educate the public about their value as service and therapy dogs.

Karen Derx lives in southeast Texas. She has muscular dystrophy and uses a wheelchair and her service dog Watkins to get around. She enjoys traveling, going to concerts (especially Rascal Flatts), helping with her local muscular dystrophy group, and researching many topics of interest.

After a freak accident in 1987 that caused permanent paralysis, **Rich Dixon** is now a freelance writer and motivational speaker, following a thirty-five year career as a public school mathematics teacher. The author of *Relentless Grace: God's Invitation to Give Hope Another Chance*, his writing has also appeared in numerous periodicals and anthologies. Rich lives in Colorado with his wife Becky and his service dog Monte.

Pat Dolowy lives in Michigan and does contract labor as a field representative for Paws With a Cause. Her dog, Partner, is a certified demonstration dog for the organization as well as a part of their breeding program. Pat's volunteer work consists of watching her granddaughter two to three days a week. She and her husband love going to hockey games.

Living on Whidbey Island in western Washington, **Shannan Dumke** enjoys being a wife, mother, and grandmother. In her free time, she likes to attend church and Bible studies, read, cook, and write letters. She just finished raising her third dog for Canine Companions for Independence and hopes to get her fourth in the near future.

Max Edelman was one of the relatively few to have dodged the Nazi rifle barrels and crematorium fires, somehow managing to survive the Holocaust. Years later, having overcome his fear of dogs, Max now enjoys a daily three-mile walk with his third guide dog Tobi. Since retirement, Max is a contributing writer to local publications and gives presentations at local high schools and colleges.

After retirement, **Lynda Enders**, a former senior technical writer for military contractors and Fortune 500 companies, moved into her passive solar home which she designed and built in central Texas. She is now working as a personal care attendant and private chef, while distilling decades of practice into a book for one-handed cooks. She is assisted with mobility issues by her aging service dog Cash and his successor Heidi.

Wendy Enos is a former medical transcriptionist who has had several strokes, leaving her with a right-sided deficit and, ultimately, impaired vision. Her fully-trained service dog Sophie had to be quickly cross-trained to guide and now performs double-duty. Sophie stops at curbs, avoids obstacles, braces when Wendy falls off balance, retrieves dropped items, is awesome on stairs and slopes, and is a super cuddle bug!

James Falsken is a 100% disabled veteran who proudly served with the United States Coast Guard. He suffers with Agent Orange exposure, spinal injuries, PTSD, a right wrist fusion, and limited use of both legs. After training his own dog with the help of Happy Tails Service Dogs Inc. to fit his disabilities needs, he and best friend Lizard enjoy taking photos and attending college together.

Dena Feller is wife to Major-select Brian P. Feller, BS, MS of the USAF and mother to Alexander (eight) and Danielle (six). She is a Type 1 diabetic of twenty-nine years, and with the help of her service dog Bailey, she is able to be an active mom and live with less fear of hypoglycemic reactions while driving and running errands. She feels that her husband, children, and Bailey give her an awesome life well worth living.

Suzanne Ferguson is co-owner of an optical company in Tennessee and works as a multimedia artist. She is a longtime member of the Lions Club and served as District Leader Dog Chair for ten years. In addition to actively participating in the University of Tennessee animal therapy program (HABIT), Suzie and her K-9 partner Schatzie are nationally certified and operational in the search and rescue of lost and missing persons.

Heidi Fernandez is the proud parent of Andrew, who was diagnosed with autism at two-and-a-half years old. She is passionate about educating communities on the services that companion dogs and service dogs provide. An advocate for people with disabilities, she has assisted with the passage of national and state legislation and served on numerous state and local boards and committees.

Clara French is partnered with her first guide dog, a lovely golden Lab named Landria, and works with children in a special-needs Sunday school class at her church. She also is a Deaf/deaf-blind interpreter. She enjoys traveling, making crafts, scrapbooking, and walking for diabetes every year.

Tracey Frost is a patient advocate, medical transcriber, and manager of a social/business chat line. Her website is www.frostmedsec.info. She also is active in the disability ministry section of her church. Her current dog is Coral, a beautiful female Golden Retriever. Tracey is from Basking Ridge, New Jersey.

Mother and advocate for her three children, **Stacy Fry** obtained a bachelor's degree in physiology with a minor in biochemistry and art. Ehlena, her youngest, was adopted from India at the age of one with polymicrogyria (PMG) which causes her to have cerebral palsy and a mild seizure disorder. Wonder, Ehlena's faithful service dog, is her hope for independence.

Malgorzata "Maggie" Galbarczyk resides in Poland, where she works as an assistant psychologist in mental health services. She is planning to do her doctorate in clinical psychology and devote herself to the field. Maggie enjoys swimming and is interested in contemporary literature.

Sarah Gales and Fargo (her guide dog) live in western Massachusetts where Sarah works at an independent living center as an advocate for people with disabilities. Her life has always included animals, from pets to working dogs and livestock. She holds a bachelor's degree in equine science and a master's degree in agriculture, and has strong interests in the areas of animal welfare, behavior, training, and nutrition.

Chassidy "Chazz" Glaze is a recent graduate of Purdue University, where she received a Bachelor of Arts in creative writing and English education. A woman of debilitatingly eclectic and constantly changing tastes, her current passions are vegan cooking, spiritual exploration, writing, working out, and reading. She is the daughter of Colleen Jessup and Bruce Glaze.

A guide dog user since 1975, **Sherry Gomes** lives in Colorado with her current guide dog, a black Lab named Olga. She works as a tech support independent contractor for a major adaptive technology company. In her spare time, she loves reading, writing, shopping, movies, and music.

On July 31, 1994, **Mike Hambly** was in an accident that left him totally blind and a paraplegic. Now, as a social worker, he operates the employment program for the Canadian Paraplegic Association and owns a company, Braille It. Mike is teamed up with his second dog Finn, and he and his wife Denise have two young adult children, Patricia and Andrew.

Elaine Harris, a radio presenter with experience in TV and print journalism, is also a public speaker, writer, and lecturer. Her third guide dog Roselle (Rosi) is named after the famous guide dog Roselle who guided owner Michael Hingson to safety from the north tower of the World Trade Center on 9/11. Elaine lives by the sea in Tasmania, Australia, with husband Chris, Rosi, and non-working German Shepherd Allie.

Katherine (Kitty) Hevener is a published author, award-winning speaker, certified world class speaking coach, and retired vision rehabilitation specialist. She is passionate about empowering businesses to generate more revenue by making their products/services accessible to people with disabilities. She also serves on the Ohio Governor's Council for People with Disabilities.

Originally from northern Kentucky, **Jennifer Holladay** now lives in Ohio where she shares her life with her current guide dog Nora, a black Lab, and her retired yellow Lab Rainy. She works for the Cincinnati Association for the Blind and Visually Impaired as a one-on-one volunteer coordinator, matching volunteers with clients who need readers or transportation. She enjoys reading, traveling, and having dinner with friends.

Raised on a farm, **Kristeen Hughes**'s love for animals and all growing things encompasses four guide dogs, gardening, and the environment. She has worked in the fields of information technology, assistive technology, and women's mental health. She lives with her life partner, a housemate, and four dogs in the Midwest.

Marla Johnson lives in west-central Florida and worked for several years as a health care administrator. After a head injury sustained as a result of domestic violence, she suffered with seizures for twenty-two years before they became disabling. Since 2003, Marla has enjoyed two successful partnerships with great dogs: Hattrick, a Shepherd/Greyhound mix, and Brie, a Lab/St. Bernard mix.

Jake Jones is sixteen years old and lives near Washington, D.C., with his mom (a retired police officer), his dad (a detective), and his sister Justine. Jake and best friend/service dog Bodie have been exploring the world together for the past four-and-a-half years. Born with cerebral palsy, Jake's life-long seizure disorder went into remission the day Bodie came into his life from Saint Francis Service Dogs in Roanoke, Virginia.

Born visually impaired into a loving family of two totally blind parents, **Ricky Jones** grew up fighting the challenges that come with significant vision loss. Now he is successful as a teacher assistant, executive director of a blind sports organization, and parent of a four-year-old boy named Jonathan. He believes his greatest success, however, may be having become a confident blind adult with Pearson, guide dog extraordinaire.

Elaine Jordan lives in central Texas on forty-five acres full of beautiful horses and cows and works the family business side-by-side with her husband. Destry, her first service dog, helps her cope with the challenges of everyday life, in spite of her disability. She thoroughly enjoys horseback riding, reading, playing with her grandchildren, and traveling with her husband and Destry.

Megan Kelly is a graduate student in New York City where she studies language and literacy. She is currently working with her first guide dog, a male yellow Labrador named Buddy, with whom she trained at the Guide Dog Foundation in July of 2008. Megan's activities and interests include reading, advocacy, writing, and teaching English, Braille, and adaptive technology.

Pam Liles lives in Arkansas with her husband Tony and service dog Jobe, a beautiful mixed breed of German Shepherd and Husky. Since Jobe came into her life, she is not so scared of being alone, having seizures, or being unable to get up afterwards because he is there to help her. Pam is very appreciative of how loving, sweet, and protective Jobe is of her.

With her degree in English and secondary education, **Caitlin Lynch** is currently looking for her dream job as a middle school English teacher. Caitlin is working with her first guide dog, a large, lovable male yellow Labrador named Laser. In the little free time that Caitlin has, she enjoys reading, writing, travelling, outdoor activities, and being with her family and friends.

Carmina Martire was born in southern Italy and moved to Rome where she studied psychology, afterward running a center for psychological and psychotherapeutic help for many years. She has been a university lecturer and has spoken at many conferences. She now works in a bank, is happily married, and enjoys traveling, reading, listening to music, and playing golf.

Michelle Massie is a freelance writer and home-schooling mom who lives in California with her husband Nick, son Cole, and Cole's assistance dog Ilia. They donate time to Shane's Inspiration (builders of universally accessible parks), The Ronald McDonald House, and Canine Companions for Independence. You can visit her blog for special needs moms at www.extrememothering.com.

Working toward a degree in sociology, **Joe Mauk** is a student in western Pennsylvania. He is an avid outdoorsman and enjoys fishing and hiking with his guide dog Roxanne when time allows. Joe also enjoys bringing awareness to others about the blind community, and one way he does this is by speaking to audiences about the benefits of having a guide dog versus the use of a white cane.

Jennifer McEachen currently resides in northern British Columbia with her second dog guide, a male yellow Lab named Nixon, from Guide Dogs for the Blind, Inc. Jennifer is involved in a variety of volunteer activities and sits on various committees. She enjoys reading, bowling, watching curling, following current events, and learning about history.

Monika Miller-Neumaier is forever grateful for the gift of "Raising Pace" as well as for the incredible family with whom Pace now lives. A former "never-ever" dog person, Monika's journey of puppy-raising turned her into one of "those dog people." Monika lives in Illinois with her husband Michael; daughter Madz; son Kai; feline sons Boy-Boy, Buds, and Tux; and grateful rescued dog Humphrey.

Dr. **Ron Milliman**, blind since age eight, is currently a full professor of marketing at Western Kentucky University. Dr. Milliman is recognized internationally for his research concerning the effects of music on buyer behavior. He is married with two boys and a girl, enjoys a wide repertoire of interests, and is an avid fisherman.

Melanie Moore lives in Ontario and is currently paired with her third guide dog Vaughn. She works in Toronto for the Centre for Independent Living as an inquiries generalist. Vaughn makes the lengthy daily commute to work much easier for her. Melanie enjoys spending time with her family (including her three-year-old son) and playing the piano.

Odete Delice Moreira lives in Florianópolis, Santa Catarina, Brazil, where she enjoys swimming and leisure walks. After becoming blind at age thirty-five, she is now, at age forty-eight, a physical therapist and ceramics artist, and is also studying transpersonal psychology. Having the love of her family as inspiration, Odete continually seeks spiritual growth.

Debbie Morgan, a kindergarten aid at an elementary school in Indiana, is teamed with her fifth Leader Dog, Ada, a lovable yellow Labrador. She is married, has a grown son, enjoys reading, likes to crochet, and is active in her church. She loves going places with family or friends and taking long walks together.

Born in Scotland, **Chris Muldoon** is manager of the Royal Society for the Blind Guide Dog Service and an international assessor of guide dog schools around the world. He has a long, illustrious career in the blindness field and is currently studying at Ph.D. level. Chris has a set of bagpipes, plays Scottish traditional music, and lives in south Australia on twenty-seven acres with a menagerie of interesting animals but…no dogs!

Kathy Nimmer is in her nineteenth year of teaching English and creative writing to sighted students in a public high school in Indiana. She is working with her third guide dog, a yellow Lab named Elias. She enjoys writing, reading, motivational speaking, following sports, working out at the gym, and playing the piano.

DeAnna Quietwater Noriega is half Apache and a quarter Chippewa. She has been a writer/poet, advocate on disability issues, and storyteller since childhood. She currently is teamed with her eighth guide dog Reno, a chocolate Labrador Retriever trained by the Seeing Eye Inc.

A retired United Methodist pastor, **Bob Norris** and his wife of fifty-one years Margie live in South Carolina with Carmen, a dog from Guiding Eyes for the Blind. Bob and Carmen have been together since September of 2008 and have very fulfilling, interesting lives. Their daily activities range from playing golf to conducting worship services or funerals.

An experienced puppy raiser, **Joan O'Neill** lives in the northern suburbs of Chicago. She has raised four puppies for Leader Dogs for the Blind and is now in the process of training her first therapy dog. She loves to travel, experience other cultures, and explore the great outdoors.

Emily Overcarsh is currently a high school senior in Georgia's metro-Atlanta area. When she was a sophomore, she became a puppy raiser for Southeastern Guide Dogs and raised and gave basic training to her first and only service dog, Trisy. Emily enjoys reading and running in her very limited free time.

Kelly Randall lives in central Ohio with her emergency medical alert dog named Jake. Kelly has recently begun speaking in the community and is striving to raise awareness about epilepsy and service dogs. She hopes to help others who struggle and has a special interest in helping young women who have encountered similar challenges.

Alena Roberts loves living in Oregon with her husband Steve and her guide dog Midge. She works part-time from home for the Sendero Group, makers of talking map and GPS information and navigation systems, and also goes to school part-time, taking prerequisites for a master's program in hopes of becoming a teacher for the blind and visually impaired. Her hobbies include knitting and playing board games.

Stephen Rodi was an inmate at JJ Moran Correctional Facility in Warwick, Rhode Island, when he was accepted into the Prison Pup Partnership Program. This is a twelve-year-old partnership between correctional facilities around New England and NEADS. The program was conceived by two correctional facility leaders in Massachusetts to provide responsibility, work, purpose, and skills that inmates can carry with them upon discharge.

Robert Routten is a retired quality control supervisor for Newport News Shipbuilding and a former volunteer firefighter. Diagnosed with muscular dystrophy in 1991, Robert continues recruiting players for the three-time women's fast pitch softball national championship team, the Virginia Legends. He currently resides on a five-acre farm in Virginia with Barbara, his wife of forty-two years, and Cocoa, his current service dog.

Nancy Rumbolt-Trzcinski lives in the Berkshires of Massachusetts with her husband and current Seeing Eye German Shepherd Yancy. She also has two other dogs and a part-time cat. Nancy is employed as the assistant program manager of an independent living center and is active both statewide and nationally in several disability-related organizations.

Michael Schiavo is now thirteen years old and lives in Virginia with his parents and sister. He was diagnosed with Duchenne muscular dystrophy—a progressive degenerative muscle condition—at the age of one-and-a-half, which led to his eventual partnership with Conan, a Lab/Retriever mix. He enjoys reading, hanging out with his buddies, and playing video games.

Nancy Scott of Pennsylvania is an essayist and poet. Her over 480 bylines have appeared in magazines, literary journals, anthologies, and newspapers, and as audio commentaries. Her second chapbook, *Leveling the Spin*, is now available.

Sixty-two years young, **Gail Selfridge** was born in Detroit, Michigan, and was mainstreamed with a resource teacher for special help during her education. A job in computer programming took her to Colorado where she worked in that profession for twenty years. She is now a freelance writer and is working with her sixth Leader Dog.

Dick and Miriam Shafner live in Massachusetts and are puppy raisers for Guiding Eyes for the Blind. Elias, present partner to the author of this book, was the Shafner's first puppy for GEB, and they are now raising their third. Both the Shafners and their dogs love sailing, flying, and spending time with their three children and six grandchildren.

Kim Shepherd used a wheelchair and a white cane for mobility most of her life, causing severe arthritis pain in her shoulders. Inspired by a blind friend's ability to travel on her own with a guide dog, she investigated the possibility of using a guide dog to regain her mobility. In 2004, she acquired a black Labrador named Scooby, custom trained by Pro-Train Institute to guide her from a motorized wheelchair, restoring her independence.

Leigh Ann Shingler and her service dog, a black Labrador named Candy, live in a small southeast Texas town. Most of Leigh Ann's and Candy's busy days are spent working for a center for independent living, advocating for the independence and rights of people with disabilities. When they aren't at work, they will likely be visiting Leigh Ann's parent's home where Candy is affectionately claimed as "their favorite granddog."

Belinda Simpson is an occupational therapist who lives in New Zealand and is partnered with her third service dog Tana, who also works as a therapy dog. Belinda enjoys volunteer work with Outreach Therapy Pets and spends her spare time training and assessing therapy dogs. Belinda is also a sailing instructor, and her dogs love to sail with her.

Robin Smith, having miraculously survived a valley fever infection he picked up on an archeological dig that resulted in a T-10 spinal cord injury, now lives his life from a wheelchair and works for the San Diego Padres as their disabled services coordinator. His service dog Chauncey has been an integral part of his survival and successes. His life is good once again, and Chauncey is more than a little responsible for his wellbeing.

Susan Smith is a former special education teacher from Indiana who is looking forward to training with her fourth Leader Dog in late 2010 or early 2011. She enjoys spending time with family, reading, cooking, and doing latch hook projects. Susan also has an unusual hobby: building large, elaborate displays using millions of Lego bricks.

Ariana Solimando was born and raised in the Bergen County community of Emerson, New Jersey, and is working with her first service dog, a beautiful black Lab named Nexus who is always at her side. She enjoys road trips, music concerts, and watching all types of sports (especially the National Football League). Ariana is active in educating the public about service dogs and their abilities to change lives. She aspires to become a motivational influence for individuals with new spinal cord injuries.

After a serious car collision in 1984 that left **Katheleen Stagg** incapacitated with many medical problems, she rescued and adopted two Bichon dogs from smallpawsrescue.org. Her family noticed one of the dogs, Summer Ann, knew when Kathleen was about to have a seizure, so they had her trained to help as a service dog. The dog that Kathleen rescued turned out to rescue Kathleen and gave her back her life again.

A marriage and family therapist, **Linda Elmore Teeple** and her husband have raised three service dogs. Grace, from Leader Dogs for the Blind, serves in Costa Rica; Faith, an Indiana Canine Assistant Network dog, helps a nine-year-old boy with Down syndrome and autism; and Hope, a career-change Leader Dog, is in animal-assisted therapy training with Linda. She and her husband have three children.

Mich Verrier lives in Ontario, Canada. He is working his first dog Dale from The Seeing Eye in Morristown, New Jersey. As an active member of his community, Mich enjoys going out to dinner and the movies, chatting online, and reading.

An advocate for people with disabilities, **Judith E. Vido** lives in Virginia with her third dog guide Maddie. Judith was diagnosed with juvenile diabetes at age eight and, because of its complications, at age nineteen lost her sight. She holds a BS degree in psychology and master's in clinical social work from the Virginia Commonwealth University and is a performing soloist with the Senior Connections Choral Group.

Deborah Wagner resides in Indiana where she enjoys outdoor and fitness activities during the warmer months and curling up with a good book or a movie with her first assistance dog during the winter. With a personality that engages people of all ages and walks of life, she enjoys an enhanced experience of other cultures through international travel. Deborah is employed in the occupational field of sales and marketing.

Although the poem in this book is about her second guide dog, **Marcie Wallace** is now working with her fourth guide dog. Totally blind, Marcie is active in her church where she has a music ministry. She also enjoys cooking and computers and is currently taking an online medical transcription course.

Katherine Walters was diagnosed with paranoid schizophrenia and generalized anxiety disorder. She is in college studying to be an animal behaviorist and has worked as a dog trainer. Katherine is also very active as an advocate for people diagnosed with or affected by schizophrenia.

Jennifer Warsing is an employee of the local Humane Society. She and hearing dog Hattie, who comes from Dogs for the Deaf, are very active in the Deaf and Hard of Hearing community. Jennifer is working on passing a House Bill (fondly known as "Hattie's Bill") which will ensure the safety of all guide, service, and assistance animals in Pennsylvania against interference, injury, or attack.

Alysia Wells has been totally blind since the age of two. When she was studying for her master's degree in social work, a good friend worked with a Leader Dog. Their relationship inspired her to pursue this kind of bond with a service animal, and several guide dogs have since enriched her life.

Paulette Wilson was born in Ann Arbor, Michigan, but now resides in Alabama. Seven days a week, she hosts a Skype prayer group, helps people with their computer issues, and enjoys her hobbies, which include music and reading the Bible. Radar, her third and current guide dog, who she got from Guide Dogs of America in California, has proven to be her best dog yet.

Married for thirteen years, Rev. **Dennis Wright**, an ordained minister who is blind and suffers with multiple sclerosis, is currently pursuing a master's in theology in counseling at Summit Bible College in California. He is on the Presidential Honor Roll and Dean's List and is working toward a doctorate in theology in counseling. Rev. Wright feels he owes his life many times over to his six-year-old service dog Sparkle, a Chihuahua.

Bill Yates is an eighty-five-year-old retiree from the California Department of Rehabilitation and is himself blind and deaf. He trained with his guide dog Barnum at Guide Dogs for the Blind in San Rafael, California. He enjoys playing chess and following UCLA sports.

Kathy Zolo is proud wife to Brian, mother to Dawn and JoAnne, and grandma to Hayley, Tyler, and Kayden. A guide dog user for thirty-nine years, she has had many different breeds and loved them all, including dog #10, obtained in November of 2009. Her hobbies are walking, reading, knitting, and talking with groups, especially school children about her life and how her dogs help her throughout her daily activities.

Training Facilities Represented in the Book

4 Paws for Ability
253 Dayton Ave.
Xenia, Ohio 45385
Phone: (937) 374-0385
www.4pawsforability.org

Assistance Dogs of America, Inc.
8806 State Route 64
Swanton, Ohio 43558
Phone: (419) 825-3622
www.ADAI.org

By Your Side
P.O. Box 272443
Tampa, FL 33688
Phone: (813) 963-3776
www.bpawsitive.com

Canine Companions for Independence
P.O. Box 446
Santa Rosa, CA 95402-0446
National Headquarters:
1-866-CCI-DOGS (224-3647)
ww.cci.org

Canine Partners For Life
P.O. Box 170
Cochranville, PA 19330-0170
Phone: (610) 869-4902
www.k94life.org

Canine Partners of the Rockies, Inc.
P.O. Box 460214
Denver, CO 80246
Phone: (303) 364-9040
www.caninepartnersoftherockies.org

Colorado Assistance Dog Education & Training
366 Rim Road
Boulder, CO 80302

Dogs for the Deaf
10175 Wheeler Road
Central Point, OR 97502
Phone: (541) 826-9220
www.dogsforthedeaf.org

Dogs with Wings Assistance Dog Society
11343 - 174 Street, N.W.
Edmonton, AB. T5S-0B7
Toll Free: 1-877-252-9433
www.dogswithwings.ca

East Coast Assistance Dogs
P.O. Box 831
Torrington, CT 06790
Phone: (914) 693-0600
www.ecad1.org

Georgia Canines for Independence
1540 Heritage Cove
Acworth, GA 30102
Phone: (404) 824-4637
www.gcidogs.org

Great Plains Assistance Dogs Foundation Inc.
P.O. Box 513
Jud, North Dakota 58454
Phone: 1-877-737-8364
www.greatplainsdogs.com

Guide Dog Foundation for the Blind, Inc.
371 East Jericho Turnpike
Smithtown, NY 11787-2976
Phone: 1-800-548-4337
www.guidedog.org

Guide Dogs for the Blind, Inc.
P. O. Box 151200
San Rafael, CA 94915-1200
Phone: 1-800-295-4050
www.guidedogs.com

Guide Dogs of America
13445 Glenoaks Boulevard
Sylmar, CA 91342
Phone: (818) 362-5834
www.guidedogsofamerica.org

Guide Dogs Victoria
Private Bag 13,
Kew, Victoria 3101
Phone: (03) 9854 4444
www.guidedogsvictoria.com.au

Guiding Eyes for the Blind, Inc.
611 Granite Springs Road
Yorktown Heights, NY 10598
Phone: 1-800-942-0149
www.guidingeyes.org

Happy Tails Service Dogs, Inc.
One West Sequoia Drive
Phoenix, AZ 85027
www.happytailsservicedogs.com

Japan Hearing Dogs for Deaf People
3200 Miyada Kami-Ina; Nagano, 399-4301; Japan
Phone: 81 265 85 4615
www.hearingdog.or.jp

Kansas Specialty Dog Service (KSDS, Inc.)
124 West 7th Street
Washington, KS 66968
Phone: (785) 325-2256
www.ksds.org

Leader Dogs for the Blind, Inc.
P.O. Box 5000
Rochester, MI 48308-5000
Phone: 1-888-777-5332
www.leaderdog.org

National Education of Assistance Dog Service (NEADS)
P.O Box 213
West Boylston, MA 01583
Phone: (978) 422-9064 [Voice or TDD] or (508) 835-3304

Oaks Veterinary Clinic
14202 Benns Church Blvd.
Smithfield,VA 23430
Phone: (757) 357-2324
www.oaksveterinaryclinic.com

Paws'itive Teams
San Diego, CA
Phone: (858) 279-7297
www.pawsteams.org

Paws With A Cause National Headquarters
4646 South Division
Wayland MI 49348
Phone: 1-800-253-7297
www.pawswithacause.org

Perfect Partners Assistance Dog Trust
PO Box 59276
Mangere Bridge
Auckland, New Zealand 2151
www.ppadt.org.nz

Pilot Dogs, Inc.
625 W. Town St.
Columbus, OH 43215-4496
Phone: (614) 221-6367
www.pilotdogs.org

ProTrain Dogs
1544 Avohill Rd.
Vista, CA 92084
Phone: (760) 749-0897
www.protraindog.com

SARA
PO Box 607
Midlothian, TX 76065
VoiceMail: (206) 376-8931
www.affluent.net

Service Canines of Montana
Box 30684
Billings, MT 59107
Phone: (406) 252-7729

The South African Guide-Dogs Association for the Blind
PO Box 67585
Bryanston, South Africa 2021
Phone: 011 705 3513/4 or 087 745 9295
www.guidedog.org.za

Southeastern Guide Dogs, Inc.
4210 77th Ave. East
Palmetto, FL 34221
Phone: 1-800-944-3647 (1-800-944DOGS)
www.guidedogs.org

St. Francis of Assisi Service Dog Center
PO Box 19538
Roanoke VA 24019-1524
Phone: (540) 342-DOGS (3647)
www.saintfrancisdogs.org

Summit Assistance Dogs
PO Box 699
Anacortes, WA 98221
Phone: (360) 293-5609
www.summitdogs.org

The Guide Dogs for the Blind Association, UK
Burghfield Common
Reading
RG7 3YG
Phone: 0118 983 5555
www.guidedogs.org.uk

The Seeing Eye, Inc.
P. O. Box 375
Morristown, NJ 07963-0375
Phone: 1-800-539-4425
www.seeingeye.org

Texas Hearing and Service Dogs
4803 Rutherglen
Austin, TX 78749 512-891-9090
Toll free: 1-877-TEX-DOGS
www.servicedogs.org

LaVergne, TN USA
12 November 2010
204633LV00001B/2/P

9 781608 447169